CHRISTIAN KYRIACOU

THE HOUSE WHISPERER

*Discovering your relationship
with the heart of home*

There is a place where my heart can rest

and my soul feels at peace...

that place is Home

First Published 2014 by Ki Signature Books

Every effort has been made to ensure the anonymity of individuals and families whose circumstances and locations have been touched upon in this book. Those people whose stories are shared have kindly granted their permission. Descriptions and any quotations relating to specific consultations typically have bearing on others of a similar nature.

Any comments made on matters relating to health are from the author's own personal experience. The intention is only to offer information of a general nature to help in your quest towards emotional and spiritual wellbeing. The author does not prescribe the use of any process or technique referred to in this book as an alternative form of treatment for physical, emotional, psychological or medical problems without seeking the professional advice of a physician, either directly or indirectly. In the event that you choose to use any of the information in this book for yourself, the author and publisher assume no responsibility for any liability.

A CIP catalogue record for this book is available from the British Library.

ISBN 978-0-9929380-0-0

Ki Signature Books
Kingston upon Thames, Surrey, England
www.KiSignatureBooks.com

Cover design by Eleni Violaris

Acknowledgements

With appreciation to the many people who inspired this book and opened their hearts to share their personal life stories within the context of their homes, sometimes in difficult and distressing circumstances. No actual names or precise locations are given for reasons of client confidentiality.

Many of the consultations in the last nine years have been carried out with Sandy Humby, who shares her unique perspective and understanding of the relationship weave between people and their homes. Expressing my love and gratitude to Sandy for her deep insights and skills in contributing to and developing the principles of *House Whispering*, and for her dedication and many gifts at all levels of our soul journey.

With greatest appreciation to Roma Harding from Dorset, for her wordsmith and editing skills, including some valued and much appreciated contributions. In particular, her patience and commitment in structuring this book for the reader, unravelling the complex realities of the multi-dimensional worlds of *The House Whisperer*.

My love to my mother Eleni, who passed away during the final stages of writing, for her open-hearted compassion and love shown to her family and friends. She has now joined my father Ioannis, who continues to guide me in so many aspects of life. He taught me the skills at an early age in the various building trades and encouraged my architectural practice.

In gratitude to those people not mentioned by name who have generously guided and advised me, and to my children Tamara, Nicky and Ed for their love and support throughout this process.

Together with respect and honour for my teachers in all realms, these experiences enable me to convey the message of *The House Whisperer* – to discover and illuminate our soul relationship with the heart of home.

Christian Kyriacou, September 2014

"In this exciting and hugely informative book, Christian Kyriacou takes us on a profound journey of discovery and healing. He shows us how the places where we live and work are far more than what many assume to be mere backdrops to their lives. By wonderfully merging the extraordinary with the ordinary, he illustrates an expanded and multidimensional view of the nature of reality, inspiring the reader to undertake their own inner journey of transformation."

Dr Jude Currivan, cosmologist, healer and
author of HOPE: Healing Our People and Earth

"Not straying from the esoteric roots of his Greek heritage, merged with his training as a Western architect and Feng Shui practitioner, Christian Kyriacou feels his way into the soul of a building. He connects with its life-long relationship to the land and her inhabitants, human or otherwise. For those people who seek his remarkable gift, he is able to guide them back to health, into better relationships, towards greater prosperity. As The House Whisperer, he reminds us of our intimate relationship to a world pulsating with life, wisdom, and possibility."

Bob Sachs, Eastern philosopher and author

Contents

KNOW THYSELF

ΓΝΩΘΙ ΣΑΥΤΟΝ

Inscription at the Temple of Delphi

Introduction

The homes in which we choose to live, reflect who we are. Many factors make up the emotional and energetic patterns that create and run the underlying purpose of our lives.

Most of us experience the stresses and strains of relationships, families and children, health challenges, career concerns, financial issues, and even haunted houses. Some people have lived for years, unable to rectify what can be life-shattering problems. They may not appreciate that the solution may well be found in their own homes.

Architect Christian Kyriacou introduces a well-grounded esoteric approach to houses in his distinctive style of communicating with the heart and soul of buildings. As *The House Whisperer* for the last eighteen years, he has developed the ability to hold the emotional space for his clients, to penetrate the depths of unseen energies that surround and pervade every corner of our homes. The subtle energies reverberating in the atmosphere left lingering from the lives of previous occupants, may have resonance to some aspect of our own lives and call us for resolution.

With his unique gifts to see what is going on in the invisible worlds of reality, to read and interpret the patterns that influence our everyday lives, he makes visible the invisible and the silent audible. He shows us why the law of attraction may draw any one of us to a happy house or one with unsupportive and destructive energies. Do our own perceptions tell us what is *really* happening?

The principles of *House Whispering* are illustrated with reference to many remarkable stories from over one thousand consultations Christian has undertaken for homes and businesses worldwide. They disclose heart rending, at times traumatised, highly charged human predicaments that lie behind every front door and to which we can all relate – of love, intrigue, compassion, betrayal, divorce, disasters, battles, paranormal activity and more.

Within the context of these scenarios, an explanation is given of the significance and reasons why certain events happen, including how most problems are successfully resolved. Using metaphysical techniques to deal with the quantum nature of time and space, he incorporates the wisdom principles of Feng Shui, Vaastu, geomancy, sacred geometry and harmonics. Interpreted and expressed through contemporary modalities, this creates an engaging fusion of science, architecture, philosophy and spirituality.

Exploring the depths of psychological and emotional issues in this extraordinary holistic process does not follow any specific recipe, neither is it an approach in the old 'give me a pill' paradigm. With the emphasis on taking personal responsibility, when we seek to identify the habitual patterns that we subconsciously perpetuate, the act of altering physical and emotional space is a profound generator for change, allowing human consciousness to evolve on many levels.

Your home is potentially your greatest teacher and companion, the catalyst that can enable transformation to occur. Understanding and unlocking its hidden power can illuminate your way forward, from the mundane to deeper philosophical questions in life. The essence of 'I Am', who you truly are, is found by connecting with universal consciousness. This path of enquiry can shed light on your unique soul purpose here on Earth - perhaps more importantly, by discovering who you are not!

In this educational and inspiring book based on Christian's own experience and understanding, intended to bring awareness and clarity of our interwoven relationships with buildings, we discover whether following a consultation people have truly listened to the messages emanating from their walls.

In a quest for peaceful harmony, creating this sustaining relationship with the soul of our home holds the key to embracing dreams and aspirations. The guidance and encouragement of *The House Whisperer* empowers us to bring balance to all aspects of our lives and achieve happiness and fulfilment, ultimately by making a house feel like home.

Whisper 1

A HOUSE HOLDS MEMORY

If walls could talk...

The Whispers

Walking by a house and hearing faint *whispers*, my curiosity is ignited. I am compelled to listen and wonder if a building really can talk. It feels as if something elusive beyond the bricks and mortar is reaching out and beckoning me. Is it the house or its occupants that I am hearing, perhaps both?

As I allow my thoughts to quieten, intrigued as to what the house is trying to say to me, I experience a physical reaction oscillating in my body. My energy fields begin to expand and contract as my emotions engage with the essence of the house, stirring up a mixture of nausea and excitement. I become aware of a misty haze of moving energy swirls before my eyes, hearing discordant notes in the air, music that is off-key as if an orchestra is tuning-up. As my vision fades into another dimension, I feel inexplicably drawn deeper into the soul of the house. My mind reaches out to touch the material structure of the building to make sure it is really there, yet an acute sense of actuality tells me this reality shift is no daydream.

I realised from a young age that I had an innate empathy with the consciousness of buildings. Whilst my initial awareness was of the physical form, my inner perception told me a different story, giving me a sense of the atmosphere within. By acknowledging its presence, a house shared with me its joy or distress and turmoil. I would re-spond and begin a dialogue with the very essence of the house itself.

Over the years as an architect, I had the opportunity to visit countless buildings and found myself being very sensitive to the

3

character of the structures that I was working with, particularly houses. The ability to see and feel the energies in a space allows me to tune into residual memories, including any spirit activity and influences from other dimensions. As a house begins to morph into unfamiliar realities of past eras, it *whispers* echoes of events that have taken place, sometimes from long ago. Shadowy people wearing the costume of their respective periods unexpectedly come towards me and pass by in rhythmic waves; their distinctive facial expressions convey an emotive story.

I recognise these metaphysical perceptions and experiences as the leftover lingering imprints of previous occupants. An energetic image shaped by the behaviours and life patterns of all those who have lived there and passed through its doors. Strange as it may seem, houses have memory just like us. It is not the general view that buildings have soul consciousness and are 'alive', that maybe they 'talk' with each other in some kind of coded language, their feelings embedded into the very soul of the house itself.

In developing a spatial awareness, I am able to read and interpret the various clues and discover what has happened in homes and workplaces, often spanning long periods of time. The intuitive sixth sense supports the familiar five senses of perception, bringing an added dimension to the all-important heart connection between people, buildings and the land. Thus, a framework evolved of my own silent communication with the veiled world of buildings, all holding untold stories waiting to be heard and reconciled.

When visiting a property as *The House Whisperer* and considering what might unfold, my initial impression of how it feels leads me to compile a memory map of its many layers of 'being-ness'. Yes, houses are far from silent; varied tones can expound peaceful serenity, quiet vulnerability or forceful aggression, sometimes very loudly indeed!

To view and listen to these memory imprints allows me to gain an understanding of the underlying messages, the inner *whisperings* of the subconscious. This is invaluable in helping me to connect with the energetic history and overall picture of the ongoing dynamics, including any spirit activity prevalent in the house. As profound revelations unfold, especially of the interwoven relationships with occupants past and present, I am aware that a house is capable of exposing many secrets held deep within the owner's psyche.

The psychology of spaces considers the fundamental question, why do we live where we do? I work from a basic premise that we are attracted by something intangible to where we choose to live. The elusive sense of the feeling of a property is what people actually relate and respond to, whether at a surface level or through a deep heartfelt connection. This is what makes one house feel good and another not so inviting.

Most of us have been inside a house that does not feel right, a bit strange or uncomfortable, an atmosphere that permeates every part of our being and makes us feel, *"I need to get out of here."* So what effect might this have on the people living there or those who may have just moved in? Will lives be influenced and steered by the cacophony of realities, memories and spirit 'presences' that dance in the invisible realms of their spaces?

These are some of fundamental questions I ask people from all walks of life, who approach me to enquire about a consultation:

Do you feel at home where you live?

Did you choose your house, or did it choose you?

Is your home a sanctuary, a peaceful place to rest where you feel energised and nourished?

Do you feel safe, secure and protected by your four walls, or do you feel a prisoner in your own home?

Do you live in a house that accommodates your physical needs alone or a home that fully nurtures your spiritual self?

Are you aware that held in the walls of your home are the emotions of joy and pain, all playing out like a video replay?

Are you living your own life or the life of someone who has previously lived in your house?

Is your home affecting your libido and sex life, highlighting the wonderment or inadequacy of your intimate relationship?

We may not fully realise the extent of power and influence that a house can have in shaping our existence. As we set up a relationship dynamic with our spaces, their response feeds back to either nourish or diminish our personal energy fields, emotions and behaviours accordingly, which in turn reflects our own temperament.

It can be devastating to feel your life being run by forces beyond your control, as this lady experienced:

"I feel the house is running my life, I just seem to get pushed around by something I can't explain."

When visiting a once magnificent country estate, I paused to take in the entirety of the original main house now converted into apartments. Feeling a tension in my stomach, I heard the *whispers* of the distressed, hurt soul of the decimated stately home: *"They did not ask if they could cut me up."* Was the lady I was about to meet attracted to buy an apartment that related to her own fragmented life?

In becoming aware of many dimensions of time and space, it is of value to listen to what our homes are trying to say to us, and look at unravelling the many reasons why they can upset lives. There are, of course, homes that carry very happy atmospheres and spiritual energies, which the process of *House Whispering* can enhance to further maximise the full potential of the health, wealth and wellbeing of a property and its occupants. Working closely together brings opportunities for transformation in all aspects of the lives of ordinary people, often with extraordinary stories to tell.

So, join me on a journey whilst I share some of my experiences, perhaps illuminating your own questioning and understanding of your relationship with home as a metaphor of life.

What Makes a Home?

My frame of reference for the stages of a consultation uses the language of the 3 R's. **Reading:** my own factual and intuitive perceptions of a house in order to unravel life's complexities; **Revelation:** sharing my findings with the client and encouraging them to recognise the underlying patterns causing their problems, leading to an 'Aha moment', the first point of potential transformation; **Resolution:** help and guidance in resolving the core issues towards facilitating positive change for occupants within their home spaces.

My reference to 'house' also includes flats and apartments. Home may not be an actual building as such, perhaps a caravan, yurt or another form of abode. Whilst our identity is usually defined by some kind of physical or social structure, the significance of our homes is far greater than providing a roof over our heads, an enclosing space for our physical protection and security. The human condition generally needs a framework and boundaries in order to express a sense of who we believe ourselves to be at any particular time and place. We all have an innate need to relate to a personal space, the same basic necessity for a place to sleep and 'hang our hats'. Even a homeless person or a tramp on the street will find a place of shelter to rest, whether under a bridge, in a doorway or on a park bench. That *is* their home, however temporary, where they may choose to relate to others in similar circumstances.

When we achieve a sense of peace and belonging in a safe space, we say, *"I feel at home."* Those who are totally at peace within their inner being are capable of feeling 'at home' anywhere in the world. For many indigenous cultures, 'home' means being part of their tribe no matter where they set up a temporary base. They take their physical homes and belongings with them as they travel from one place to another, their families, friends, vehicles and animals perhaps being more important aspects of their identity.

Most of us, however, need a physical building or familiar space from where to come and go, which mirrors back to us who we perceive ourselves to be. For the most part, the perceived degree of security of our externalised house is a projection of our own inner sense of Self. Architecture and home spaces are not isolated concepts. By no means are we separate from the spirit and soul of buildings; they exist in terms of our co-dependency and influence on all aspects of our being. The hidden psychological and emotional patterns that control our lives are illuminated by the outer reflection of our inner world of self-beliefs, desires and intentions.

When looking to find a home, we make a decision often in the same way as we choose to be in an intimate relationship. Initially, a resonance or sense of familiarity leads us to feel, *"I could live here."*

Although location and price are important factors when buying or renting a property, no matter what our financial position, social class and personal values, we usually choose a house by how it feels. This attraction comes from the heart rather than being a rational decision.

The way a space feels is what creates equilibrium between the individual and the material. Even if we have the best house or apartment we can imagine, that does not necessarily mean we will feel at home. Ultimately, the true sense of feeling 'at home' comes from heart coherence, when our own heart-waves synchronise with the heart of the house and merge into one. With no disparity or fragmentation of the energy fields, we can be at peace in that space and at home in our hearts. This is similar to recognising compatibility with a partner. When we are in love, our feelings are expressed through coherent heart-waves that synchronise with one another.

The *House Whispering* process can certainly help to improve our relationship to our homes. However, if the fundamental 'feel good' factor is not there in the first place, no matter how much work takes place to transform our space, we will rarely be able to experience the total heart coherence that brings the highest level of connection. If a building doesn't speak to us and light up that elusive, magical spark, giving the exquisite feeling of home, it may be that we are just not in the most favourable place. Our choices never lead us to the 'wrong' place, as where we are drawn will always relate to our life path.

Our buildings can show us how the physical layout of our living and working spaces shape and mould our lives. Our homes have a direct correlation with our quality of life and reflect back to us our experiences, ingrained patterns and learned emotional responses. They communicate much about our attitudes in general, analogous to a relationship with an intimate partner. Just as our cars, artefacts and treasured possessions have much to say about our inner beliefs and personal values, our homes convey our social, professional and financial aspirations, a statement of how we relate to the world around us and how we wish to be seen by others. Thus, the stories and hidden secrets embedded within our homes tell much more about us than we might imagine. Like a book to be read, each chapter represents a unique and conceivably mysterious part of our being.

Owing to the constantly changing dynamic of this mirror imaging, any physical alterations that we make, from internal décor to building an extension, will directly impact on certain areas of our life. The way we furnish our homes and arrange our artefacts also correlates to our inner belief systems and the value we place on ourselves.

When you move into a house where someone else has lived, soft furnishings and carpets are best replaced or at least deep cleaned, as every fibre soaks up physical odours and energetic imprints like a sponge. Someone who chose to live for eleven years with the old carpets, curtains and decorations, rather than putting their own stamp on a home, said:

"It felt like I was treading on eggshells, not sure if I really belonged."

Everything that happens within our four walls is an expression of some part of who we think we are, whether we are consciously aware of it or not. When we seek change in our lives, this inner desire is expressed through some kind of outward adjustment to our homes. Our home is therefore an absolute externalisation of who we perceive ourselves to be, projecting every dream of existence from childhood, our likes and dislikes, failures and successes.

With life in a constantly evolving state, if we are to maintain our heart connection with where we live to ensure that we always feel at home, our buildings need to remain aligned with changing personal demands. The individual rooms of a house, each with a different purpose and ambience, correspond to the interior facets of life. This metaphorical reflection of the multifarious aspects of our psyche, we often unknowingly fragment and compartmentalise to the detriment of soul unity.

My work as *The House Whisperer* is all about listening to the individual at all levels and communicating with the soul essence of their home, interpreting the positive and negative effects that any aspect can have in this interwoven relationship. The familiar concerns that people voice range from a wish to improve their lives in a general way, to more specific problems involving health matters, finance, moving house, issues with children or relationships. The common factor leading a person to take action is a significant event that acts as the catalyst to declare, *"Things must change."* In asking for help, they may initially offer a short factual description or more usually, a lengthy explanation of their perspective of the problems they are facing. *The House Whisperer* is often called in when matters have reached the extremity of physical expression and discomfort, as shown in some of the stories in this book.

The process is one of illumination, bringing to light and helping people to recognise what is going on through the vehicle of the house or apartment where they have chosen to live. Much of what we explore is about yourself, your inner home and the personal patterns you take with you wherever you go. To reconcile challenges brings the potential for greater contentment and happiness, enabling people to live in a peaceful, tranquil heart-space within their homes.

The Quest for Sanctuary

We should feel our home to be a totally safe place at all times, a sanctuary that provides refuge and comfort. The front door is our protector from the outside world; its physical solidity denotes the degree of security we feel within. Just as the windows are the eyes that look out and shine to the world, the main door is the mouth that breathes in the wind through which we nourish the soul of our home. Our mood as we enter will echo the energy of our day and feed into the material substance of our spaces. The degree of nourishment depends on what and whom we invite in, offering sustenance that may be meagre or abundant. The compass orientation and view from the front door are most relevant to the quality of energy we draw in. It is these positive or negative vibrations in the spaces where we live and work that influence and shape our everyday reality.

A house is a living organism with conscious presence and has a degree of free will, yet cannot easily alter by itself. Our homes need human interaction to morph and change, to be able to support and nourish us, so that in return we can nourish the soul of our homes. Influenced by the whims of all who pass through its doors and look through its eyes from within, the consciousness of a building is aware of those who enter. Houses remember their occupants and even their visitors. Does your front door send you out into the world fully empowered for the day ahead and welcome you back to refresh your soul? Are your windows watching you as you leave, eagerly awaiting your return? A homecoming welcome is like a dog greeting its owner, whether a chihuahua or a rottweiler. Is the sunlight able to charge up the energy particles of your home during the daytime, and the shining stars bring serenity at night? What do you see, hear and feel as you connect deeply with the soul of your home?

Each room has a particular significance in our lives and has some awareness of every other room in the house. Whether perceived as separate spaces or as part of the whole will have a bearing on our wellbeing. If all parts are not in unison, the resulting fragmentation will be mirrored in disintegrating aspects of our personal life and in the health of our physical body. We all have the choice to ensure that our homes hold our essence and that our breath does not seep out through the walls, denying us the rightful solitude and dream space we might seek. When your house is empty, do spectres of the past lingering in the air come out to play, creating havoc or even obstacles in your path? Do your boundary fences keep you safe, supporting and enhancing your wealth and status as well as your role in the wider community? These questions, all deemed worthy of contemplation, are considered in my role as *The House Whisperer*.

What you do in the rooms of your house matters. The activities that take place and the company you keep all influence the atmosphere. Creative hobbies, cooking, playing music, in fact anything you enjoy and love, will raise the vibration and consciousness of your spaces. Whether high-tech 'state of the art' or a simple, rustic edifice tagged onto the back of a cottage, the kitchen is the generator of nourishment within the home. The vibration it sends out will affect the molecular structure of the food, enhanced by the people preparing it and absorbed by those who eat it. To prepare meals lovingly can perhaps only truly happen in a nourishing space.

Even those abandoned rooms that may feel dismal and uninspiring can be made to feel better if you use and energise them. A basement of a public building was transformed from a gruesome dungeon into a place of sanctuary when designated for community activities. After playschool came in once a week and regular yoga classes began to take place, the atmosphere perceptibly lifted when the building and the earth itself were given more love and joy.

The energetic gifts your home can offer flow only in accordance with the depth of the well and purity of the water bringing life to the ground on which it stands. The degree of life force we absorb is largely a matter of choice, determined by many factors relating to the energetic configuration of our spaces. Our homes merely respond and mirror our soul as they accompany us on our life's journey.

So, what *is* your relationship to your home? Will your house make you a prince or a pauper? Are you its master, the queen or king of your castle, or the servant in the basement? Is your home a tribute to the pride of your endeavours, reflecting the values and self-respect that shine through your soul? You can only be as large as the physical and energetic space held by its walls, as clear and pure as the shining floors and polished surfaces. Yet, the walls hold the visual illusion of our general concept of 'home', whilst the etheric heart centre is the true reality, silently nurturing our soul or not, as the case may be.

If we fail to search deeply and examine our motivation to create a loving, heartfelt relationship with our home, in seeking freedom its spirit may outgrow the walls. On occasions, a house will shake its shoulders and react back at the owners, sometimes fiercely – when this happens, there is trouble! This yearning is expressed by your home manifesting all kinds of challenges at subtle levels and more evident problems with the physical structure, from leaking roofs to blocked drains and all else in between. As one woman said:

> *"It feels like the house is fighting us, as if it's angry and unhappy about something, and our health is suffering."*

By recognising and choosing to release any restraining shackles, your house can feel loved and appreciated. Treated with love and respect, your home can be a powerful friend.

Are You in Resonance with Your Home?

Most of us seek a nourishing place to live that we resonate with at a soul level. People often refer to various ways in which they choose to bond with their homes, whether through a love of music, books, art, soft furnishings, gardening, or just an overall feeling of connection. However we perceive our relationship, the identity of a building is influenced and moulded by the land upon which it stands and the character of the locality and country where it resides.

To varying degrees, we identify with the emotions of a space from the aura of a building. Whether it feels light and happy or heavy and oppressive makes it possible to identify the attitude of a property. The message it sends out may be, 'welcome, enter' or 'go away, don't come near me'. People are often aware of strange sensations or odd energies in their spaces, but are unable to rationalise, quantify or express what they feel, let alone know how to deal with them:

> *"…my house feels a lot of sadness, especially in the lounge and our bedroom above. I am left feeling uncomfortable, stirred up and not quite knowing what to do."*

Without the experiential framework or skills to interpret what they are sensing, people often remain vague and will merely say:

> *"Something is just not right, it doesn't feel good."*

When the underlying patterns and stories are unravelled, exposed and illuminated, most people do then recognise what is going on and can relate their current situation as mirroring past circumstances, childhood issues, or perhaps other aspects of their lives.

Several books and films in recent years have inspired us to look at life from a spiritual perspective, helping us to understand that we create and influence our own reality through the choices we make and the focus of our intention. In spite of such tools and tips for self-help, no matter what some people do, things still feel stuck:

> *"I need some help 'clearing' my living space in order to bring more flow into my life. There is a sense of inertia here."*

Whatever a client says, I pay particular attention to the sound of the voice, as this carries knowledge of deeply held ingrained attitudes and beliefs. By tuning-in to the core of their being in order to feel and perceive their energetic blueprint, this helps to identify what needs to be dealt with. In reaching the periphery of human consciousness, gauging emotions and weighing-up issues by making that crucial connection through the eyes, engages and acknowledges a person at a profound level. This can frequently unleash a range of emotions as the journey begins towards resolving issues and traumas, held in the depth of their soul.

As an architect, whether working on a new build, an existing house, a conversion or corporate project, I aim to design in order for people to find a harmonious relationship, peace and sanctuary within their spaces. When a house is fully in balance, the occupants will be in peaceful accord within themselves, in total resonance to their home. To find the heart connection that epitomises a healthy home and nourishes the soul is what I call true architecture. Whilst a house can be tuned to an individual or family, it may not necessarily resonate or create the same degree of comfort or support for your relatives, friends or even future occupants. It is very much about making an individual connection that is unique to your own energy blueprint, and offers the potential for achieving your utmost dreams.

Over the years, I have noticed that when people own rather than rent a property, this gives them a more grounded sense of connection to the earth. We are, of course, only caretakers of the land belonging to Mother Earth. In my experience, when no landlord or other party owns the land that your house is built upon, it allows for a deeper connection with the structure of your home, providing a more secure sense of support. I find this to be more important for a woman, especially if her personal astrology is ruled by the lunar feminine and she is seeking the dynamic of masculine balance in her life.

Lives in turmoil have no rest. If you are not truly feeling at home where you live, then the house is just a building serving your physical needs alone. This Canadian man feels that he has never really lived in any of his homes, and relates this to not being at home in himself, in his own body:

> *"I have owned several houses and have never really lived in any of them because the sense of home was not present. They were all projects in progress, but as I completed them I would sell, usually out of financial necessity. The idea of a 'home' just remains an idea. I notice that I am not at home in myself, in this body, in this world. I often feel like an alien awkwardly trying to fit in."*

Without stillness, how can our 'inner home' find peace? Every part of our material space should ideally reflect and remind us of our connection to the cosmos and to the beauty of the natural world around us. Each aspect of our individuality then has the opportunity to be at peace and at home. The right balance, clarity and energy flow brings full empowerment and support to our lives. The process of maintaining this soul connection is through simply being rather than doing. Thus, any form of accessing the memory of who we truly are and where we come from is of value. Whether in the form of yoga, meditation, contemplation or prayer does not matter. It is our intention to search for unity in our relationships that holds the power to allow us to truly focus on our inner and outer lives.

Many religious and philosophical discourses inform us that unity is ever-present, but we tend to forget to recognise this and can spend our entire lives searching for something that we already have. Our real spiritual work is perhaps to realise the illusion of what we are not, thereby allowing our true nature to shine forth. This is the path that the *House Whispering* process endeavours to follow, to reach and assist with the journey of uncovering and illuminating the often painful and difficult parts we do not wish to see, feel or acknowledge. We are then free to aspire to greater wholeness and fulfilment.

Matching Patterns

Did you choose your house or did it choose you? At another level in this fascinating symbiotic relationship, you may be drawn or led to a house because it sees *you* as the perfect matching partner. It is not so far-fetched to believe that a house has a part to play in choosing its own occupants!

Because our homes carry a flavour of what has happened in the past, we often find matching patterns in the lives of current occupants to those who lived there before, sometimes long ago. This can also show up in the personal relationships we are unconsciously drawn to through resonance. Patterns typically repeat themselves in families, which may even link back to previous lifetimes. How often does a woman marry a man who replicates certain characteristics of her father, or a man find himself with a woman who reminds him of his mother? When analysing an individual's Nine Star Ki (Whisper 7), I find that the energy numbers of a partner frequently match those of their opposite gender parent. A woman may choose a man whose Ki numbers replicate those of her father, whilst the man may relate to a woman with numbers similar to his own mother.

The aim of my work is to identify the relationship between the soul of the house and its current occupants. I will always look at why a person has chosen a particular property in the context of their on-going life story. Finding the underlying reasons why this match has been 'tapped into' holds the key to unlocking and resolving many of the issues that may be creating obstacles in their lives.

When a couple are looking for a house together, it is often the case that only one partner will have a pattern match to the property they choose to share. This match may be to just one or two particular aspects of the many stories that are lodged in the memory of the house. This recognition activates upon first viewing and explains why usually one partner more than the other feels, *"This is it, I could live here."*

What happens after purchasing a property or signing a tenancy agreement is that any other previously hidden stories then come out to play. Until that time, any challenging energies left lingering will remain active only in connection with the seller, the current owner who retains the soul contract with the property until sold.

On many occasions when seeking a house of my own, I have found myself in the right place at the right time, guided by a sense of knowing. I found my present home by being drawn to a certain road in Kingston upon Thames, sensing a house calling me. Within a few weeks of moving in, the original owner from when the house was built in 1939 visited me 'in spirit'. She had worked from the house at a metaphysical level and wanted someone to continue along similar lines. Many potential purchasers seemed to be blocked, but she allowed *me* to buy it, which was indeed a privilege.

The significant thing is that we choose our home or work location through the law of attraction. Just as we may recognise another person as a reflection of ourselves, the same applies with a house. The ancestral history of the house and the land are in most cases relevant to the bigger picture. We arrive at a certain place or property owing to some degree of awareness of a resonance with our own life story. It is as if our soul is guided towards the next step on our journey, revealing aspects that may have remained obscured or deeply buried.

It may feel like there are energies in your home that you perceive as external and unrelated to yourself, although a sense of something familiar will certainly relate at some level to your inner patterns and life stories. Paradoxically, this tends to make it harder to see clearly the psychology at work, especially when those energies may be detrimental or even malicious.

We can explore the idea that the patterns we bring to our present home were formed through our life experiences in previous homes, especially the environment where we lived during our early years. In the nature-nurture debate, we are not just a product of our inherited genetic make-up and conditioning. We will discover that through the imprint of previous activities that have taken place in a building, its unique energy signature influences us too.

Many cultures believe that at some deeper soul level we choose our moment of birth and the parents to whom we incarnate, and thereby play a part in determining our environment and exposure to certain tendencies and life patterns. With this understanding, we can then gain a better idea of why we may be drawn to a home where its ambience, created largely by the history of previous occupants, leads to what is aptly termed 'fatal attraction'. This recognition means we are no longer at the mercy of fate, or lay blame for our own ills on other people, places or circumstances. We may also gain insight into the many interwoven layers that make up our lives. To draw on the past to inform the present but not be restricted by what went before, empowers us to be active participants in co-creating our future.

Should we feel that any patterns manifest through external influences unrelated to our homes, then consider the possibility that the home we have chosen to live in *is* the perfect space, in the right place at that time for whatever needs to unfold - pure karma! Many people end up living in a particular house that totally reveals the karmic patterns that play out the personal blueprint of their lives. Either way, all is for the purpose of recognition and healing.

Listen with an open mind to the hidden messages of your home and be aware of your own subconscious patterns. What may be revealed can help to highlight areas of your life that are not working as well as they might be and would benefit from improvement or change. The key is not to hang onto the past as a template for the projected future, but to discard any outmoded patterns and retain those that continue to nourish – at least for the moment. They too will become outdated as the wheel of life continues to revolve. By identifying and unravelling the matching patterns that run our lives and shape our future, it is possible to learn how people interact with the land and buildings in a fusion of past and present purpose.

Pandora's Box

"The secret of change is to focus all your energy not on fighting the old but, but on building the new." (Socrates)

In taking responsibility for every part of your home, any room that is ignored is a reflection of some aspect of your life that you may be reluctant to look at. There can often be apprehension or fear attached to opening the proverbial Pandora's Box. When we do not address certain issues in life, constantly finding reasons to put off those things we know need dealing with, this will manifest as some kind of externalised expression in the place where we live.

So, if a particular secret is kept secluded in our past, we may find a room in our home that is untidy, cluttered, trashed or even out of bounds, kept locked from the outside world to prevent others from seeing it; perhaps we do not even go in there ourselves. In some instances, entire rooms have been blocked-up, only much later to be discovered as time capsules. Woe betides anyone who should attempt to raise the subject of anything deeply sensitive we may hold in our shadow. As this person explains:

"...and the weird thing is that I am so blocked in dealing with it. I have known for the past ten years that I have to address aspects of the house which are affecting our lives in a negative way, and somehow the house, our life, my inner reality are so intertwined."

By daring to examine any issues kept suppressed in our psyche, the lid comes off and this individuation archetype journey begins. In the Greek mythical story, Pandora was urged not to open the jar (pithos) as it contained all the evils of the world, yet at the bottom lay the magical ingredient, the vital spirit of hope. The opportunity for positive thinking and behaviour can never be taken away from us. To free and release the soul of your home can be of great benefit, as it too can suffer. If we are brave enough to step into the unknown, the process that unfolds may be uncomfortable but is guaranteed to be both challenging and life-changing in a good way.

A lady attending one of my *Journey Home* workshops said that she experienced flooding in all of her homes. The final ruin was sewage filling her ground floor bedroom one night, right up to mattress level. During the guided visualisation, she saw seawater closing in from both sides and remembered for the first time since it happened, the occasion during her early childhood when she attempted to cross a beach to a nearby island at low tide, but the adult with her miscalculated the tides coming in. As this memory programme was still active, she recreated her subconscious fear of drowning and brought this devastating reality into every home where she lived.

These invisible programmes, often buried in subconscious depths, have the creative power to manifest in the physical world, causing similar catastrophes. Once so clearly illuminated, it was possible for this lady to release her inner fear, giving her the opportunity to live wherever she chose without recreating her recurring past pattern.

To shine the light of consciousness on any issue is often enough to dispel or at least loosen it up. We are likely to find that no matter how long we have maintained our strength of belief, its validity can often turn out to have been fear-based or simply an illusion. Whilst there may be nothing further required in terms of inner processing, letting go of a long held conviction can lead to a sense of loss, as if there is some kind of gap. A period of adjustment to a new framework of reality may then be needed.

During *The Journey Home* visualisation, people will often access their inner homes in a very different way than anticipated. With our eyes closed we use different faculties of the mind; the act of engaging with our inner eye helps to detach from familiar patterns of perception, enabling us to view beyond three-dimensional physical reality. A very different picture can emerge of what a person may have thought their home actually entailed, which will be related in some way to their own self-beliefs and filtering systems of the mind.

Certain rooms can turn out to have a significant meaning that we may not even have previously been aware of:

"I can see in my mind that I have a room in my house that doesn't actually exist... there is a dark window in this room..."

This perception points to a part of her that this lady does not wish to address; perhaps she is in denial of a certain aspect of her life, unaware that a certain part of her shadow self even exists. Similarly, this man felt:

"It's a very cold room; it's got this damp problem... I psychologically just think it's not there."

Some people find they cannot even get through their own front door, or instead use the side or back door:

"The house will not let me in through the front door, it does not feel inviting, something is stopping me from going in."

Sometimes they end up coming in through the roof or a window, or somehow just appear in a room. On occasions, they cannot get inside the house at all; it will just not let them in! It is very significant indeed when a house refuses to allow a person to enter his or her own home. I am led to question what aspect of themselves is preventing access to their inner home, to who they truly are, effectively blocking them from finding inner security, peace and tranquillity.

Further exploration usually reveals the cause to be due to some degree of past trauma and sustained fear lodged in the heart. There is also the possibility that an overlay of spirit activity may have its own agenda in trying to prevent a person from entering their house. This paranormal aspect is further considered in Whisper 3.

Do you feel that the house you live in is really yours? To this question, another woman responded by saying she realised for the first time that it was not, and recounted her disturbing visualisation:

"In the living room I saw a big spiral going towards the ground, the floor disappearing and showing me a huge dark well. The doors closed as I was trying to go to the other parts of the house, sometimes not letting me in at all. But the scariest part was when the house suddenly pulled me down, deeper and deeper into the ground."

Only when we begin to recognise what is going on and release the fear and tension that keeps us on hold, can we make informed choices from a place of conscious discernment. We are then in a position to change the less beneficial aspects of patterns that do not serve us. This is especially pertinent in cases of predisposition towards victim or martyr patterning. Unless we take active control, we are likely to become the product of where we live. Victims of our own illusion or delusion perhaps! We only have to think of those who 'against all the odds' of upbringing and environment make a success of their lives. In the universal school of life, in accepting the lessons and challenges of our karma, we may through ignorance and pride pretend not to have problems. To release buried fears from our inner home is a brave move indeed.

We often avoid our darker side, but delving deeper to embrace our shadow can offer immense healing and teach us much more than we might have ever imagined. The question remains, why were you attracted to a property with a certain resonance in the first place?

Inherited Predecessor Energies

We are drawn to certain properties that remind us of something familiar. This feeling of recognition or comfort will match certain aspects of our life, but whether that particular home will necessarily benefit us is another matter. That depends on what aspect of us, or the house, did the initial attracting. Whatever the reason, this resonance will, nevertheless, take us on the next part of our soul's journey.

Every building embraces the patterns of activities and emotions of all those who have occupied that same space. Past happenings, good and bad, happy or sad, will leave an energetic imprint, an ambience absorbed by the walls that lingers in the atmosphere. A house therefore holds memory of both the physical and metaphysical activities that remain in the fabric of the building for others to sense and feel. New people moving into a property will then be affected by these old energy blueprints from the past within a matter of days or weeks. This established 'predecessor energy' holds memory in the form of subliminal messages, informing all those who walk into a space of what happened before they arrived – assuming they choose to listen!

The lingering energies of previous occupants, whether alive or dead, come packaged with the emotional residues of their life issues and challenges, loves and losses, successes and failures, which can seriously affect people living there now:

"I feel there's something going on in my house, it doesn't feel good."

Because this established blueprint is accessed knowingly by consciously 'reading' the space, or unknowingly by the subconscious mind, this means that painful memories, emotions and trauma can influence and impinge on your life. I have encountered many varied instances where human thoughts, behaviours and feelings, the characteristic uniqueness of individual past experience, all show up as a reflection of those currently living in that place now.

If a person's life is not feeling energised or inspired, we need to look at what went on before they moved in. If the previous occupants went bankrupt, this can have the effect of leading them down the same road of diminishing finances. One man's business failed within weeks of moving into a new house, before he discovered that all previous occupants had experienced financial difficulties. Similarly, when a relationship has problems, we rarely consider this could have come about due to the interplay of lives with the old stories of the house. No matter how close a person might be in their relationship with a partner, the quality of any previous relationship dynamic lingering in the air of the new property will undoubtedly affect them.

A couple who moved into the North London home of a jilted, divorced woman had their relationship condemned to failure, and were subsequently drawn into the depths of a divorce. One man's expression after choosing a house with a challenging history:

"I'm not even sure she's hearing me!"

In my experience, just like a person, a house is capable of having multiple personalities. Many soul fragments can accumulate as the house soaks up various characteristics of all those who have lived there and passed through its doors. The stories embedded in our homes are the silent reminders of inherited predecessor energies, the hidden patterns that 'play out' in our spaces just like a video clip replaying in the background, the walls holding the programmes. Thus, the residual memory codes that continue to emanate within a building can influence the way current occupants think, feel and act. This brings with it the danger of life patterns repeating, as the residual memory compels us to re-enact past events, disastrous scenarios that may have nothing to do with you – or do they?

Exploring our own patterns that may need restructuring will open up many forms of enquiry in the search for true 'home'. When you move to a happy house, you will likewise experience great joy emanating from the walls.

Not only do we programme our spaces through our thoughts and actions, we also create further memory packets as predecessor energies for others to inherit. So it is good to be mindful of the nature of our thoughts and feelings, as whatever we send out into the atmosphere will create the vibrational imprint for others to experience in the future. Remember, the walls are listening!

The Ki Signature of Buildings

In the same way as human beings carry a DNA soul imprint for this lifetime, we each have our own energy signature or Ki Signature as I term it. This vibrational code or blueprint, similar to our unique fingerprint pattern, is what defines us. Just as a dog will bark, a duck quack, all differ in the behaviour of their inherent nature, reflective of the individual patterns fashioned by personality and experience.

Each building and surrounding land also has an energy blueprint embedded within it. This is the core software programme that will run during its lifetime, unless reset or erased (Whisper 5). To achieve a sense of truly feeling 'at home', our personal karmic blueprint or energy map should ideally correlate to that of the house and the land on which it stands. This is how our home mirrors who we are and endorses our path to achieving our full potential. The extent to which our Ki Signature is in accord with that of our home will determine the degree to which we are in harmony and influence how we interact with our spaces. Those areas of life on the periphery of consciousness merely cloud our original coding, confusing and scrambling our purpose and life path.

A healthy home or building requires the natural cosmic energies to flow cleanly and unimpeded. If the house and garden are not in accord and singing to the same tune, with nourishing land energies permeating every space, this may indicate blocked or misaligned energies. It is then much harder to find a common reference point for our own energies to merge and synchronise with all areas. For this reason, we find some people spending most of their time outside in the garden, seldom wanting to be indoors, or vice versa.

When a person moves back to the house where they lived as a child, perhaps inheriting the property from parents, they will confront the memory patterns left behind many years ago. All material items such as wallpaper, carpets and furniture are remembrances that may feel like a comfort but can actually be a hindrance. Likewise, some people are content to stay in the same place forever, obliviously unaware that the connection they have with their homes, however healthy or otherwise, is where they choose to embed themselves. They may travel the world, subconsciously trying to discover their true identity, only to return to the same place to find that their soul essence has not moved on. Their lives can then become a merry-go-round as they head off to another seductive place, return to the same life-work pattern, and the ongoing cycle continues. What is missing is the ability for the heart to truly settle and rest, to sit still and face their inner demons; to explore any buried aspects perhaps perceived as somewhat scary. The homes of such individuals are likely to reflect and compound their unrest, thus perpetuating a sense of disconnection for those who may live there in the future.

My goal as *The House Whisperer* is to find the relationship between an individual's soul contract and the soul of their house, to guide them to achieve a harmonious connection within a life-work balance. It may not be enough just to feel you love your home. Listen to the messages it may be sending out, as your home also wants and needs to love and nourish you in return. Again, for this to be possible, what is required is to look openly at the issues that may need facing-up to. Understanding the lessons we can learn from our personal energy blueprint is invaluable to our spiritual progress.

As with any form of personal development, it is the responsibility of the individual to embrace and take steps to bring about resolution in order to move forward. By tuning-in and considering those buried patterns, we have the opportunity to locate the source of when and where any 'damage' might have first occurred. Be open to the possibility that this could be from other lifetimes. Unless the root cause of a problem is consciously addressed, assuming you recognise there is one in the first place, any unhelpful or damaging patterns are likely to remain subconsciously buried or deliberately ignored.

My approach is based primarily on metaphysical principles of energetic transformation. I find this process to be a potent way of achieving deep clearing, transformation and realignment of space, leading to a most successful connection for a person with their home. Resolution is to be found at the deepest level of the zero point matrix, where the knowledge of any intention is held (Whisper 5). This can be likened to a germinating seed that holds the potential of a plant to grow. The point where happenings have become locked into the invisible energy fields, and importantly from where they can be released, is replicated at the heart centre of the home. It is from here that I will connect with the consciousness of a building.

In acknowledging that a building has consciousness and a heart, my aim is to identify events or aspects of a person's life that correlate with the underlying story and character of their home. To understand the complexity of what is happening, the background of the house and locality will help illuminate the bigger picture. Just as a psychotherapist endeavours to assist in bringing clarity of awareness, I aim to facilitate recognition of what is going on in the deeper realms. To empower a person gives them the opportunity to take responsibility for any significant life changes they may then choose to make.

Many factors influence the quality of the spaces in our buildings, both internally and externally. When we can connect with and read all these aspects that operate on many complex levels, our buildings will respond and truly speak to us. There is much to be gained by encouraging our homes to respond with nurturing arms, to open our eyes so that we may see how our own personal journey correlates with all those who have chosen to live there before.

For self-empowerment and full connection to where you live, I frequently use a visualisation to bring the breath and heartbeat into resonance with that of the house. Merging the common harmonics, wavelengths and frequencies gives the potential for total synchronisation of a person in relationship to their home (Whisper 5). Making this personal connection at a heart level allows your home to serve and support you beyond being a functional roof over your head. This is the crucial difference between a house providing for your physical needs alone and a home that fully nurtures you emotionally and spiritually. This heart merging makes it possible to experience a true sense of harmony. The typical response that follows is usually, *"Ah, I feel at home."* Any further traditional Feng Shui cures and enhancements, together with other chosen therapies and treatments, then have a greater chance of being much more effective.

How Does a House Hold Memory?

"Fundamental to the amazing chemical and physical properties of water, its unique hydrogen/oxygen electromagnetic energy bonds enable a high level of information to be imprinted at a molecular level." (Dr Jude Currivan)

Much contemporary research exists around the concept that memory imprints of events are stored in the molecular structure of the natural mineral world. This is the fundamental premise of practices such as homoeopathy. Experiments of exposing water crystals to human emotions show that sending out loving intent allows the crystalline molecules to resonate to their innate pure hexagram geometry and form beautiful harmonic patterns. Conversely, negative emotion will distort the geometry and create a fragmented chaotic arrangement.

Human beings are largely composed of water, which has unique properties to retain and transmit information. Our minds register and link-up life events and translate experiences as emotive memories; interaction with people and their emotions is inseparable. So how *does* a house hold memory in its walls? All building materials contain some degree of water, or would otherwise turn to dust. Thus, the moisture content in physical materials and the surrounding land retain a degree of memory. Embedded and encoded in the walls, and in artefacts and furniture for that matter (Whisper 3), are memories of human experiences and emotions that when activated are able to replay in our spaces. Everything can influence and shape our lives without us necessarily realising it.

What about memory in the air that we breathe, the space itself? Water molecules are accountable for varying degrees of humidity, so one could say that the higher the level of humidity, the stronger is the memory potential. But what if a strong gust of wind blows through the house and clears the air – does memory in that space disappear? Not totally, only what is going on there and then at surface level is likely to clear from the atmosphere. There is, nevertheless, a deeper level of imprint. The invisible matrix of space may be likened to the memory in a computer or information on a hard drive, whereby anything recorded and saved can be retrieved and replayed. Unlike a computer where information stored can be erased, within the etheric matrix it is generally not possible to delete or wipe out what has already been imprinted. However, with a paradigm shift in consciousness, it is possible to access and transform this information.

As the life stories in this book demonstrate, when an established event takes place or different people move into a property, the emotive memories of human activities affect the nature and feeling of a building. These memories become firmly embedded as a blueprint in the etheric matrix of third and fourth-dimensional space. Just as we can see the molecular structure of cells through a microscope, exhibiting interconnecting geometric shapes, this is how I see etheric space in my mind's eye. Imagine a cube with transparent lines forming a lattice frame. At each corner junction are node points holding the harmonic codes. Like computer software, these vibrational codes have an ability to be programmed or shaped by an emotion, thought or action, and hold memory of all that is left lingering from previous occupants of our homes. Whilst memory retains information that will impact on us, what really matters is our response to the emotion it triggers as a consequence. Are we interpreting life in actuality now, or allowing past actions lingering in the memory fields to influence experiences that are not necessarily a part of our own reality?

All information, including activities, memories and dreams, are imprinted and held in what ancient texts refer to as the Akashic Records. Akasha in Sanskrit means 'space' or 'ether'. Contained within the invisible yet audible structure of the etheric matrix is all knowledge, the beginning and end points: alpha and omega. We perceive the essence of Akasha by listening to the silence within the stillness. The codes held within the seed points are the harmonic keys. As we shall see in more detail, the harmonic codes are activated through the intention of the mind to bring an object or desired action into manifestation. These human thoughts and intentions are propelled forwards through sound and vibration. Whilst we all have the ability to think and share the same universal language, it is within the Akashic field that the sound vibration of thought becomes translated into the language of our native tongue.

In the circle of nine points of the Vedic teachings, Akasha is located at number five, midway between the inner world of universal Self and mind, and the outer worlds of the four elements: air, fire, water and earth. The library of knowledge contains information of everything that has ever been: of *all* events, activities and emotions, not just with people and buildings but also of entire communities, cities, countries and the world. We can all use our innate capacity to tune into these records, depending on the degree of honing our inner vision in order to achieve good and clear perception. For the most part, we do this naturally without even realising it. We are all listening to each other's unspoken natural language at some deeper level. To truly listen in the present moment to the silence within a space offers the potential to harness what is commonly termed telepathy as a normal mode of communication.

Over the years, with sensitivity to metaphysical realities, I have developed techniques that allow me to access any knowledge needed in any given situation. There is no standard formula: simply to be in the present moment, the 'now', means dispensing with all peripheral thoughts and sensations, to simply focus and 'just be'.

This connection to Source gives access to whatever is needed for the next moment to unfold. There is no need to store vast volumes of information in our minds, but just use the ability to tap into and read what is already written in the book of universal knowledge. Choosing to tune in and direct the mind and heart to whatever you wish to see and hear will allow precise knowledge of an event within any particular timeframe to reveal itself. An unfocused mind can be assailed with the entire bandwidth of history, thus scrambling the information needed for whatever is being sought.

Whisper 2

RELATIONSHIPS AND LIFE ISSUES

Behind every front door is a story of people's lives

Home Affecting Intimate Relationships

If you are unhappy with the circumstances of your life, your home could be a contributory factor. Whilst not always the cause, a house has immense power in influencing our wellbeing and relationships. The clarity of our home spaces will allow us to embrace a healthier emotional connection within ourselves as well as with others.

Our interaction with our homes can be seen as analogous to a relationship with a personal partner; we can feel close and intimate or isolated and even estranged. In the dynamic of a couple living to-gether, if either or both individuals are out of alignment with their house, it can feel as if the house itself is another person in the rela-tionship. This will then interfere with their intimacy with each other, and at worst lead to disassociation to the extent that they do not recognise the person they live with, or even know who they truly are themselves. On more than one occasion, a partner has been told:

> *"You have changed since we moved into this house; I don't recognise you as the person I knew from before."*

This not uncommon situation of an entangled relationship triangle directly impacts on the quality of the lives of all who live there, both now and in the future.

The power of the natural world revolves around the free-flowing cycle of energy exchange. This is why the art of giving and receiving are both vital factors in the success of all aspects of life. To give too much in compensation for an emotional expectation or trade-off is equally as unbalanced as the inability to receive or seek help from others when needed.

Another biscuit? Conversation over a cup of tea is a good way to listen and gain a general picture of a person's life story in relation to their house. On one occasion, whilst sitting in the home of a woman in Surrey, she recounted in detail about her life and marital relationship. She told me that it was not until about twenty years into their marriage she discovered her husband was gay, *"...another biscuit?"* she interjects, passing the plate. This being one of my early *House Whispering* consultations, I was not quite sure how to respond or even if she was at all concerned and wanted resolution on the matter, so I took another biscuit!

This house is a metaphor of our relationship This was the expression of one man whose home reflected the push-pull dynamic of the couple's lives, mirrored in the uncomfortable, subtle energies in some of the bedrooms. Communication of the most basic kind needed in sharing a space together did not exist. Their personal rapport was externalised both in the house and in separate disjointed decisions about many aspects of family life. Although I was able to clear the space and align the house to its highest potential (Whisper 5), it remained for the couple to look at their inner patterns that required change and resolution.

Polarised lives In a south of England coastal town, this couple led separate lives, spending most of their time at opposite ends of the house. The atmosphere in the husband's den room was very heavy and dense, which was not helping matters. He was carrying some quite unpleasant energies and she had become dependent on a lady friend in the spirit world for company and protection from him. Having dealt with his menacing influences, it was time for the woman in spirit to be released from the wife. This was quite an emotional letting go, yet she knew it was necessary and agreed for me to assist in the release process. The couple were then left in a better position to face-up to and work through their relationship without the self-imposed barriers of co-dependency on otherworldly beings.

Releasing a relationship Once her house was space-cleared and aligned to who she truly was, this woman in Wales realised that her partner was hindering her life vision and not providing the support she felt that she needed:

"I feel like my flame is going out."

Her partner was taking over and dishonouring both her home and personal space, with no respect for her privacy or overall wellbeing. It took much courage on her part to persuade *him* to 'go out', but afterwards her feeling of moving forwards with life was wonderful.

Relationships Between Children and Parents

The energy of a newborn child is one of delicate vulnerability, its need to be nurtured usually bringing out our natural instincts. When we look into the eyes of a baby or young child, we see many qualities reflected, including the features of the parents and sometimes grandparents. Some children look simply innocent and cute, while others appear to have come into this world with a wealth of knowledge and experience; they imbue the wisdom of the ancestors at the deepest level, perhaps from another dimension. Have they been here before is the question? If so, what is the relationship to their parents, land and country of birth, even to the house in which they are born?

Part of my work in rebalancing the home is also to help children to feel safe and secure. Balanced emotional development allows fulfilment of learning potential. When blocked at an early age, perhaps through a missing factor such as an absent parent or fear due to unwanted spirit residents, this will discourage confidence and hinder the expression of inner vision and perceived reality.

The connection that we have with others in a close relationship clearly goes far beyond physical characteristics carried by the DNA alone. Emotional bonds are inextricably linked in time and space through the Akashic memory field that connects consciousness of all happenings. Those to whom we are bonded sense our thoughts and feelings, each responding according to their own level of awareness and degree of emotional attachment.

Cutting ties Emotional connections with family members or a previous intimate partner can activate at various times in our lives, especially if a particular event ignites the memory link. Unfinished business with others equates to ties that 'hook in' to our personal energy fields and can often manifest as an illness or discomfort in a certain part of our physical body. Such emotional scenarios, experienced as a controlling influence, are often initiated by the most dependent person in the relationship, albeit subconsciously. What is being highlighted is the opportunity to look at and deal with their own deeper issues, or perhaps even choose to ignore them, while at the same time allowing the recipient to explore the underlying lesson. There is always something of value to be learnt, but it is then best if unhealthy ties are broken so that all can get on with their lives.

The important thing with attempting to cut anything or anyone from your life is that unresolved issues will find another way to come back at you. This concept has parallels to space-clearing a property: unless the ongoing story embedded in the house is addressed, it will find another way of expressing itself. When endeavouring to cut ties with another person, they may not necessarily be aware that you have distanced yourself, although something intangible will have alerted them at a subconscious level. This may then ignite their memory to send out an intention to reconnect and cord back into you. People ultimately have free will and if it is not possible to reconcile matters, despite your own willingness to attempt to do so, then the only recourse may be to consider personal protection of your auric field. Shielding techniques are especially helpful if negative energies projected by others are harming your life (Whisper 7). If it is possible to resolve the issues that caused the problem in the first place, which may in itself present challenges along the way, the cords will dissolve naturally of their own accord.

Whilst we cannot change what has happened in the past, we can change our emotional response and reaction to the memory of that experience. Forgiveness of oneself is part of the process of forgiving another and involves far more than simply being a reasoned mental construct with a repetition of words such as 'I forgive you.' Whatever approach we take, whether through an internal restructuring of our thoughts or ceremonies such as the Hawaiian *Ho'oponopono*, a true sense of lasting forgiveness comes from within our heart. To honour an experience without holding onto the emotion entailed can bring us to resolution and a sense of peace within ourselves.

Relationship with mother   One woman distressingly told me:

"I feel like I am becoming like my mother, behaving with all her mannerisms and it frightens me."

Another lady had a deep underlying and unresolved issue in her relationship with her mother. As we began to go through the process of clearing stagnant energies and realigning the space in her London flat, it felt natural for her to cut what she felt were unhealthy cords. Within minutes of attempting to do this, her mother telephoned from abroad to see how she was. This clearly indicated a strong link between them, confirming that resolution of certain matters was most definitely needed.

Mother in spirit sets chair alight   After walking around one particular house with incense during a space-clearing process, I left the burner safely smoking on the dressing table in the rather dense master bedroom which was in need of a good energy blast, then went downstairs. Whilst the owner was telling me with angry undertones how she hated her mother who had passed away some years earlier, I suddenly began to smell burning and rushed upstairs. The charcoal in the burner had somehow jumped out onto the chair next to the dressing table, setting it alight. The owner gasped in astonishment:

"That was my mother's favourite chair."

The mother had certainly made her presence felt and her attitude towards her daughter known!

Child's perception of home   There is no better example of how children perceive their lives and homes than through their paintings. Every brushstroke is a visual expression of their inner language as they interpret the world around them.

At a consultation in Portugal, a six year-old child loved her house. She painted the sun in the sky and flowers on the green grass, but the upstairs windows were black, indicating that perhaps something was worrying her. She was a bright, happy child, but her father was not living with them and she yearned to relate to masculine energy.

Keen to join me in the task of space-clearing and realigning the energies of the house, she took hold of the dowsing rods and showed incredible sensitivity and accuracy as we walked around the rooms, her rods responding similarly to mine. The house was experiencing many difficulties, including builders having trouble in completing various renovations, several mechanical and electrical breakdowns, also some very bad egg smells, all of which are typical of paranormal activity that was affecting their health. On the darker side of the girl's awareness was her grandfather dying in a fire up on the first floor of their home. He chose to remain in the house in spirit through his love for the family, wanting to protect and keep them safe from the threatening malevolent energies that were still active when I arrived, and had contributed to his death.

Procreation Influenced by Environment

A child is born of spirit. The balance and weave of male and female energies is crucial when seeking to bring a new life into being. The structure of a house can be seen as the masculine-holding framework, containing and protecting the feminine inner sanctuary or womb-space (Whisper 7). These sacred spaces also need to be protected and nourished, so getting the quality of the external structure and internal space to the highest purity and alignment with life's purpose allows the best chance of successful conception. When all are healthy and in balance, procreative energies have a better opportunity to flourish.

The procreative factor is generated from the same energy vortex spin or chakra point in the human body as the creative impulse. Whether expressed through having a baby or applied to worldly creative projects for recreation or business purposes, the success of any new venture requires a unified heart connection. An optimum free-flow of natural energy will vitalise creativity. Conversely, when blocked through emotional issues, relationship problems or clutter in our home spaces, life can feel like we are pushing a reluctant mule uphill, or simply going round in circles like a hamster on a wheel.

On a metaphysical level, the soul is said to incarnate in the etheric realms at the moment of conception or at around the twelve-week stage of foetal development. It is unusual in the West to adopt the cultural view that successful conception depends on the soul of a child choosing to come into the world through particular parents or even deciding to be born at all, which may account for some parents' painful experience of a stillborn baby. It may also be that an adult needs to go through the experience of learning to love and lose in order to further his or her own understanding and experience.

Despite the perceived reasons often given for a woman wanting a baby, if the relationship between a couple is not close then there is little chance of igniting the fire, the magic spark for a new soul to emerge. When conception is proving difficult, a couple's sex life can tend to revolve around ovulation and temperature charts, inhibiting the spontaneity of passion in the relationship. The issue of IVF can dominate some couple's lives and finances, bringing up all kinds of energetic and ethical dilemmas.

There is of course the biological drive for a woman to give birth, but many overlays can create confusion in the energy fields. It is well documented how the effects of geopathic and electromagnetic stress deplete our immune systems (Whisper 6). Many opportunities for conception are lost owing to geopathic stress in the underlying land and the influence of unbalanced or negative energies in the home, adding to the general stresses of life. Equally, the quality of life force that a person is able to absorb and sustain will be severely depleted if unhappy past events or paranormal energies are still lingering. When a house has a history of no children, successful conception may be difficult owing to the memory imprint of the house holding that pattern. Any inherent programme running at a subconscious level can interfere with the female/male union, the vital yin/yang of creation and alchemical fusion needed for conception.

In my experience, when a pregnant woman spends time in dense, heavy atmospheres or encounters paranormal activity, this will affect her general health and is unfavourable for the developing foetus. Underground spaces and basement areas with diminished flows of chi, poor quality light and air, are especially prone to heavy, treacle-type atmospheres. Whilst being mindful of the quality of energy in our own bedrooms, we also need to be aware of detrimental energies prevalent in hotel and guest rooms where many other people have slept. A couple wishing to conceive or a woman in the early stages of pregnancy should therefore take great care in their choice of living and sleeping environments. Essentially, any space can affect you for good or bad; the build-up of people's issues, attitudes and emotional baggage can accumulate just about anywhere.

Misaligned energies in the home or workplace are a common cause of the cry, *"I just can't get pregnant."* Once detrimental issues are identified, the situation can be addressed to allow the best propensity for conception to happen. There is always a solution. Where it is not possible to alter your physical working environment as decisions for change are controlled by others, to become pregnant or prevent miscarriage the only option may be to change jobs or location.

In working with couples having difficulty conceiving, their homes will often reveal the reasons why this has not occurred. The important thing here is that the house, a reflection of a person's inner state of mind, will mirror their attitudes and beliefs concerning children. A home that is unhygienic, disordered or impractical to raise a child, such as living with family members with no space of one's own, may not be conducive to conception. In contrast, an environment that is almost too clean, sterile or sparse can be unfavourable for nurturing a new life. The five elements of water, wood, fire, earth and metal, all play a part in procreation at physical and subtle levels: fire is the vital ingredient that ignites passion, necessary to bring into being a new soul born of water.

Homes that are clear of energetic debris allow the sacred space to come into alignment with the same healthy vibration as the fractal resonance of nature. This natural geometrical expression relates to the vibration of the heart and the golden mean ratio, which gives and sustains life in pure nourishing harmony (Whisper 7). Both the health of the man holding the seed and the woman carrying the egg to be fertilised are vital for successful conception. Maintaining a good, solid energy-holding spatial framework to nurture a developing baby in the mother's womb, the child's first 'house', is crucial.

Getting the external environment ready is indeed relevant. The key, however, is to resolve any personal issues that might inhibit the coming of a child. Aspects of *House Whispering* can enhance your home and work environments to maximise the full potential for fertility and conception, and to nourish yourselves both now and in the future.

Actively fertile land energies Where you live and work has an impact on your sex life. The degree of raw energy generated at a core earthy level has influence on a person's base chakra and will enhance or diminish libido accordingly. In some regions, fertile earth energies in the land have a potent aphrodisiac effect. They activate our physical and energetic bodies, waking up the vital organs to engage in sexual activity and maximise the chances of getting pregnant. One such place is Cerne Abbas in Dorset, where the chalk hill figure of the Cerne Giant is reputed to help women to conceive.

Fertile land energies will soak up through and imprint buildings, making them libido charged houses or workplaces. In one commercial building, when I became aware of the strength of earth energy in a particular spot in one of the offices, I was told:

"Every girl who works in this area of the office always becomes pregnant!"

Supermarket pregnancies There are several documented cases concerning different British supermarkets, where many of the girls working in particular stores have fallen pregnant within weeks of sitting at certain cashier aisles. In one instance, the management decided to remove the culprit chair after the 13th girl fell pregnant! Dowsing would have indicated high levels of fertile earth energies.

Fertile house I advised a young female celebrity searching for a new home in London that she was likely to get pregnant if she moved into the house we were viewing, because it carried a very high fertile energy. As she did not want children at that time, she declined to buy that house. What had attracted her was the opportunity for a creative space to enhance her singing career, creativity coming from the same chakra region of the physical body as procreation. A gynaecologist had told the woman selling the house that she was unable to conceive owing to fertility problems, yet soon after moving in she miraculously fell pregnant. Exploring its Feng Shui aspects, I noticed that a small extension housing the central heating boiler had been built in the compass sector relating to procreation and children. Any projection from a building will enhance and intensify the energy of that life sector; the fire element of the boiler further activated the procreative impulse, creating a potent house of high fertility

Sterile home environment Approaching a house in Middlesex, built in the grounds of a former country estate, faint *whispers* of children playing could be heard, voices from another world. The young couple living there already had a history of miscarriage, yet their house was so sterile that it felt as if nothing would choose to grow or survive. The dining room, representing nourishment for a family, was particularly devoid of human warmth. Perhaps a child wanted to arrive but was waiting for a more nourishing and supportive environment. In the nursery, the cot was positioned under the wardrobe top-box, a 'cutting chi' damaging energy for an adult, let alone a baby. In the kitchen, only one of four rings on the hob was working and the oven did not work at all, no bun-in-the-oven!

The house was duly space-cleared of unsupportive energies and aligned to their personal energy blueprint, with nourishing procreative energies activated. Once their reasons for wanting a child were addressed at a deep subconscious level, they both reached a sense of peace over their concerns about having a family. Within one month of working with this couple, the rekindled fire element had reawakened the passion in their lives. The woman was delighted to become pregnant and went on to deliver a healthy baby.

Baby clutter inhibits conception A woman wanting to get pregnant had a nursery set up in readiness for a baby. Ironically, her baby clutter was blocking the procreative impetus, with the cot stuffed full of bags of new and second-hand baby clothes. In subconsciously 'numbing out' to the truth of her dysfunctional marriage, she was unknowingly impeding conception. Following the consultation visit, her husband was pleased to report:

"My wife cleaned her mess in the baby room. The bags have been organised and she just needs to discard unwanted things and put the rest away. So it definitely feels like a new dawn, with things feeling fresh and different."

In the old tradition, which some would consider old wives' tales or superstition, a nursery would not be set up until a baby was on the way. It was deemed very unlucky to bring the pram into the house. In the days when families lived in close proximity in the same village or town, it would remain at the home of the expectant mother's parents or a close relation until the baby was safely delivered. Today, some baby supply stores provide a holding service.

Hoarding illuminates dilemma   The night before my visit, a lady dreamt that she was pregnant and giving birth. My feeling was that she was in a dilemma over whether to create in terms of career or to procreate a child. Moreover, she was being held back by the considerable amount of clutter piled-up in her flat. With her willingness, it was possible to help her to recognise the unconscious issues that had created the mess in the first place. Deep soul searching is needed in such common circumstances, where a person's 'stuff' represents the restrictive aspects of life that need acknowledging before they can begin to be addressed. With clarity and resolution, the chosen creative path can then flow naturally and smoothly.

Tension and miscarriage   This lady had lost her baby son during pregnancy and his spirit remained around them in their apartment. On the mantelpiece, which in Feng Shui often symbolically represents one's future vision of life, were two stuffed foxes facing away from each other with a gruesome looking mask in between. Images of separation are not the most propitious symbol of a close and harmonious relationship. When I pointed out that this did not bode well, irrespective of how much they may try for a baby, they realised the significance and replaced the objects with a statue of a couple with the mother holding a child in her arms. My sense was that the clarity of reconnection with their son in spirit was sufficient to bring their emotions of deep loss to some degree of resolution, perhaps without the same intensity of yearning for a possible replacement child.

Safe space for a child's cot   Having brought a life into this world, nurturing a baby in a safe space is of paramount importance. Many people do not realise that not only the choice of room, but the position and orientation of the cot also needs to be taken into account.

Placed in unpropitious areas or danger zones can cause a baby's fragile body to take a greater hit from misaligned or geopathic energies, which can result in illness and even cot death.

At a house in London, a child spent most of his time in three different 'negative' areas: the cot in his bedroom, and play areas in the living room and garden. His recently married parents felt they needed to have a child, but I questioned whether they really wanted the child at all. The location of these unfavourable zones indicated that perhaps at one level they did not. Although they loved their son, in a strange way and by no means deliberately, they put him in harms way.

Loss of a child in a past life   This lady attending one of my workshops recalled a past life in which she had lost a child, and felt she could never love again as the pain was too much. *"To love is to lose"* was her mantra. She could not even bring herself to love her pet cat. By recognising the core of her loss, revisiting her painful past experience and doing some deep inner work, she began slowly and gently to release this fearful pattern and began to love again.

Do you really want a child?   I will often ask this question of someone who appears to be desperate to have a baby. Exploring the fundamental motivation that is driving them can often bring up aspects of their lives which illuminate their longing may be for the 'wrong' reasons. Sometimes a couple may feel that trying for a baby is the next expected step. One couple both believed they wanted a child until delving deeper revealed the reason why she could not get pregnant. They only really wanted a son to continue in the family business; neither of them truly wanted a child for the child's sake.

Do you want a child with your current partner?   In heterosexual relationships it can sometimes be the case that although a woman may yearn for a baby, she is holding back at a deep emotional level. Some women are reluctant to procreate with their current partner for reasons they don't wish to admit or keep subconsciously buried. Perhaps she does not trust that he is the man she wants to take care of her child. She may not feel she is in the 'right' relationship, that it may not last, or she does not want to become a single parent.

One couple supposedly wanting a baby were making all the right noises superficially. On delving deeper, it turned out that the woman did not really want to be with her husband at all and was constantly having affairs with other men. During the consultation, I could hear her thinking:

"I can't wait to leave this marriage."

It also happens that personal habits can put some women off becoming pregnant, especially if she discovers that her partner is an addict, alcoholic, gay or transsexual. When a woman has experienced the trauma of rape or non-consensual sex, this too can affect her attitude towards pregnancy. Patterns may also emerge reminiscent of an unhappy relationship with her father or some other unwelcome trait of an ex-partner. Some couples are just not meant to have a child together for reasons of genetics, karma or simply chemistry. In other instances, couples come together primarily for the purpose of pro-creation but later separate; perhaps realising they married for the 'wrong' reasons and then divorce. People are often surprised at what comes out of the closet once *The House Whisperer* is engaged.

Exploring the Workplace and Business

In the world of business, I look at matters ranging from why an individual or company may be suffering or heading towards bankruptcy, to enhancing the workplace for a thriving business wishing to achieve even greater success. My approach relating to the all-important heart connection with our homes applies equally to the workplace, with some specific added parameters. When a business requests my guidance, I often recommend working with the key people in their homes to ensure that their living and working environments are brought into alignment.

Whether self-employed, working from home, or for a company at their premises, we will all at some time or another encounter situations where sharing space can present challenges. In our interactions with colleagues we need to find a common ground, a mutual reference point. This may mean trying to adjust our own resonance to that of another person or space to find a place from where we can communicate and work together effectively, perhaps as part of a team. People are our most valuable commodity, so it is essential that they should be healthy and happy, with optimum energy levels. A holistic approach can only be beneficial for harmony with our fellow beings.

All aspects of our lives, particularly those connected to our work or job in the outer world, relate to the energy of our homes. If we are not achieving our goals, we need to find the reasons that are holding us back. When a problem manifests in the workplace, it can often be traced back to something not quite right at home – a mirror image of personal patterns and aspirations. On a bigger scale, if we do not take up the reins and come into true alignment with our life purpose, we can find that any imbalance not only creates stress within our bodies and disharmony in our homes, but also gives rise to challenges or even disaster in our working lives.

The success matrix One of the most important areas to examine is the energetic structure of the success matrix. This can make or break a business, from a sole trader to a corporate company. Many people attending my workshops find benefit from adapting their management style to consider the energy matrix:

"I've just realised that the session we had might have been a major catalyst in the shift with my business."

It is possible to re-evaluate negotiations, presentations or meetings within certain parameters to change an undesirable outcome. By re-programming the energy matrix, we can achieve a different result. This quantum shift created beyond space-time is very powerful and needs to be handled with great care. The focus of intention should always be for the highest good rather than imposing our own will to the detriment of others, as energy has a way of rebounding.

Rebalancing the office For the benefit of any workplace and for those who work there, it is important to ensure optimum business efficiency by keeping the premises both physically and energetically clear and harmonised. After clearing and rebalancing the workspace of an American real estate client, she was delighted to report:

"The energy clearing in my basement office continues to produce improved results... the most active I've been all year."

Clarity of purpose Rather like a natural stream that needs to flow unobstructed to reach its final destination, it is crucial for the energy flow of our personal and working lives to run smoothly and efficiently, otherwise obstacles can impede our main goal. As with honouring the land and asking what it needs (Whisper 6), we should consider doing the same in the workplace and then align our intentions for that purpose. In commercial proposals or when making a bid, the need for our inner thoughts to match our outer expression can make or break a deal.

The office of a self-employed man, working from home in Greater London, was very cluttered with a heavy atmosphere that hampered clarity of purpose. As our external environment is simply an outer projection of our inner reality, copious wall images conveyed mixed messages and an uncertain sense of direction. My recommendation was to remove all of the pictures and replace them with just one power image. This would help eliminate confusion and focus clear intention on what the business was all about.

The desk position should also be considered in accordance with Feng Shui Landscape Form School principles (Whisper 7). His desk up against the wall created a block in future vision. Having his back to the door was symbolic of turning away business opportunities, which people are inclined to do when in sabotage mode. By taking my advice and deciding to turn the desk around, his actions reflected an inner intention to move into a more amenable, positive frame of mind. After my visit, he was delighted to report that making changes and a new attitude resulted in a long awaited surge in business:

"The whole of the next day was spent cleaning and rearranging the house. My office has been de-cluttered and rearranged as you suggested. I will be ordering the wall print for the office, buying a mirror and a chair that will be a throne fit for a king! Already just sitting here I feel the energy is different. I feel lighter and free, less inhibited, and can see out as I don't have my back to everything. The following day, I confirmed substantial business and the next day a sum a little higher. Then as soon as I took down the images and

cleared the power wall, two other jobs were confirmed within days. I don't know if it's a coincidence or something has shifted – either way, I am happy!"

Communication breakdown The main problem affecting the success of a company in Germany was the inability of the two key people to communicate together effectively. It transpired that both had throat cancer. Their weakened throat areas were absorbing the workplace stress, creating a self-perpetuating cycle. After clearing the accumulative stagnant energies from the thick atmosphere in the offices, I then worked with them to illuminate the issues that were holding each other back from speaking their truth. This brought clarity, opening-up a better way of dealing with matters needing resolution and gave an opportunity for improvement in their health.

Past life fears One lady in Dorset was struggling to get her business out into the world; whatever she did, her efforts remained unseen. Further exploration uncovered a previous lifetime when she and her sister lived in the same locality making natural herbal remedies. This was at a time when the 'authorities' viewed the deep wisdom of herbalists and healers with caution and tried to discredit their abilities as superstition and old wives' tales. At worst, they were hunted out as witches. As the sisters resisted, they were accused of fraud and charges were made against them.

This deep psychological memory was the reason for her expression of mixed messages in her current business and explained why she felt persecuted by men in authority, threatened by her knowledge and power. To remain unseen meant she was safe, but her hesitancy to become visible made her very unproductive. Having returned to the same location in this lifetime, resolution was only possible by bringing these past patterns to light. Once she had experienced the Aha moment allowing the possibility of transformation, she was able to release her past trauma connected to the area. As a result, her now flourishing business could expand out into the world, with no further fear or retribution.

Blocked front doors impede careers The front door of a house in Essex had been removed and the opening walled-in, with the path from the road grassed over. This made it appear rather odd and sad. The couple accessed the house through a side door, thereby changing the compass orientation of the original main entrance, which inadvertently dishonoured the spirit of the house. In Feng Shui, the front door is the mouth of chi that draws either nourishing or detrimental energy into the house from the outside; the path leading up to it represents the flow of life's journey, in worldly terms denoting career and business opportunities. With no footpath and a blocked off main door, the couple were experiencing diminished business success and lack of prosperity. After heeding my advice to reinstate and use the original front door, their lives changed for the better.

At a home on the south coast, another couple chose to use the side door and entered the house through the kitchen. Their front door was blocked from inside by a rats' cage, an old television set and other family debris. A large motor home, regularly parked on the drive directly outside the main door, blocked the natural chi flow into the house as well as their personal energy potential. Consequently, career opportunities were not good for either of them.

Arriving at the house of a couple in Surrey, there was no reply when I knocked on the front door. Appearing from down a side path, the client told me they had sealed the front door from the inside because it was too close to the road. One of the main issues I was to address was lack of trade in his building company. When I pointed out the significance of the front door in relation to career and business, he immediately decided to unblock the door and use it. After checking back with him some weeks later, he told me that he had blocked up the door again as too much business was coming in! So I prudently suggested he dealt with the increased workload by taking on more staff rather than once more blocking his front door.

Importance of a successful location On my visits to business premises, it is often very clear to me which companies will be successful as opposed to those who are likely to struggle. There is often no rational explanation for this, other than a purely intuitive sense of the combined effects of location, earth geomancy, predecessor imprints, and the personal energies of owners and staff.

We often find that certain businesses change hands on a regular basis; after an initial surge of interest, customers seem not to return.

Any new venture opening in refurbished premises which previously met with repetitive patterns of illness, trauma or bankruptcy, are likely to experience a similar scenario.

At each end of a shopping parade in Putney, London, is a restaurant. The one on the far right serves great food and has a thriving business, whereas that on the far left constantly fails and changes hands. Just as a house can be reprogrammed for optimum function, a business can be space-cleared of historical imprint. To remedy an old failure pattern will neutralise any damaging potential and give the best opportunity for success (Whisper 5).

Harnessing positive earth energies   Other factors that influence the essential dynamic of a business include the natural earth chi of the underlying land that charges-up or depletes the energy of the space accordingly. In one a particular office building, the main client meeting room was located on a powerful earth vortex that harnessed positive energies (Whisper 6). It was found to be a good place to finalise financial deals, which always had a positive outcome.

In contrast, a British business was suffering owing to negative earth energies affecting the building in which all other previous ventures had failed. Although the main problem with the underlying land was resolved, the owner took my advice to relocate to a more auspicious building nearby. He was delighted to report:

"We have secured the supermarket business that we targeted which is great for us and are talking with other potential customers which is very positive indeed. We are moving to the office unit that you recommended, and even this fell into place as it was not actually available when we spoke. I also had a very positive meeting with the financial authorities and it could not have gone any better considering where I was with them before! Such simple but powerful changes that you advised have resulted in the most dramatic shift!"

Sharing a building   Where more than one business shares the same premises, energy work on the entire building can be undertaken to give each a sense of identity as well as 'zero out' any past events having a detrimental effect. A commercial company in London, located over two floors, was lacking a sense of unification and awareness of each other, so what was needed was to break down the barriers of separation and energetically merge them. Programming crystals with the intention of togetherness was most effective in giving each area harmonious connection. Despite being on separate floors, the company became united both in the unseen world of intention held within the space and through the employees renewed sense of awareness of their colleagues. The crystals were left as a gift, the people thereby holding in their own hands the vibration of connection and success.

Hotels The communal nature of hotels, where many people pass through and sleep in the same beds, accumulate many thoughts, feelings and emotions. These linger in the atmosphere, soak into the walls, fabrics and soft furnishings, the mattresses especially, and can then latch-on and affect the next person sleeping there. As this intensity compounds over time, the rooms themselves would benefit from routine space-clearing and an energy recharge. Hotels where I have consulted on this basis have gained both a feeling of wellbeing and an increase in room occupancy ratio, excellent for business.

Airports Airport environments have a most interesting mix of socially concentrated energies in one location, with the need for diverse requirements within different spaces. Having had the privilege of designing numerous interior schemes for most UK airports in the 1980s, the principles that apply are very different from homes, offices, hotels and other commercial premises.

Some spaces such as rest areas need to hold stillness, whilst others are very active. Shopping areas need alertness to encourage people to buy, whereas cafés, bars and restaurants entice you to sit or perch with a degree of comfort, but prohibit truly settling in. When I was involved in these kinds of briefs, I always erred on the side of subliminal suggestion rather than overt manipulation, as I questioned the integrity of being asked to influence the traveller in this way.

Getting to the flight gate requires a design that activates chi flow in order to get people to move faster towards their departure point. The design components of the walkways therefore include active shapes and colours leading through to the departure gates. The build-up of emotional tiredness and frustration from endless queues of people all negotiating seemingly senseless ribbon lanes of passport control, could certainly benefit from regular space-clearing. The same applies to baggage halls, which can appear to carry a sense of futile anticipation as people wait to identify their cases on slow-moving conveyor belts. Whilst the customs hall tends to feel more like an abandoned area these days, we are nevertheless aware of the invisible lingering eyes that watch our every move.

Care homes   The nature of multi-occupancy homes of any kind is complex, with many individuals living as a family unit or occupying several mini-homes within a bigger set-up. Whilst individual responsibility is integral to the process of successful space-clearing and re-alignment of energies, in situations where the lives of many residents and staff need to be taken into account, it may not be possible for all to be involved. More importantly, the residents themselves are not always asking for help or seeking change in their lives.

When I was called in by the owner of a Surrey care home, because it was inappropriate to undertake any form of psychotherapeutic process with the residents, my scope of input was limited to a general space-clearing and sweeping of stagnant energies. This resulted in lifting and brightening the atmosphere for the benefit of everyone.

Large workforces   In buildings that occupy a large workforce such as factories and industrial units, the recurring energetic effects of mechanistic operations, repetitive tasks and constant noise can dull the senses and lead to boredom. When managers and employees are themselves aware of the importance of their environment and consciously work to alter the mood, a new upbeat approach will create a more vibrant and productive operation.

Secluded homes affect business   At certain times in life, a person may choose to retreat and live in solitude, sometimes yearning for deep personal healing. They find a cosy cottage, tucked away in a secluded place perhaps, or may even leave the country for a while. Whilst an isolated place may be protective and give comfort, it can also cut them off from the world. When in a low-ebb period, they may shut down psychologically from the outside world, reflected in their attitude towards personal and business affairs also. I often see this pattern within a person's Nine Star Ki time-cycle (Whisper 7).

Although this reticence to be active may be appropriate for a specific time, problems can later arise when that person is ready to shift into a high-energy phase and wants to become more outwardly visible. Should they continue to live in the same place that holds the established shutdown seclusion blueprint, this will hinder any efforts and enthusiasm for expansion. To collapse and zero out a redundant pattern will remove any restriction and allow movement forwards and outwards.

Conversely, when in a high energy, outward-going phase of a cycle, we want to be fully visible in the world and will find a living space reflective of openness, light and space. Our business attitude will likewise project a more open and generous approach.

Sharing Spaces with Our Animals

The purpose and value of our relationship and connection with our animals is close to my heart. The quality of our interaction with our pets has significant influence on our spaces. Sensitive animals such as cats, dogs and horses will intuitively sense any problems being experienced by their owners. Horses particularly will scan our energy fields to see if we are centred in our hearts.

If we do not listen to their *whispered* warnings, this can result in some form of illness developing in our physical body. Our animals can literally smell dis-ease on their owners, who are sometimes unaware of what doctors have yet to diagnose. In protecting us, their consciousness and intelligence will try and find some way of alerting us when an aspect of fragmentation of the heart occurs. Although this is part of the quintessence that many domestic animals share with humans, unless our own personal 'stuff' is dealt with, any long-term unresolved toxic residue from our emotional processing will make our pets sick and can ultimately kill them.

When people contact me owing to ill-health or unrest with their animals, I find the cause inevitably relates in some way to the owners themselves, further compounded by any issues with the underlying land and within their own homes. Any perceived problems caused by barns or stable buildings for example, are likely to be a reflection of happenings in the lives of the owners.

Horse reflects owner's fears I was called to work with a lady whose horse had become lame within a couple of weeks of moving to a new house. Surrounding the property was a feeling of persecution; numerous locks on the front door from the previous tenant echoed a sense of entrapment. On taking the owner through a process of sensing her relationship with the house and the land, she clearly saw and felt a past life connection of being chased by a gang of people through a forest. In sensing her anguish, her horse had taken on her distress in the form of lameness, so the situation could no longer be ignored. After working with her to illuminate and resolve the underlying trauma, miraculously within one week her horse recovered and she was able to ride him again. The owner had been called to the resonance of this environment that reflected her deep subconscious fear of persecution so that it could be brought to the surface. Perhaps the previous occupant had been drawn here for similar reasons. She was then able to continue working through this aspect of her soul journey, reaching deeper levels of resolution.

Canadian herd roaming wild At *Equinisity Retreat Centre* in British Columbia, Canada, I was honoured to come into contact and work with a herd of fourteen horses. Free to roam this vast sacred land, each morning they worked with people needing healing. As a team, the horses would line up at certain angles towards an individual lying flat on a healing table, connecting with and scanning the person's auric energy field. They would then physically touch, nudge and breathe on various areas of the human body. When I lay on the table, I experienced an extraordinary sense of heart connection with their empathy in total giving, free from any judgement or expectation of receiving anything in return. I was aware of how their innate intelligence was weaving the geometric energy matrix fields around and through my body, facilitating a specific personal healing process.

The horses also needed healing from the effect of residual trauma still resonating in the land from an indigenous massacre many years ago (Whisper 5). Drawn back to live in the same place in this lifetime, to reclaim her power the owner needed to face certain issues from her past life as a local tribe member. Soon after reaching a degree of resolution of the devastating events that took place, the health of the equine herd in her care improved greatly.

Equine space healing   As a result of working with horses, my method of *Equine Space Healing* has become a recognised way of helping to prevent and overcome illness in our four-footed friends. As was apparent in the previous story, intrinsic to the process is the relevant underlying life story of their owners. In a therapeutic sense, profound change and healing is then possible for people and their animals as well as for buildings and the land. As so often happens in life, by helping to heal others, we are healing ourselves – which could well be why we are called to do this work.

Neighbour Conflict and Boundary Issues

Is there such a thing as unpleasant neighbours, or do we draw them towards us gift-wrapped in numerous layers as a surprise offering to show us something about our own lives? It certainly does seem to be the case that we can sometimes unknowingly activate a challenging situation to create an opportunity for resolution.

The dreaded fences   When a woman chose to buy a house in Nottinghamshire that had issues with neighbours and boundary fences, she was aware of potential problems when she first viewed the property but chose to disregard them. In hindsight, she realised that her actions were sustaining the familiar pattern from childhood:

"It'll do you, you're never good enough, you don't count."

Although her compromise sits in the subconscious, the emotional patterns that reinforce her low self-esteem are kept alive; the house is a perfect mirror for this process. After illuminating the situation for her, with increased self-awareness she is likely to make healthier choices in the future that place greater value on her own self-worth.

Persecution room   This man had difficulty going into a certain room in his house due to a protracted two-year boundary conflict:

"I call it the persecution room, partly because it was infiltrated by the family from next door..."

I suggested he changed his language to alter his perception of the space, otherwise he would always associate the room with his issues concerning persecution or ill-treatment. For another person who might move into the same house, the neighbour scenario would not necessarily engender the same emotional response. The degree to which any animosity is triggered largely depends on the pattern match between the individuals concerned.

Disturbance in the walls This woman had noisy neighbours and considerable disturbance within her flat:

> *"Although my flat is now a sacred space, the flat on the second floor above me seems to have a life of its own. The previous occupants were drug dealers. I cannot describe the levels of noise and distur-bance, which affects the whole of the first floor. The people who live above spend their time shouting and banging doors, yet the rest of the building is calm apart from the woman below me, so yes I'm sandwiched between the two! As I work on myself to clear what in me was drawn to this, I could do with some help, as it's now become too much to bear. If I were able to get on with the neighbours I would get a circle together and drum it clear. It feels like something as powerful and visceral as that is what is needed."*

Two aspects here need addressing: firstly, to identify why and what were the attracting factors in coming to the property; and secondly, to find resolution with the conflicting issues, which is why the occupant is asking for help. Although she suggests 'drum it clear', I would not recommend this approach. You cannot resolve something just by 'clearing' it. In attempting to do so, unless the core issue is addressed, the problem will be temporarily calmed (or made worse in some cases) and will inevitably return with a vengeance.

I would never advise people to simply move out of a property and leave problems behind. To escape a situation is usually of no avail, as the next property chosen is likely to mirror similar issues. The reasons that attracted them to their current home will continue the call for resolution. Having come to a particular place through the law of attraction, there is a potentially valuable lesson to be learned, no matter how difficult the situation may seem. In spite of genuine injustice at times, we tend to think the reason for conflict with neighbours, or anything else for that matter, is because of something or someone else – we too undoubtedly have a role to play.

Past life neighbour revenge A desperate woman contacted me owing to noisy neighbours in the flat above her. The main culprit was angry and abusive towards her when they met in the communal areas. When I suggested she look back at her own part in contributing to the situation, she could find nothing. As I took her further back into the layers of time, we both recalled a previous lifetime where she was a member of a village tribe that sold *this* woman into slavery. Whilst it was very unlikely that the upstairs neighbour consciously remembered this, the original hurt held in her cellular memory reactivated in now finding herself living above her protagonist and wanting revenge!

As my client took on board the reality of the situation, I suggested she make apologies in her mind to the woman she had once wronged. To attempt this face-to-face was not a good idea in the circumstances, and how could she possibly explain her past life actions? For a while, things between them calmed down, but enduring peace was not to be and battle resumed. For full and mutual resolution to take place, the neighbour would also have to understand the true reason for her actions and come to terms with what might be considered a strange set of circumstances. The solution to prevent further conflict was to create a metaphysical isolation shield between the two flats, so that neither could 'see' each other (Whisper 7). This again bought peace for a while until the intensity of the neighbour's anger broke through, continuing the onslaught of revenge. Matters then had to be taken to a more potent, robust level with *The House Whisperer* pulling out the next level of defence shields to achieve a further degree of resolution.

Prisoner in the priory In a West Country village, a woman beset with legal battles following a boundary dispute with neighbours, is unable to sell her home. Entering a secluded and peaceful courtyard, as I strike the door knocker, a blunt echo emanates from the hallway. Momentarily aware of a cloud of uneasy melancholy from another age, the heavy door creaks open. Confronted by a rather formidable lady in her late sixties, casually dressed in dark hues, spectacles precariously balanced on her nose and looking rather like a mother abbess, she welcomes me into her home. Without delay, she tells me in a well-spoken voice that she cannot seem to attain release from this village, and feels as if the surrounding courtyard is holding her prisoner. Looking out from her upstairs living room window towards the tombstones in the churchyard, she reflects:

"I don't want to end my days here in this house and be buried in that churchyard."

I learn that her house stands in the grounds of a former priory, believed to have been founded by the Normandy monks of Mont St Michel in the 11th century. Later wars between England and France during the Middle Ages interrupted their contemplative lives, when they were expelled from the priory on several occasions.

Entering the dining room, a musty odour and feeling of heaviness engulf me. Sensing an odd atmosphere not of this time, I 'see' men wearing black tunics sitting around a table, plotting and deliberating as they wash down their meal with jugs of ale. The owner tells me that every time she opens the dining room door, she senses that *"someone is there"* helping themselves to her drinks and hospitality. She feels uncomfortable with this oppressive male presence lingering.

Working together to explore and resolve some of the complex interwoven issues between her present circumstances and the overlay of history surrounding her home, a recurrent theme of battle emerges with resonance in her own life.

In our conversations over the months that followed, the owner explained that her legal issues had been resolved to the extent she was now free from the constraints that prevented her from moving. The atmosphere in her dining room had lifted and remained clear. Many aspects relating to both her life and within herself had begun to change for the better, although the story continues.

Ancient lights In the 19th century, the entitlement known as 'ancient lights', the sacrosanct zone around windows, came into being. These areas had to be kept clear to prevent the neighbours' natural light from being encroached upon. The concept of preserving the flow of energy into a building is the relevant deeper aspect here, a human right for sustaining nourishment. By painting the walls white opposite the protected windows, this would maximise the reflected daylight. Although the law of ancient lights no longer exists as such, the principle of the right to light remains.

The Symbolism of Art and Artefacts

The energetic imprint carried in all forms of art, whether a painting, sculpture, piece of porcelain, item of furniture, in fact any object that has resided in a home, sometimes for centuries, will echo all that has previously gone on in those houses. The canvas of a painting, for example, may to a degree reflect the ethos and personal life of the artist, perhaps an enlightened person or a depressed, sad individual. Added to the blueprint or underlying symbolism of the actual painting or object itself, this compounds to create an inherent atmospheric feeling that will influence our mood, and evoke emotions ranging from an ecstatic response of great joy to uneasiness owing to dark and destructive vibrations.

The pertinent question is, why did you choose a certain object or piece of art? Investment is indeed a rational decision, but another more pertinent reason applies. The significant factor, from my observation of people and their homes, is the matching pattern with their own personal past, be it recent or ancient. In just the same way as the familiarity of our homes makes us feel comfortable, we see a reflection of some aspect of ourselves in our artefacts, particularly in the objects we put on our walls. They may give us pleasure, a sense of security, or simply a feeling of being at home. This resonant frequency draws us like a moth to a flame to whatever we are attracted that carries either a more subtle or blatantly direct message.

The issue here is not about 'good' and 'bad' art. It concerns the immediate elusive feeling experienced when we stand in front of a particular painting, image or sculpture; the subjective impression it makes on us at an emotional level, reaching deep unconscious recesses beyond its aesthetic appeal. Thus, being comfortable with a work of art we buy it, usually without considering whether it will support us or take us on a journey of destruction. What *is* for certain is that a piece of art has influence at a fundamental level, whether we are aware of it or not, and can enhance or destroy the atmosphere of our spaces, with a direct effect on our finances, health and relationships.

Have you ever walked across a room and been aware of a portrait with eyes that follow you? The consciousness of the person in the painting, or perhaps of the artist themselves whether still alive or dead, seems to have an energetic live-feed to the actual image. Either way, a connection and thereby a relationship exists between the portrait, yourself and the house it hangs within.

Walking into the living room of one particular home, a portrait caught my eye. It was of a gracious lady from some hundred years ago, the spirit of the past having a significant hold on the owner's life. By keeping each other active in their memory fields, their interwoven relationship led to issues on both sides needing to be reconciled.

Feng Shui not only considers actual objects themselves, which become precious despite any intrinsic monetary value, but also looks at the symbolic significance of what we place where in our homes. This will indicate an individual action of success or one of sabotage in relation to specific areas of life. Whilst we are regaining some of our long lost understanding of this ancient knowledge, much conscious reasoning has been forgotten and our sense of direction is often disconnected from Source.

Symbolism is an unspoken language, embodying silent codes of power. The symbols themselves evoke subconscious memory and activate an emotional response specific to an individual or cultural group. The hexagram, for example, is the geometry of the six-pointed star, a very stable energy, more recognisable to many people as the Flower of Life or the Star of David. Another symbol is the swastika, a word that originates from the Sanskrit *svastika* meaning 'good' or 'auspicious'. This powerful symbol of life and good luck in Hindu, Buddhist and Tibetan cultures, represents to the Western mind a dark time of 20th century world war history. As with other evocative symbols, we have the choice as to how to deploy that inherent energy in either a responsible or destructive manner.

Different symbols come into our lives at different times, holding a certain vibration with an association that may be both universal and personal. Problems arise when we wish to move from an old phase in life to perhaps a new home or relationship. Hanging onto paintings, artefacts or symbols from the past that have little or no meaning in the present can keep us stuck in old belief systems. Belongings then become little more than excess baggage, making it harder to move on.

When a woman announced that her husband had just left her and taken the paintings with him, his art collection represented such a big part of himself (and his financial investment) that he could not leave the paintings behind. Clearly, they meant more to him than his wife.

If a work of art has truly been painted from the heart of the artist, then it will touch the heart of the viewer and is more likely to bring forth a sale. Art galleries can, of course, be more successful if their spaces are clear of any negative or damaging energies, and optimised with vibrant chi flow. Creating a pure quality of atmospheric space applies equally to our homes. In essence, the art in your spaces can potentially affect any aspect of your life; you can change your life by changing the symbolic significance of any of your artefacts.

Making room for love When someone wishes to be in a close personal relationship and it's just not happening, we can look to the symbolism of pictures, paintings and artefacts in the home, in fact anything that carries symbolic significance. Soft toy animals such as teddy bears in the bedroom, for example, are often substitutes for an intimate relationship. Likewise, a bed jammed-up against the wall allows no physical access or symbolic invitation for a partner.

Just as where we choose to live, our chosen relationship status sets-up a dynamic pattern in the etheric matrix of our homes. We find typically that a single woman will have images of single females on her walls. Indeed, when she moved into that particular property, she may have just left a relationship and intended to remain single for a while. Whilst her personal choice of pictures relates to her life at that time, subconsciously reinforcing her status, problems are likely to arise when she wants to move into a new relationship. The already set programme that constantly replays the *"I am single"* mantra will impede her, compromising the prospect of any suitable partner coming along. If she happens to meet someone whilst still resonating in single mode, any relationship is unlikely to be of a permanent nature.

Changing the energetic code by changing the pictures to images that hold a different symbolism, perhaps of two people together, will reinforce her clarity and determination to bring a new person into her life. Her pictures alone will *not* achieve this, what matters is her intention to let go of being single and sustain her desire to draw someone close. Care needs to be taken in what you ask for in your chosen images, as you are highly likely to get those qualities and all that they entail. Finding an image that embodies the emotions she wishes to experience will solidify her intent, projecting out into the ether her aim of attracting a person with the qualities she seeks.

Single man A young first-time buyer in Bristol was unable to find a partner, but has he made room for love? The dominant painting he has hung in his flat is of a single man and the objects around the place are of contented solitude, reflective of his subconscious status of being alone. Now, even if he wishes to embrace a relationship, in order to change the old ingrained pattern running in his home, he will need to bring outmoded issues and feelings to a close. By taking them right back to zero point, he then has the choice to erase old attitudes and entrenched belief systems, specifically concerning his preconceived notions towards relationships. From this neutral blank canvas position, he can then re-programme his intentions and broadcast out to the world his request for the ideal and perfect partner. As he begins to change his artwork to reflect the feelings and emotions he aspires to attract, this gives him the best opportunity for a desired relationship to come forward.

Working with another man concerning his difficulty in finding a partner, the point at which he felt a total heart connection with the concept of relationship, two birds appeared and danced playfully together in the air in front of us, representing the sacred male and female weave of nature's powerfully synchronistic indicators.

Invisible relationships This woman living in North London was unable to find a partner. Her house was one of many in the area designed by a well-known local architect in the early part of the 20th century. At the time when she moved in, she had just come out of a relationship and was content to be on her own for a while. As we sat talking in her living room, I became aware of a 'stuck' male presence. She had at a subconscious level chosen a safe relationship with the old architect who had passed away seventy years ago; both seemed quite happy with the situation. The problem she now faced in wanting a live partner was the necessity of letting go of the man in spirit.

In agreeing to release him from her home, she then had to deal with the feeling of emptiness and loss of his company. Only then would the space and opportunity arise for a real man to come into her life.

In a similar scenario, a woman who had separated from her previous partner chose to be single for a while. When she was ready to commence a new relationship, nothing seemed to happen. Whilst working with her, I became aware of a male energy around her. It transpired that through her ancestral history, she had drawn to herself an elderly male relative in spirit. In his concern for her, he took on the role of looking after her. As she was now seeking a partner, his presence prevented a real man from manifesting in her life.

Another young woman recently out of a relationship was drawn to move into a flat with the trapped spirit of a single old lady. Owing to her wish to be single for a while, she felt a real connection with the spinster. The problem came when she wanted to move into a new relationship but could not find a partner. Illuminating the situation enabled her to recognise that her home had slipped into the pre-existing atmospheric single woman imprint. After thanking the spinster for her company, this allowed her spirit to release and the pattern was broken. She then met a new partner soon afterwards.

The House Whispering process is not about insisting people alter their images, but to point out the symbolism they reflect. In the following examples, art and artefacts mirror various relationship dynamics:

Relationship to self　One lady believed she wanted to stay single following a distressing divorce. Her sabotaged sense of self was symbolically represented in a pair of upside down full-size female statues placed in her relationship sector of the Feng Shui life-map (Whisper 7). This reinforced the significance of the mixed messages she was giving out, with little chance of a man coming into her life.

Lacking togetherness　The art in this home lacked any symbolism of togetherness. Some of the images were vague, others grotesque, few depicted a peaceful atmosphere, a perfect mirror of the couple's relationship of mistrust, with little real communication. Despite being aware of the shortfalls, at one level they were content with the way things were, unwilling to alter the status quo by making any changes.

Crossed swords In a well-to-do apartment in Central London, this couple's relationship was compromised by two crossed swords that lay on a table in their Feng Shui relationship area. Was this the cause of the uneasy feeling carving up their marriage, or did they merely reflect the subconscious animosity between them that led to the swords being placed in this location in the first place?

Bedroom on a Greek yacht The use of a Feng Shui compass here was not feasible, as the positioning of the Ba-Gua would depend on which way the boat was facing at any moment. Analysis therefore required the Tibetan Black Hat method of orientating the life-map from the 'front door' (Whisper 7). Most interesting was a large mirror behind the bed, which traditionally in Feng Shui energetically draws a third party into the marriage. Although his girlfriend wanted a monogamous relationship, the yacht owner was open to other options. There are occasions when no solution satisfies all, especially if one party only wishes to see their own reflection!

Yearning for home A couple living in suburbia had an uneasy relationship. A large picture poster of the American city where the wife was born, hung on the chimney-breast of their lounge, the area Feng Shui often associates with future goals. Not feeling fully at home in England, she was not fully engaged in her marriage. On pointing this out, the couple realised that her yearning for home was affecting their lives and wanted to work towards changing this. The foremost thing here is that it is *not* the picture itself that was causing the problem, but what the chosen image represented – the wife's subconscious desire to return home to her birth city. Thus, the necessary change was an inner one, for her to attain peace and a sense of true home within herself and with her husband in their current home. The act of finding a new picture, more symbolic of stability and togetherness was the first step towards embracing this; things would slowly begin to unfold from there. His feedback was unexpectedly encouraging, confirming a shift in their relationship. He was most intrigued as to how things could feel so different based on the consultation.

Renewed attraction is not an uncommon result of helping people to reconnect to the original essence of what drew them together in the first place. Love *is*, after all, the attractor factor.

Whisper 3

GHOSTS AND THE PARANORMAL

The effect of living with presence

Living with Spirit Residents

I often ask people at a consultation or in a workshop, do you feel at home where you live? In many instances, I find that other influences are preventing them from being fully settled or in charge of their own home. Not only do we find ourselves inheriting predecessor energies from the lives of previous occupants who have physically moved to another property, we may also encounter various spirit beings living in the shadows that have not even moved out.

It soon became apparent to me that if I was to understand the reasons why some departed souls became stuck between this world and the next, I had to listen to their *whispers* and discover what they needed in order to facilitate their release. Even more intriguing, I wondered if there was indeed any relationship between the current occupants and those spirits calling for help; did either have any connection to the soul of the house itself? So my life entered a new phase of strange and curious realities, talking to houses and listening to them talk back. This is how *The House Whisperer* came into being.

Spirit presence can become perceptible in many ways. We commonly find an accumulation of stagnant energies in just part of a house: a hallway, landing, library, and often in the bedrooms. Areas that feel especially heavy, cluttered, unusually cold even in summer, or are simply uncomfortable places to spend time, can draw attention to areas of our lives that are likewise becoming problematic:

"There's one room in my house I won't go into."

When people die and get stuck in between worlds, this often indicates a degree of trauma or sadness in their heart at the time of passing. Their spirit may not have fully released and as a result can get entangled in the web of fragmented non-sacred geometry in the energy matrix of our homes. Like the fly unaware of an approaching spider, they await powerless to initiate the next step themselves.

A departed soul may still be attached to their home or a family member, or simply chooses to hang around through an emotional resonance with the current occupants, sometimes sharing quite uncanny synchronistic aspects of their life stories. A trapped soul is not actually confined to the past and neither is their presence necessarily a memory replay from their previous lifetime. Although they may have passed away many years ago, their soul remains very much in the present moment of the space-time continuum. This explains why discarnate souls can be seen, felt and communicated with in the now, yet behave with all the characteristic mannerisms of their former personality. Why one person may be able to sense or see them and another not, depends on their degree of sensitivity and vibrational resonance to each other. This is not the same as receiving guidance from those in the spirit world who have transitioned from this life through to the next stage of their journey.

For myself, I sense spirit presence with both my physical and etheric bodies. Depending on the density of the veils that separate my perceived reality, the degree of transparency varies. Sometimes I glimpse shadows dancing in the light of day, or see a faint vaporous mist blowing gently in the wind. Spirit can be as elusive as a watermark on paper, or as solid as a real person with sharp, clear features, dressed in the costume of their own era. Finding out more about the history of the house can often confirm their identity.

It is not always necessary to release spirits or ghosts; to simply acknowledge lives on both sides of the planes can often be sufficient resolution in itself. Well, at least for the moment.

My name's Joe Even when not actively engaged in working with houses, perhaps at a social event, I may find myself being shown around the host's house. On one occasion, I became aware of a male spirit wandering the first floor of a house in Somerset. The homeowners were happy to accommodate his presence and at ease with his company, so I was not being asked to deal with him in any way. As the last in line going back downstairs, I felt an otherworldly tap on my shoulder and heard a voice saying, *"My name's Joe."* My reply, *"Hi Joe"* carried with it the recognition that he had once occupied the house. Content to share the space with the current owners, this was enough for Joe to feel acknowledged.

Don't be silly darling, it's only your imagination We often hear this familiar phrase when a child mentions an encounter with the paranormal – a nightmare, imaginary friend, or sensitivity to an atmosphere. Even if the parent knows something unusual is going on, they may be reluctant to consciously acknowledge something they don't understand, or are simply afraid to consider anything that may open a 'can of worms', let alone know how to deal with such matters.

Suicide wanderer This family lived in a wing of an old Oxfordshire mansion, where a child complained of being unable to sleep. His bedroom had a very heavy atmosphere, overlaid with the presence of a ghost man who was particularly active at night. I watched his vaporous shadow draped in a full-length black raincoat, aimlessly walk slowly down the long, dark, narrow corridor. My description of him to the owners apparently matched that of the previous male tenant, a depressive who had committed suicide. Trapped through the guilt of his desperate action, his spirit clearly needed help. Following our compassionate connection with him, through his own inner resolve he was then able to release from his former home and move on. The lady owner reported:

> *"Today, the house feels so different. The sun is pouring in the windows and it feels so calm and tranquil. I feel the love is back in the house... Your visit did not only have an effect on our house but also a huge effect on us as well. As a family unit we feel stronger than ever. We are so much happier and much more comfortable. I now feel that it is my house. You had an amazing effect on us all."*

In another home, the radiator in one of the bedrooms never worked, despite various plumbers attempting to fix it. Although the room was south-facing, an unusual chill in the air could always be felt, resulting in the child sleeping badly until the prevalent spirit energy was released.

In the following two examples, the parents were well aware of spirit presence and did not dismiss its purpose for being there, allowing their child's creative, imaginative faculty to flow:

Surrogate spirit mother   A young girl was aware of an old lady appearing in her North London home, particularly whilst she practiced at the piano. Far from causing any problems, fears or concerns, the lady in spirit was in fact taking care of the girl, who lived with her father and desperately needed a mother figure in her life. Did she unknowingly call in this presence, or was her father led to move to a house with an unseen helper ready and waiting?

Co-dependent spirit   In a house in New Jersey, USA, a child often mentioned sharing his bedroom with a visitor, a spirit man who was usually there at night time. They were happy to have each other's company, so his presence was no real problem; clearly each needed something from the other. In this situation it was inappropriate to attempt to release the man in spirit until the reasons on both sides for the co-dependent relationship could be identified and resolved.

Waiting for a loved one no longer alive   It is sometimes the case that a deceased person trapped in spirit is waiting for something or someone, usually for a loved one to return, unaware that their spouse or partner may have left this Earth plane themselves. There was a sadness surrounding a house that I visited in the Cotswolds. From a top floor window was a faint glimmer of a man in spirit, looking out with a pensive waiting gaze. As I connected and communicated with him, it was clear that he was waiting for his wife to come home. This could never happen, as he did not realise that she too had passed away, so his wait would be eternal. By letting him know she was no longer in her physical body allowed his spirit to release, giving this loving couple the opportunity to reunite in another dimension.

Spirit perceptible through scent   It is not uncommon to smell the scent of perfume in a house, worn by someone who once lived there.

Walking through a house in Surrey, a perfume pervaded the air. The owner said it was not hers, but that she too had been aware of this scent on many occasions. She soon realised that the previous occupant was making her presence felt, especially in the main bedroom. The electrical appliances would often switch on-and-off of their own accord, a classic indication of paranormal activity. By acknowledging the spirit of this elderly lady, it was possible to help her release from her former home, and reduce further visits by mystified electricians.

At another Surrey home, the owner was also aware of the odour of a previous occupant:

"Quite a funny thing in my house, I love my house, I've lived there for over twenty years and in our bedroom among the wardrobes, I can smell an odour that nobody else can."

Unresolved issues holding her prisoner In some situations where resolution of a specific event requires the actions of others, it may not be possible to free a spirit trapped between worlds. When I visited an empty house on an island in the Pacific Ocean, the last lady to live there was born and died in the house where she spent her entire life. She continues to occupy her home, walking the corridors in search of resolution and redemption. Her spirit asks me for help, but there are matters that first need to be addressed by others who hold the key to unlock a chain of events before certain aspects of her life can come to peace. If resolution can be achieved and she can be released, this will bring about healing for all those people, both living and ancestral, involved with her troubled soul.

Sisters' active memory portal Not always is the sense of others in a house necessarily of those who have passed over; it may simply be the energy links of former occupants. Whilst staying overnight in a thatched cottage in Cambridgeshire, I became aware of two young girls of about five-years old bouncing happily on one of the beds. My sense was that they were sisters who had lived in the cottage around eighty or so years ago, and were still alive and living together nearby. They had happy, cherished memories of the home where they grew up, a familiar connection which they kept active and to where they returned in their minds for comfort and fun.

Departed Souls Influencing Lives

It can be devastating when previous occupants of your home have passed over, but you find their influence still very much present. To unconsciously soak up the mental imprint of energies from other realms will impact and shape your life, leading to the realisation that you have bought a house and ended up living the life of another.

As mentioned, a deceased person stuck in spirit will continue to hold the values and beliefs from the time they passed over, perhaps many years ago. When a new owner or tenant comes along with good intentions for looking after the house, the deceased may still see it as their home and judge the actions of the present occupants from the perspective of their own timeframe, not appreciating the different generational approach or recognising cultural variations.

Becoming the previous owner In a small Dorset town, the current owner had occupied her house for the last twenty years. Her partner had shared her home for the past three years, but had never felt entirely welcome. It transpired that the previous owner, from 1937, was still around in spirit. Information from neighbours revealed that she was a strong character who gave her husband a rather hard time. He would escape her wrath by going down the pub on a Friday night for a pint of *Henpeck*, as the current owner's partner jokingly called it. The amused couple both realised that she was playing a similar role, treating him with the same attitude. They also realised that Friday night was when they tended to get into arguments, especially after a glass or two of wine, thus repeating the ingrained pattern. By releasing the attitude patterns around men held in the memory of the house, within a short space of time the present couple were then able to see what aspects of life were really theirs and not those of the previous owners. The peculiar feeling of extreme cold in the house, felt by the current owner around her legs and feet, also soon disappeared.

Similarly, a woman in London was displaying character traits that were not her own and she knew it. I could see another's aura around her, shaping her sense of reality. She described the previous occupant exactly as she was behaving herself. When this overlay pattern was released, she could gradually revert to being her authentic self.

Not in control of my home   At the house of a couple in Oxford-shire, the lady had never felt entirely in charge of her own property, like a visitor unable to take free rein of the estate. After walking around the house, we entered the master bedroom where I could clearly see a woman in spirit sat upright on the bed, wearing a Victorian white lace dress with a black trim. Alongside her lay her dead husband, dressed in a black and white pinstriped suit. Within this extraordinary theatrical scene of the spirit world, in their own time zone she was 'alive' whilst he was actually 'dead'. When checking the dates of this event using dowsing rods, we both got around 1860. Later that evening, the owner discovered from doing some historical research that the male owner of that time had passed away in 1860 – a wonderful confirmation of the dowsing.

Connecting with the elderly lady in spirit and holding a gentle *whispering* conversation with her, an understanding unfolded that she did not trust the current owner to run the household in the way she had done. One of her concerns was that the milkmaids in the old dairy were being neglected, even though they had passed away some 150 years ago, but in her timeframe were still alive and milking! After giving her some assurance that the house and all within would be cared for, something quite unexpected happened. The woman on the bed next to her deceased husband stretched out her arm and handed the current owner a key – *the* key to the house. It was a surreal and magical moment, watching her symbolically pass on ownership of the property in its fullest sense. The present owner was then finally able to fully take charge of her home.

Husband's grandmother running the show   At a family house in Lisbon, Portugal, the husband had a successful job. His wife wanted to return to the business world but felt shackled with their two children in the role of housewife, bidding the wishes of his grandmother. Before passing away some five years ago, she was adamant:

"This house is for my grandson and you are to look after it… and my plants!"

Unable to escape the constantly active live programme enforced by the grandmother from the other side, the wife felt trapped. Following

67

my guidance, she took the courage to have a few carefully chosen words with grandma, and while respecting her wishes told her in no uncertain terms to back off and allow her to run her own home.

Ancestors Prevent Owner Running Own Home

Standing in the kitchen of this mid-40's couple, I asked the wife:

"Who are the old ladies over by the cooker?"

Looking bemused, she said she could see no one, so I continued:

"Well there are three of them here, dressed in shabby, black Victorian clothes, nattering away and clearly in charge of the household."

The expression on her face, as sudden realisation dawned, showed a glimpse of why she never truly felt as though she ran her own home. She felt like the kitchen girl, just another servant in the house, which was causing her a lot of grief.

It had taken me a while to find the cottage, tucked away in a small Somerset village. A local, elderly lady eventually pointed me in the right direction, towards the entrance of an unnamed lane with no indication of any dwelling. I finally arrived at the property after passing scattered outbuildings, several chickens, cats, a dog, and some curious nature spirits. Difficulty in getting to a property typically indicates that the overlay of energies on the soul of a building and surrounding land do not wish me to arrive, let alone to enter the house; they know their comfort zone will be shaken up!

This lady asked if I would visit, as something felt very uncomfortable in her home. She did not feel settled even after living in the cottage for many years, admitting she just didn't understand what was happening. Her husband was totally at ease, seemingly unaware of his wife's distress. Looking at his demeanour, I could sense that he was straddling another world, holding the essence and patterns of his ancestors who had lived in the cottage for several generations. This familiarity allowed him to be comfortable with his surroundings and perceive the quality of the space quite differently.

It became clear to me that one particular matriarch was very definitely in charge, running the household from another dimension. The focus of these spirit ancestors was the kitchen, where the mind-chatter head noise was cacophonously loud. Their presence dominated the space, leaving no room for the wife to even think her own thoughts, let alone fulfil her role in taking control of the household, a prerequisite for any keeper of the hearth. To feel blocked of her rights of feminine power touched on what was to be the key to unlocking her anguish and distress.

When I connected with these female relatives, it was obvious that they were unhappy with the present wife's ways and making things as hard as possible for her. She explained to them that her natural gifts with herbs and nature were much the same as theirs, but understood things were done differently in their day.

Most of us will have ancestors or living relatives whose physical lives were out of necessity task oriented, with little time and space to analyse and reflect on perceptions and feelings; most likely regarded as a modern indulgence as they look on contemporary lives through the veils of time. Nevertheless, there was no conflict in truth and the wife just wanted the best for her family, the house and land as well as the nature spirits, all very much part of the ancestral lineage they shared. She acknowledged the ancestors' important role in maintaining the house and garden, and honouring the value of the natural world. She gave them her thanks and assurance that she would continue to work with respect for their traditions.

As a result, it was possible for the three old ladies to release, allowing the wife to finally feel fully empowered to take her rightful place in the family dynamic as the woman of the house. She said:

> "I felt that in many ways my intentions for the house did not flow with ease as they should and did in all other areas of my life. Since I arrived seven years ago, I've changed things beyond recognition, especially in the kitchen... The presence of the previous inhabitants speaking loudly were very much a part of my reality.
>
> "During the consultation I meditated and saw a young lad in spirit with a cap on, dressed in Edwardian attire. He was in the corner of the kitchen, and said, 'Sorry Missy, we know not of your ways.' I gave my love but did not allow myself to get emotionally

entangled, so I asked the archangels, angels, and spirit guides working for the highest to guide them on for the greater good. It was ethereal and the veils between the worlds felt thin and tangible. I felt like I could at last hear my thoughts, and wherever I went on the land or in the house I felt at peace with myself and with my home."

She reported on how things were progressing:

"I cannot believe the transformation of this house I could cry... I feel so content, the kitchen feels wonderful and I can hear myself think. I feel no obstacles or restrictions and my body feels lighter... Being a Feng Shui consultant myself, I realise getting in help is also very beneficial, as it is often difficult to see a situation clearly when you are in it. If there are malevolent spirits creating chaos around you who will not leave because it's their house, not yours, things cannot flow without back-up to hold the space in a neutral zone to allow healing and for their departure to take place. Amazing!"

Spirit Presence in School Buildings

The design of new or renovated buildings for nurseries, schools, colleges and universities that incorporate Feng Shui and other holistic principles, will benefit an environment allowing the delivery of an enhanced quality of education. The design of healthy school buildings imbued with love and care will indeed reflect in the experiences of all who use them and contribute to the health and wellbeing of children, young people and mature students, as well as teaching staff and administrators. Achieving the sense of feeling 'at home' applies equally to the places where we work and study; augmenting our spaces ignites mind, body and soul, nourishing every aspect of our senses and cognitive faculties.

Of greater significance is how the human aspect of what has taken place in our buildings can influence the ability to learn. Many existing spaces, particularly school buildings, were at some time in the past adapted and used for other purposes. Leftover lingering energies leave an atmospheric imprint in the emotional world, affecting all those who subsequently spend time there. In many instances, the architectural design is of little consequence compared to the overlay of human emotions and spirit activity, which continue to influence the lives of those in the present.

When working at a sacred site, house, school, or sometimes when attending funerals, a departed soul may choose to merge with my own aura, as in this next story. It is important to take care to ensure that any spirit deciding to release in this way has your permission, and that you allow it to happen only if you recognise a purpose or value to the lessons needing to be learned for either or both parties.

School controlled from another dimension   Many disturbances at a school in Derbyshire were the consequence of energies lingering in the wide main corridor. In my mind's eye, I could see beds lined up on either side against the walls, with a walkway through the centre. Most disturbing were the images of sick soldiers lying motionless with blood stained bandages. This scene had been imprinted into the memory of the building from when it was used as a temporary hospital during World War II. The stagnant yet active emotional energy affected both teachers and children unknowingly, not a favourable atmosphere for any building, let alone one for education.

Walking around the school, I became aware of the spirit of the original headmistress and soon came to sense her essence very clearly. She was a single woman, a Miss Jean Brodie type of character, with very fine delicate features. Her lack of relationship experience made her apprehensive and mistrusting of men. She was unhappy to allow the present head teacher a free rein to run the school because she disapproved of her methods and did not trust anyone else to adhere to her own high standards held in the 19th century. The school was therefore being run from another dimension. As those present acknowledged her concerns that the school should be run in an excellent way, something very strange and unexpected happened. She decided it was time to hand over entirely to the current head teacher. Sensing that she had been seen and accepted, she chose to release her connection from the school through a man's body, mine! This was a most curious experience, a tingling sensation gently vibrating throughout my entire being. She hovered for a while as if wanting to sense my masculine energy and then very gently departed upwards towards the light, free to go wherever her soul was called.

The head teacher's feedback a few days later was most encouraging:

> *"Having been back in school for the last few days, it is settling down well after a few blips, and feels much better and people appear calmer. The change is substantial and will definitely support learning within the school and its ethos."*

She also conveyed that they looked back in awe at the consultation day and as they continued to talk about it, more and more fitted into place. The sound in the main corridor was much clearer and when people spoke their voices echoed rather than being muffled by etheric debris and paranormal activity (Whisper 7). She later passed on a message from an individual present that day who had received 'contact' from the original headmistress, saying that she realised she was wrong to have stayed and had not only held the school back, but herself as well. She wanted to thank me for showing her the difference between a male and female energy.

Childrens' homes   A children's home in Surrey, converted from a spacious Georgian country house, felt a gloomy and dismal place. An oppressive intensity echoed through the corridors from the mixed emotions of happy and sad children from the past. Not surprisingly, the basement was full of dark entity energy, feeding off the distressed emotions of these children, a form of energetic food for such beings. This compounds and creates a sticky atmosphere that gets thicker and heavier, experienced at some level by everyone. After carrying out an energetic space-clearing and realignment of the entire house (Whisper 5), the feeling of clear space brought great relief all round.

At an institutional building for handicapped children in Austria, the sense of resigned lives was palpable. Resonance of abuse and injustice echoed in some of the rooms. A gentle process of space-clearing dispersed the stagnant feeling to some extent, but this only addressed the top layer of the problem. The distressing memories of emotional traumas still lingered in the deeper recesses of the consciousness of the building. Once compassionate connection was made with those vulnerable children and their experiences acknowledged, the emotional threads of past memories were able to unravel, allowing their soul fragments to be set free.

Spirits at play   At another educational building, the teachers and children were experiencing some strange disturbances due to spirit activity. One particular member of staff was carrying a male spirit attachment in her energy field. It transpired that he was a man who had been killed on the site in a tragic accident some years earlier.

In these kinds of situations, to free and release energies that are not truly part of an individual's own soul will usually bring a sense of liberation for everyone concerned.

Ghosts and Paranormal Activity

In my early days of experiencing subtle energies, I was unable to rationalise or really understand what was going on, but just felt uncomfortable and sometimes quite scared. After immersing myself in exploring sacred sites, esoteric and philosophical studies, my framework of relating to these energies began to expand and develop. Little did I know that some twenty years later, my architectural and design consultancy would be drawn into the world of Feng Shui. Personal consultations provided the opportunity to visit many houses and come face-to-face with a broad spectrum of paranormal activity.

Chased by country pub ghosts   In the early 1970s, I accompanied a prospective purchaser to an unoccupied country pub in Essex, which he intended to convert into an educational establishment. In spite of wonderful rural views, this rambling property was rather sad and forlorn, full of uncomfortable undertones. After looking around, we headed back to the car and noticed a window had been left open in the observatory tower. I was casually asked to return and close it.

Aware that the building held other types of spirits other than in the empty bar, I dreaded the idea of going back up alone to the tower, but put on a brave face. Striding up the many steps to the top, I watched my back as many vaporous beings appeared from doorways along the corridors. After closing the window, I did not relish the thought of returning back down again, yet a worse fate may have awaited me had I become trapped in the tower. Pausing apprehensively to get a sense of the ghostly residents, quite happily living there rent-free and not wanting anybody to buy the property, I contemplated my exit strategy. With no alternative way out, avoidance was to no avail. So, I took a deep breath and sprinted as fast as I could down the several flights of stairs and through the long corridors, being chased by the mob. Emerging out of the front door a little dishevelled, I pondered whether to share my harrowing experience with the others, but pride got the better of me and I just grimaced. I still wonder to this day if we did actually leave the observatory window open, or whether it was an otherworldly prank.

Interacting with ghost world   In my present work with houses, I do not deliberately seek out trapped souls, but am often asked to help in situations where the deceased have not departed this world and continue to cause disturbance in the lives of others:

"Something is going on, it's getting frantic; our house spooks everyone who comes here but gets to me most of all."

I find that listening and understanding their plights and stories helps to release trapped souls from people's homes, freeing them to move on with their own journey whilst at the same time liberating the current occupants. This does, however, require the occupants to be actively involved in the release process, as resonance to the spirit presence in relation to an unresolved aspect of their own lives is likely to have drawn them to the property at the outset.

Fragmentation in the human energy field can create a schism, resulting in portals opening-up into other dimensions. This formation of energy can sometimes be seen or may be sensed as something reminiscent, an uncanny familiar feeling encountered before. This is the reason for many peculiar activities taking place such as footsteps on the stairs, strange sounds and knocking, or unexplained atmospheres. It can be most unsettling to find plates falling off walls, objects quite literally being spirited away only to reappear in a different place at another time, and other bizarre happenings. Assuming that no other reason exists to explain these strange occurrences, experienced by many people who will often not admit to it, then it is usually paranormal – meaning phenomena that the rational mind cannot comprehend or does not concur with recognised scientific theories, understanding or belief systems.

Interaction with the spirit world is through resonance with the shadows. These ghostly beings, often from long ago, whether simply mischievous or maddeningly destructive, are in fact disembodied souls – those who have passed over, but are trapped through trauma or some unresolved life issue. Thus, ghosts are holding aspects of wounds to the heart they are unable to release on their own. They may not even be aware they have passed over. Most of the time, in appearing to invade our spaces, they hang around and seek our attention, crying out to be heard and acknowledged. As they await resolution and the possibility of release, they will only get louder and more insistent if we do not listen to their needs and help them.

Shattered aspects of the psyche can be mistaken for entities or attachments. Time and distance are of little consequence in the spirit world. Frozen in time through accidents, violence, murder or other forms of trauma, these trapped soul fragments interact with our peripheral energies within the etheric psychoactive grid. They too have a distinct vibrational blueprint; it is our individual harmonic code or 'musical note' that attracts any one of us to their resonance. Even a group dynamic can make a connection without always realising the subtle underlying reason or undertones.

I encounter many situations where electrical fields have created a vortex that enables ghostly or darker energies to enter and access a building. Numerous instances of electrical or computer malfunctions relate to a synergy between spirit activity and digital technology. When a space is neutralised of otherworldly presence, equipment tends to return to normal function. In some cases, physical repairs may be needed to rectify damage caused.

If the distressed energies of departed spirits and other discarnate souls that disturb our peace are not addressed by balancing the entire building, it is likely to remain in that condition. The constantly generated cumulative effect will be reflected in the negative and agitated state of the people, to the detriment of their health and wellbeing. Similar overlays of unbalanced energies can be found in entire towns, particularly in many European cities, some of which are very dense, intense and dark indeed.

Spirits in bars and restaurants   Many buildings where alcohol is served engender spirits of other types – haunted bars and restaurants abound in many cities. Chester is supposedly the most haunted city in England; it is not difficult to sense why if you choose to spend a night out, eating and drinking in some of its establishments.

In my home town of Kingston upon Thames, from the doorway of one old pub you can catch sight of men in long black boots, wearing tricorn hats, carrying their tankards up the steep, narrow staircase.

Balls and chains in the corridors Whilst teaching in a monastic building in Salzburg, Austria, the ladies attending my workshop who were sleeping in the dormitories at the top of the building, reported hearing balls and chains being drawn through the corridors at night. Even more alarming was that several of them complained of being dragged out of bed during their sleep by something sinister pulling on their feet!

In the Oak Rooms in Dorchester, Dorset, a court house of Judge Jeffreys in the 17th century, the balls and chains of condemned people awaiting hanging can quite literally be heard in the upstairs panelled hallway by those waiting for tea to be served.

Hotel built on a graveyard As I lay in bed unable to sleep in a hotel in Prague, I became aware of some very active spirit energies and watched the ghostly traffic wander through my room all night long. Sharing my experience the next morning with a local man attending the conference at which I was presenting a talk, he told me that the hotel was built on the site of an ancient burial ground.

Total recall Past events triggered by living in a New York riverside apartment, turned out to be a mixed blessing for this occupant. Soon after moving in, memories began to surface of sexual abuse by her brother when she was seven years old, which had remained deeply buried for the past forty years. No one, not even the cat, ever wanted to go into the empty main bedroom, furnished with just a sideboard and a solitary chair in the corner. I could see the replay of a man violently attacking and sexually assaulting a woman on the bed in this room, before he murdered her. My sense was that at a subconscious level, in needing to bring forward her traumatic childhood experience, the occupant had chosen this apartment that held a resonance to her past. What was required was to clear and release the embedded blueprint of violent actions from the bedroom and reset the space to a high positive vibration. She was then free to move forward with her life without the active memory replay in her apartment constantly pulling her back into her painful past experience.

Girl crying in cottage In an 18th century thatched cottage in Wiltshire, the memory replay of a woman being pushed down the stairs was tangible, as were the cries of a little girl heard at night. Whilst it felt to me as though they were separate unrelated incidents in different timeframes, their release was a relief for the departed souls as well as for the current occupants.

Protecting the animals In the front garden of a London house, three sisters hovered around in spirit. The building was once used as a veterinary surgery, where they continued to see their role as protectors of the animals who came in for treatment. These female spirit presences were unaware they had passed over, or indeed that the building was now actually somebody's home. When told that their role had been fulfilled, they were content to leave.

Compelled to push her down the stairs A well-heeled woman had found her fortunes dwindle due to her ex-husband's gambling habit. Since moving house she had ended up in poverty, living alone. At the top of the stairs leading to the basement, I had a vision of a man pushing a woman down the stairs. She plummeted down so violently and lay motionless across the bottom step, where she died a slow, agonising death. As the owner switched on the basement light, I had an overwhelming sense of wanting to push her down the stairs, but resisted doing so – not good for client relationships! The active memory replay still resonating powerfully in the house created a vibration that propelled me to want to re-enact the man's behaviour.

Whilst space-clearing down in the basement, a book literally fell off the shelf. I picked it up to find it was a novel about ghost stories set in an English country house, and opened it at random to a page describing a man who killed his wife by pushing her down the stairs. Sharing this insight with the client, she paused for a moment before divulging that this was exactly what happened in her house – an historical fact reported in the local newspapers some time ago.

Why the financial issues? Held in the memory imprint of the house was the psychological pattern of diminishing the value of the feminine. This had been created or was exacerbated by the trauma of the murdered woman, and could even have been due to an event from long before that time; this pattern clearly needed diffusing.

Our perception of time and reality becomes more elusive as metaphysical experiences increase, especially if you have entered otherworldly realms from a young age. Many time layers can open up, igniting memory links that transport you to events still active in the etheric field. As with past life recall, this can happen spontaneously even when not tuning-in for a specific purpose:

Witchfinder General In a small suburban town in Pennsylvania, USA, I experienced a strange incident of memory replay whilst sitting in a local restaurant. As three men burst in through the double swing saloon doors, my body was immediately drawn into a defence position. The central man stood hands on hips, the other two on either side and slightly behind him. I did a double take as I watched him weigh-up the place, looking slowly from side to side as if searching for his victims. Drawn into a time portal from the past, I could see him dressed in dark period costume from the days of hunting out women whose powers were considered a threat. Yes, he was a 'witch finder'. As our eyes met, we both recognised and knew his purpose. For a moment there might have been a fight, a chase or even death in the air. Breaking the locked gaze and snapping back into current time, all three men walked on past to the food counter at the rear, where each ordered a slice of angel cake and glass of fire water.

As I reflected on this experience, it felt as though I had lived through and known the happenings that took place over many years of time, yet in terms of normal reality only about a minute had passed. I couldn't help but sense that I too may have played a part in that past era and if so, wondered what role that might have been?

We sometimes encounter ominous energies that seek to create more darkness and chaos, with a vested interest in keeping people and their spaces 'bad'. These dark, lower astral energies have no soul as such and, as demonstrated in some of the following consultations, are dissolved and dispersed in a very different way to those trapped spirit or soul fragments needing release with love and compassion. Nevertheless, approaching any 'negative' entities in the knowledge that 'All is One' is of paramount importance, even if a battle stance is necessary. The attitude of detachment is exquisitely portrayed in the story of Arjuna in the *Bhagavad Gita* (Whisper 7).

Vortex zigwhol In a European city apartment, an earth energy vortex had opened-up a portal into other dimensions. This allowed open passage, a *zigwhol* I call it, for beings from a darker world to enter the bedroom and create havoc. As a result of using metaphysical techniques to close the portal, the owner's life affected in more ways than one, improved dramatically as did her quality of sleep.

The feeders In many instances when people are ill or weak, dark murky entity energies will feed off them. In a house in London, the quality of life and health of the paraplegic son in a wheelchair was not helped by the intensity of threatening energy sucking the life force out of him. This was dealt with by firstly disengaging the dark energy attachment from him, then giving the house a thorough space-clearing before charging-up his environment to give it more vibrancy. It was then programmed for invisibility to darker forces.

Spirit presence with attitude Opening the door to the husband's den room in a house in Germany, I was repelled by a 'Mr Blobby' filling the entire space. The aggressive attitude was most definitely, *"Do not come into my space!"* The husband would get very angry, almost to the point of becoming demonic, having soaked up this dark energy which he expressed by throwing beer cans at the television. After diffusing the blob, the man's behaviour changed for the better and the atmosphere in the couple's home began to settle down.

Video games open dark portals In a room where a teenage boy played some pretty horrific video games for many hours, day and night, a thick dense atmosphere of dark energies accumulated. This then fed off him creating a very destructive cycle so that he often appeared like a zombie. Once the sinister energies were pulled off him and his room cleared and neutralised, he was given breathing space to reconsider his activities. Whilst his mother had called me for help, only if and when her son decides to take responsibility and change his habits, would he no longer attract these dark forces.

Film-maker scripts own death Working with a woman in her house, the atmosphere was heavy with dark, ominous energies, especially in the lower ground floor areas. Her husband had written and produced a film on aspects of black magic and paranormal activity, where the protagonist ends up dying. He chose to act this part himself and fulfilled the reality of his own script when he died during the final stages of filming. The question is, did he manifest his own projected reality or was he manipulated and coerced by desires from other realms in creating this sinister and dangerous film?

Memories and Spirits in Artefacts and Furniture

Further to the symbolism of art and artefacts (Whisper 2), any lingering ghostly energies, particularly in ancestral paintings and other heirloom or tribal objects, can have serious and unexpected consequences. The message of the following stories is beware of the history of furniture, or any artefacts for that matter:

Destructive energies in paintings Having a significant influence over the lives of this couple in their apartment were a collection of paintings that carried some very dark, destructive and fragmented energy. The question was, which aspects of their dramatic lives were playing out through the emotive connotations of their chosen art? The powerful imprints in the images continually bolstered their personal dynamic, making it difficult for them to change aspects of their relationship even if they wanted to.

Painting of deceased friend In the bedroom of another couple hung a large painting of a deceased male friend of the wife. Whilst we may love and miss someone and wish to honour their memory, we need to be mindful of the location of images. As the bedroom represents our intimate relationship with a partner, any piece of art, especially a portrait, will symbolically and energetically bring that person's energy as a third party into the relationship, even when they are in spirit. The wife chose to move the painting and hung it on the landing wall outside the bedroom, close but more suitably located.

Painting of a battle   Upon entering an apartment in Malta, what first struck me was a very large, old painting, hardly visible from many years of atmospheric pollution. The closer I looked at this depressing and energetically dark image, the more detail began to emerge. It was a scene of fierce battle and death called *The Plague of Malta*. Being hung in the area of the Feng Shui life-map associated with relationships, it was adding an emotive flavour to the couple's lives. I suggested they might look at why they had hung the painting there in the first place, and perhaps consider donating it to an arts museum. This they did, where it was restored to its original condition and former clarity, giving their relationship a refreshed vision.

A Greek tragedy unfolds   At a house in Athens, old oil paintings of family ancestors that had previously hung in a heavily haunted house belonging to the lady's parents, carried the embedded energies of many ghostly dark souls. The owners subsequently called in a local priest to exorcise the demonic energies that were causing serious disturbance to their lives. The priest chose to employ the traditional method of fighting evil with the sword of Archangel Michael, but his actions resulted in the daughter's dog taking the hit and being fatally thrown off the roof. As a natural protector, the dog died in an attempt to save the little girl's life. The entities in the house were aggravated by this approach of attack, rather than being acknowledged and heard. Even active, evil energies are part of the unity of creation and can be brought to rest by compassionate means. These dark entities took out their revenge on both the priest and the family who had called him in. As is often the case for *The House Whisperer* in such circumstances, time was of the essence in reaching an understanding with these angry, unwilling spirits and a family reluctant to let go of the past. Resolution was eventually achieved with the release of these ghostly beings, finally bringing clarity and peace to the household.

Artefact causes sudden illness   A previously healthy man from Surrey was afflicted with a sudden illness. He was soon at death's door, the medical profession unable to identify his mysterious malady. In the centre of his home was a carved wooden mask, recently brought back from abroad, which carried a very demonic energy. Placed in the health area of the Feng Shui life-map, this exacerbated the damage that a perilous object can cause. Being familiar with similar circumstances, I told his wife to bury the mask. This she did and her husband miraculously began to improve and was better within days; doctors had no idea how he recovered so quickly from a life-threatening illness. Some days later, his wife contacted me as she fell suddenly ill whilst out shopping. On returning home, she found the children playing in the sand pit where the mask had been buried, but had somehow uncovered itself and was out in the open doing dam-age again. This time I told them to burn it, which broke the 'spell' of the artefact so it could no longer cause harm to the family.

Ghosts in the furniture   Items of furniture are occasionally found to carry ghostly energies. A couple in London bought a second-hand bed that came with a man in spirit still lying in it. This did not make for a restful night's sleep or indeed help their relationship. A metaphysical eviction order was therefore needed!

In another scenario, a lady bought two armchairs from a charity shop. The manager received a call complaining that she wished to return the chairs demanding the shop come to collect them. Insisting on knowing why they should take them back, the purchaser replied:

"There are a couple of old ladies sitting in the armchairs who won't go away, so I don't want them!"

Russian man in the chair   A couple returning to England after working in Russia wanted to sell their house, but viewers were reluctant to go into the living room. Upon entering this space, I could sense at the far end a very ominous energy. Looking deeper into the layers of the unseen worlds, I noticed an elderly Russian man sitting comfortably in an armchair brought back by the owners from their apartment. Having come with the furniture so to speak, well entrenched in the familiar comfort of his chair, he was quite unaware that his presence might deter potential buyers. Knowing that I must be as tactful as possible in approaching this complacent and slightly confused elderly gentleman, I needed to find a way of telling him that he was no longer alive and had to leave. Already with his feet up, smoking a cigar, I decided to sit with him and share a shot of vodka to sensitively broach the subject. I began my delivery:

"Mr X, I have some news for you."

He leaned forward, curious as to what I had to say:

"You happen to be in the wrong country... and what's more, you're dead!"

Rather surprisingly, he didn't seem the slightest bit perturbed and looked me in the eyes as if to say he knew this all along. Taking another sip of his vodka, he then casually got up and strolled off. Having released his hold on the chair, this freed-up the unusually odd energy overlay on the property, which sold soon afterwards.

Heart connection with grandfather clock In an apartment in Lisbon, Portugal, stood a grandfather clock graciously ticking away, the pride and joy of its owner. When he was admitted to hospital with a heart problem and fell into a coma, the clock stopped. Despite his wife winding it up, it would just not tick. After a month when he came out of the coma, with treatment and his condition no longer critical, the clock began to tick again of its own accord.

This is a perfect example of a person so connected to a much-loved object that it becomes attuned to them at a very deep level, responding acutely to its owner's consciousness. Mechanical and electrical devices notoriously respond both in sympathy and even erratically to human emotion and paranormal phenomena, especially in tense, stressful atmospheres that fragment the energy fields.

Traumatised Cars and Vehicles

In many garages and workshops, we find the souls of traumatised cars from road accidents and crashes. If the overlay of human shock and trauma is not released and discharged from the vehicle, the existing or new owner of a repaired car will soak up the intensity of emotion from the accident. Even worse, the event may replay whilst they are driving that same car, so they find themselves involved in the inevitable consequences of a similar accident. This principle is comparable to an accident blackspot, which holds the memory of an event that keeps happening in the same location (Whisper 6).

At a car breakers' yard in Newcastle, the emotions emanating from crashed vehicles arriving after an accident were primarily of fear and distress, imprinted at the moment of impact. When these car parts have been torn away from the main vehicle, they comprise a mass of distressed and isolated mechanical limbs, heart valves and other body parts, making up a stock room resembling Death Valley. Many vehicles were also holding a resonance of the various countries of their make of origin, adding to the confused sense of disorder. Once these soul fragments were released and the disturbed energies of fear dispersed, the spare car parts were able to 'communicate' with each other and could rest with greater ease on the storeroom shelves. As a result, the very next day business markedly increased and on the second day, the phones didn't stop ringing.

Spirit release from a vehicle The fragmented soul parts of a person who dies in an accident can overlay the soul of the vehicle, whether a lorry, bus, car or motorcycle. This is exactly what happened some years ago, when a local collector purchased the motorbike on which the well-known Lawrence of Arabia (T E Lawrence) was killed, in May 1935, in Dorset. When he invited his friend to see his new acquisition, the now retired reverend gentleman in question was unable to go anywhere near it without feeling the distress that emanated from the machine. As a healer, he could feel the 'stuck' energies and 'see' Lawrence still attached to his *Brough Superior*. After working painstakingly for some time, communicating gently with his spirit and explaining that he was to be freed, prayerfully thanking him for the work he did whilst inhabiting his body, both rider and motorbike were released at last. After the accident, at one stage during restoration the handlebars had apparently sat on the desk of a workshop mechanic for a year. The *Brough* went on to fetch considerably more at auction than had been paid, even without its more recent provenance. It was thought that it had gone to America, but was later discovered that Lawrence's restored motorcycle was proudly on display in the Imperial War Museum in London, the only exhibit with its own room.

Attachment and Spirit Release

Any spirits or soul fragments already residing in a house will cause greater disturbance when an occupant has a history of 'attachment' with a person they have been unable to let go of or may have inadvertently allowed to hang around. This can happen when a person has a fragmented or leaky aura owing to past trauma or abuse. Problems are compounded in the event of severe shock, which can upset the system at many levels and create a greater propensity for spirit activity. This applies both to the person at the time of passing who may attempt to re-establish a union, and to the recipient open to experiencing an attachment or even to be taken over by another. This is usually someone with whom they have an emotional or ancestral connection and have empathy, even if not in a good way.

It can often take years for people in this situation to recognise what is going on, let alone know what to do about it. Yet at some level they may have always known, but were unable to talk about it or find the right person able to help. Even though a person's issues may interact with the predecessor imprints in the home, they will be far more affected if their past carries a resonance to a matching story that will activate what is being held dormant in the building. This touches on a not uncommon condition that I have come across in working with people; trauma follows you wherever you go until it is released from the person. This is really important otherwise it will sabotage everything in your life, not just the home you live in. Why this happens to some people and not others may be part of the karmic soul lesson or contract they have chosen in this incarnation. Living with an attachment to one or more aspects of a deceased soul is quite different from moving into a house where a disembodied spirit already resides.

Communal living Anywhere condensed patterns of physically, mentally and emotionally challenged individuals reside – retirement and residential homes, community centres, hospitals and units for psychiatric patients – are prime host targets for paranormal activity and intense forms of emotional distress. In older hospitals especially, we find wards of the 'walking dead' wandering around waiting to take up residence in a new physical body. When under anaesthetic during surgery, the human body is vulnerable to invasion by discarnate beings seeking a host. We sometimes hear:

"He/she was never quite the same after their operation."

When a person acquires an attachment, they will display characteristics of the invasive personality. In extreme cases, someone who is totally taken over by a spirit entity is referred to as a 'walk-in'.

Attachment of unborn child   A mother was concerned that her teenage son had acquired a spirit attachment whilst under anaesthetic during an operation, which had caused him problems since puberty. Although hospitals are rife with spirits seeking a host, there was something more to this situation. As I guided her to connect with her son and the energy attachment, we both sensed a black amorphous 'being' near his head. Dropping into her heart, a deep sense of compassion overcame her. I wanted to ask if she had ever lost a baby, but held back and waited. I then saw a cord linking the two together getting longer as the 'being' began slowly to draw away.

After a few minutes, a feeling of euphoria was perceptible; we both opened our eyes knowing that the spirit had been released. The mother acknowledged her need to protect this other male energy, and was sad for it to go. She then told me of a dream the night before she miscarried at four months pregnant, giving her a boy's name. Her pain and sadness from that time resulted in her unconsciously looking after both her children; her teenage son and the younger lost baby attached to him. With a poignant sense of peace and relief, she knew that both her boys were now free.

A love triangle   The unfolding of this relationship revealed a complex situation between a married couple and a young girl who was tragically killed. When the husband was six years of age, he saw his brother's friend, a girl classmate of eight years old, run over and killed by a bus, and recalled looking into her eyes after she had been hit. Since the accident, fragments of her soul remained attached to him. He had 'taken on' the girl through a sense of compassion and looked after her in another realm, acknowledging that he watched her in spirit every night as she actually shared the marital bed. He had been living out a fantasy relationship unbeknown to his wife, with unforeseen consequences to his marriage and his own health.

Jilted woman's anger ingrained in the bed A wedding bed in a secluded English country house was causing much disturbance to guests who slept in it. The bed was a gift but came with a history of anger related to the original owner, a furious jilted wife who had unconsciously created an active live link, a type of curse generated from anger rather than any conscious intent. Once the intensity of her emotional energy was disconnected and dissolved through a metaphysical process, this active link to the bed was broken.

Fear of dying A deceased man was afraid to let go of life and his loved ones, and so clung onto his house and to his wife whom he deeply loved. She felt him around her much of the time, which on occasions made her feel quite uncomfortable. She was consequently beginning to exhibit personality traits that were not entirely her own but more like those of her husband. Having connected with him and resolved his concerns, he was then able to release his link to the house, leaving him free to visit in spirit should he so choose.

When someone is fearful of dying, they can cling onto aspects of what they had in life and continue to inhabit their house just as they did before. Their presence in a parallel dimension can cause problems for the remaining spouse, partner or family members, and even for new owners who may have since moved in, making it difficult for all to fully embrace their home and get on with their own lives.

Helping the person in spirit to understand and come to terms with their fears and concerns, which are as real now as when they were alive, can assist their soul in resolving issues so they can release towards the light. One might consider this approach as psychotherapy from beyond the grave, yet it is no different to sitting in a room with a person and guiding them to consider their issues towards finding resolution.

Ghost busting or addressing the story My work is not about going around releasing 'stuck' spirits simply because they have ended up in 'ghost-land'. Spirit release should certainly not be carried out for the sake of sensationalism or without permission. Very many paranormal films only seem to focus on a sensational portrayal of certain features of a storyline for entertainment value. The media rarely uncover the entire backdrop and usually fail to address the fundamental reasons why a departed soul became trapped in the first place. Worse still is the heartless approach to the concept of ghost busting that exposes spirits only to leave them screaming, fearful and angry, causing a violent trail of destruction and all kinds of chaos in their wake. Because being treated in this way leads to further fragmentation, soul retrieval will at some stage be needed in order to piece back together the splintered parts of a damaged soul.

Before any spirit or soul fragment can be freed and released from a place, object or person, the bigger picture needs to be addressed for the benefit of current occupants, the spirit beings themselves, and the building in question. Understanding the reasons why they were drawn to a particular place and became stuck or attached to a house or person, are crucial to establish. Just moving them on or trying to get rid of something only moves the problem around and resolves nothing. Inevitably they will either return and cause further problems or create an imbalance elsewhere.

Spirit beings co-existing with current residents are not necessarily aware of each other or even that they have passed over, and may not always be asking for help. Should a person be unable to resolve their deep need for perhaps security or comfort, they may very well take on a co-dependent presence in the form of a departed soul, as with the *Invisible relationships* and other stories (Whisper 2). This can be what has happened to people diagnosed with multiple personality disorders, which can then entrap both parties and may hinder the release of a spirit that wants to move on. Healthy resolution can only be achieved by addressing why the dependency first came about.

My work as *The House Whisperer* is to find the true narrative as to why a deceased person hangs onto some aspect of their departed life, and to facilitate resolution followed by meaningful and compassionate release. My usual approach is to gently activate a shift within the vibrational frequencies of the geometric matrix of the space, which is like a crystalline web holding human thought patterns. This loosens up the emotional bonds and allows enough movement for those who are inextricably involved to become consciously aware of their own personal connection in the wheel of life. It may be that another person is hanging on to the deceased through their emotional attachment, making it harder for its spirit to let go, especially when in turn it is 'tagging on' to someone living in the present. In these circumstances, to initially involve them may only compound the problem, although they are a necessary part of the process. They may first need to resolve karmic issues in their own life relating to the departed soul, which may illuminate their role in why its release has been restricted.

If the issues are very deep and intense, it may be too traumatic to attempt to resolve them in one go, and can give rise to paranormal happenings along the way. Therefore, resolution and release in stages may be needed with all those involved, otherwise this can result in the traumatic shattering of a soul that is trapped between worlds. As with ghost-busting, the shaman or energy worker then has the task of soul retrieval, gathering up fragmented soul parts through dimensions of time and space in order to reunite them as a whole.

Exorcism As we have seen, when a stuck or wandering departed soul is searching for company and finds an empathetic emotion, its spirit can lodge into a living person who carries a familiar resonance or emotional need. By loosening up the energies in a property, as well as the personal energy fields of souls both living and in spirit, this gives both sides the opportunity to recognise the nature of any co-dependant relationship. They can then choose to deal with releasing the emotional bonds between them and be set free of one another.

With any consultation involving unwanted spirit energies or an attachment, if the stuck soul is reluctant to let go or refuses to leave through various cord-cutting techniques, an exorcism may be appropriate. This does not need to be a violent, distressing or sensational course of action, as so often depicted in films.

All types of spirit energies seek resolution and release. Even the reluctant malicious ones have the desire at some deeper level to re-integrate with the unity of creation. Compassionate recognition that we are all but a reflection of universal Self is far more powerful than attempting to force further separation or soul extinction. Physics tells us that as a form of energy, there is nowhere for these beings to go other than for their soul essence to be transformed or transmuted. Successful resolution comes about as a result of the skill of the practitioner and their philosophy of life. One can either fight evil with the omnipotent sword, or approach a situation knowing that unity exists within all of creation and assist in releasing a departed spirit or soul fragment with compassionate action. This is no complacent process and requires experience and focus to prevent negative energies from rebounding, as in the earlier account of the *Greek tragedy*.

The need for protection Many people ask how I protect myself. Ultimately, even when working with dark, destructive lower astral energies, if one is totally connected to Source, there is no separation in truth and thus nothing to protect from. But in the theatre of life we so readily drop into duality, so before any work is carried out there is value to consider invoking a degree of protection using coded shields (Whisper 7). My approach will depend on the nature and degree of danger that I am walking into, such as psychic attack from other realms. I have developed some refined intuitive and metaphysical abilities in this specialised field of spiritual work, which I deploy as appropriate. It is certainly not advisable for those without experience of working with soul retrieval, spirit release or entity removal, to attempt this on their own. It is not an activity for the fainthearted!

Awareness of a full range of vibrational energies, from the higher angelic to the lower earth energies is required. Universal law holds that higher vibrations can interpenetrate the world of lower vibrational frequencies, but not the other way around. Higher vibrational beings can read the lower ones, which cannot themselves see the higher ones even though they may be drawn to their resonance.

If a feature of your own life resonates to the matter at hand, the emotionally vulnerable human tendency can lead to a strong temptation to be drawn into the matching story. So, to prevent finding yourself lost in the shadows or immersed in the drama of others, my suggested approach is to maintain a high vibration, remain detached and not become deeply involved. There is, however, always something of positive value to be gained by understanding any matching resonant patterns that may relate to personal issues in your own life.

Whisper 4

BUYING AND SELLING A PROPERTY

What do we want from moving home?

Why Do We Move Home?

In deciding whether to move house or make changes to the home we already live in, we are likely to be seeking some kind of change in our lives, perhaps in our intimate relationships also. Likewise, we express change in our lives through various aspects of our homes. This energetic connection is very often synchronistic.

We move house for a whole host of reasons, including the rational and financial aspects of life. Sometimes where we live just doesn't feel right any more or we simply don't like the neighbours. Maybe the location is no longer appropriate for work, school or some other factor. We may feel the need to settle, want a bigger or smaller space, our relationships change through separation, divorce or death of a loved one. In other instances, we may want to experience life with a new partner, or just want to improve our happiness and wellbeing. Whatever the reason for our decision to move, it is usually because our home is out of alignment with our current circumstances or even life purpose, so we seek to realign ourselves in a different place. Finding ourselves in the 'wrong' place, we are likely to feel disconnected from both our home and our lives. This leads to a fracturing of our energy fields and can put the immune system under stress, which can eventually shut down, affect the heart and cause serious illness.

Many people say that they moved to where they now live as a short-term temporary measure. They never intended to stay long and have never really felt at home there. Years later, they wonder why they have been unable to move out and move on with their lives:

"My home was meant to be a stepping stone, I never intended to stay longer than a year, but yet here I am after eleven years and still don't think of it as home."

For those who live in more than one place and perhaps spend time at a weekend cottage or a boat, it may take time on returning to reconnect with their main home. The ability to flow smoothly between various homes will depend on the sense of heart connection to each place. Just as when planning a business trip or holiday, we find that a few days before departure our energy body has already gone on ahead, several days before our physical body catches up.

Those people who live in numerous places and have no fixed abode as such, spending time house-sitting for others, staying with friends or family, camping out, volunteering in a community and so forth, can find their lifestyle makes for unstable and ungrounded relationships. This may have started out for a variety of reasons, perhaps due to not having the funds to start again with a mortgage after a divorce, not finding the right place when a tenancy came to an end, or a job involves going somewhere they do not really want to settle. In many instances, however, people simply cannot find a house that fits all their perceived requirements.

Unable to find a house When people have been looking for months or even years, have viewed countless properties and yet still cannot find a home, something is very fundamentally wrong. This person expresses the sentiment of many:

"Have been looking for ages and seen hundreds of houses but cannot find the right one!"

For an individual or a couple seeking a home, success in finding the perfect property is dependent upon the clarity and union of their desire for what is wanted. One couple could just not agree; each disliked aspects of the properties that the other was drawn to. The problem was that their individual vision of life was not in alignment with each other or their relationship. Both were projecting their desires of the ideal house onto what the other partner was seeking. This created confusion in their thought transmission check-list, inhibiting them as a couple from attracting their perfect dream house. Once their heart connection comes fully into alignment with each other and they send out a unified message, the right house will respond and is likely to appear very shortly afterwards.

Buying Your Perfect Home

Individual needs and desires are expressed and translated through the homes in which we live. Most of us want to enjoy living in spaces that feel comfortable as well as look pleasing. The aim of developers and property agents is to sell houses easily in a short space of time, essentially to make a profit. During challenging market cycles it is therefore even more important that homes 'for sale' have the edge with the 'feel good' factor. Alternatively, being able to make our existing homes more comfortable, nourishing and harmonious places to live, takes on an even greater importance.

When making the decision to move to a new house, apartment or business premises, we need to know what to look for. What creates that 'feel good' factor, leading us to feel we can truly make it our own space? Given that we choose our homes according to our attitudes, belief systems and past patterns, our inner emotional issues are to a great extent projected towards finding the ideal place to live.

We have seen that people's lives are affected and influenced by the spaces where they choose to live and work, and by what happened there before. The significance of many of these factors relate to the energetic patterns that drive our motivation and run the underlying purpose of our lives. We may feel we are not in control, but that is not necessarily the case.

Whilst the important considerations tend to be location, price and suitability, we can be drawn to a house for many other reasons. Most people are attracted to buy or rent a property because it 'feels' right. The eyes can confuse. The heart is the magnetic attractor, vastly more powerful than the mind, which along with our gut instinct tells us this is the place for us. We may not be able to consciously explain how or why we chose a particular home, but it is usually because at some level we love it. I suggested to one lady that she stood in the house, closed her eyes and 'viewed' it with her heart. Having done this with her partner they bought the house, moved in and just love being there. Another couple who followed their heart, said:

"We just felt this was the right house and I know I'll be happy and feel safe here."

This elusive feeling, often more subconscious than rational, is how we perceive the life force of a building. Sharp skills of perception are needed to uncover numerous pre-existing layers that mirror our perceived reality. To consider whether a different house is going to benefit or hinder your life can be just as crucial, if not more so, than simply liking it and whether or not the furniture will fit.

Resolving life issues in relation to your current property will give you a much better understanding of the suitability of a potential new home. Without resolution with your current home, you are likely to find that your next property will carry the same familiar matching patterns, forcing those issues to be faced yet again. The purpose of illuminating the process of house searching is to help in the smooth transition to your new home from the outset. In essence, it is about the soul's journey back to Self, often as long and tortuous as Homer's *Odyssey* with a series of personal challenges and obstacles thrown in.

When seeking to move, I will check that a residential property is propitious for your next stage in life and identify any hidden issues in the building that may need adjusting if and when the transaction goes ahead. Also considered is the level of stress on the land, the dynamics of previous occupants, orientation of the building and your personal astrology. Then there is the crucial matter of timing – is your next house actually available for you to occupy?

New house for a new relationship   A fresh start can be beneficial for a couple seeking their first home together. Moving into a partner's current house can create problems owing to existing patterns of ownership and lifestyle, as this person recognised:

"When we got married we felt it important to start our relationship somewhere new that we both shared together... somehow this feeling of territory is quite important, setting the foundations for the relationship otherwise you're always in somebody else's space."

It can be particularly devastating when an ex-partner has moved out and the new partner is expected to replace them. In one situation where the new wife moved into her husband's existing house, she never felt good enough, always being treated and compared as if she had to live up to the ex-wife.

A house waiting for you   It is not so unusual to believe that a house will often wait for a suitable owner. The right house will be there for you even when it has been 'sold'. It will sometimes reappear after many offers have been made; something leads to the sale falling through or the owners take the house off the market until you are ready. This strengthens the concept of a house choosing its occupants. When contracts are exchanged, the new owners will invariably say:

"This house was just waiting for us!"

This is just what happened when a house in Somerset with several acres of land had been on the market for some time. It eventually sold to people who were keen to establish a permaculture centre, clearly in alignment with the consciousness of the land.

Hereditary pattern match   A young lady wanting to buy a house in Sussex sent me the property agents' details for assessment before purchase. I had recently carried out a *House Whispering* consultation for her parents, at a house her mother had chosen. The astounding thing was the pattern match of both properties. The daughter had chosen a house that was visually, characteristically and energetically similar to the home where she grew up. This scenario is not unusual between parents and children or in relation to our previous homes. It is most fascinating, however, when similarities encountered span several generations, especially when spread over different locations.

Just had to buy it back!   In a small New Jersey town, a lady regretted selling her house. She desperately needed to buy it back, so that's exactly what she did. Her connection with this house is quite fascinating. She was to discover evidence that her basement was once used as an early 20th century drinking den, to the stern disapproval of the local priest. One fateful evening when partying was in full swing, he locked the entrance trap door from the outside. Unable to escape, many of the guests perished in an accidental fire.

This consultation was being filmed live whilst we were working in the basement. I placed the incense burner used for space-clearing on the concrete floor as we sat and considered the energy of the space, the memories held in the walls and by the old charred beams. Shortly thereafter, the camera woman accidentally kicked it over as she stepped backwards, but as the charcoal had extinguished there was no concern about it being a fire hazard. Minutes later, I could smell burning and began to cough, yet could see no visible reason for this. Then those present also began to cough. Within moments we were all choking as if the basement was filling with smoke. Realising that this was actually taking place at a metaphysical level for the purpose of recognition and acknowledgment of past history, we remained calm. After ten minutes or so, our sense of reality returned to the present and the atmosphere regained a clean, fresh feeling. We all looked at each other in disbelief at what had just taken place.

Our intention for revelation and resolution was the catalyst that reactivated the catastrophic event of a century or so ago. The deep ingrained blueprint had manifested in the physical world so that the memory patterns and distraught souls could be released. My sense was that the current owner was one of the women who had died in the original fire. She may not have fully consolidated her experiences in that era, which is not uncommon when a person dies suddenly in traumatic circumstances. This may explain why she was compelled to buy the house back, purchasing it twice in this lifetime.

The Power of Dreams

> *"Your vision will become clear only when you look into your heart.*
> *Who looks outside, dreams. Who looks inside, awakens."* (Carl Jung)

Few people are consciously aware of the more subtle implications of the choices they make regarding the place where they spend huge amounts of time and money. Considering that we spend around one third of our lives at home in bed asleep, processing the substance of our inner realms, the psychology of the house is an intriguing arena that leads to all kinds of dreamworld questions. Are the dreams that you have your own, or generated by the residual activity of those who have passed through and dreamt in that space before?

Integral to my work as *The House Whisperer* is illuminating the hidden patterns that affect our dream spaces. The use of analytical systems to understand and unravel dream symbolism can be invaluable. Daydreams are also a rich source of creative imagination and help to bring our relationship with home into more conscious focus. Many cultures believe that during a dream, the soul travels to other dimensions. My own experiences make me very aware of this, both at night and when working during the daytime. Our dreams reflect a multitude of realities, fears, loves and externalised desires, perhaps unrequited. Expressed through the symbolic language of theatrical metaphor, dreams can show us our creative potential. I believe it is possible to unite our outer expression with the ultimate desire of the heart to be 'at One' with the universe, our true inner home.

At Epidaurus in the Peloponnese region of southern Greece, the most celebrated healing centre of the Hellenistic classical world, people went to be healed from many ailments. One modality was through dreaming. After taking certain herbs, they would spend a night in the Sleeping Hall near the sacred mineral springs. The healer god Asclepius would visit them in their dreams and tell them what they had to do to regain their health. Around 300 years after the Romans banned the practice in the first century BCE, the sanctuary enjoyed a new upsurge, ironically under the Romans. Epidaurus became a Christian healing centre until the mid-5th century.

In late 4th century Gloucestershire, England, the Romans built a healing temple dedicated to Nodens (Nudd or Lludd), the Celtic divinity after whom Lydney takes its name. An inscription on a fish-covered mosaic was found to refer to 'Victorinus the Interpreter', believed to have been an interpreter of dreams.

From the inner patterns held in the unconscious higher mind, it is possible to dream and co-create our perfect home. Our way of thinking will determine whether we decide to manifest a castle, a stately home, something more modest, or a cardboard box under a bridge. Just as the homes we choose to live in, our dreams reflect our conscious and deeply held subconscious attitudes and beliefs, which influence all aspects of our lives.

For some people, nightmares emulate the dark underworld, defeating every effort to escape. Paralysed by fear, they can only glimpse the seemingly irrational stories of their homes as they unfold behind their eyes. Holding in its walls the quintessence of your desires, your house *whispers* into the darkness of your soul, magnifying your fears and aspirations that it too can feel. In the corridors of perception and our collective unconscious, we process events and correlate reality with dreams, which we release in the light of day. Just as in the hero's journey or a love story, we reinvent our myths and find that a common thread from many lifetimes begins to reveal itself. We come back to the same theme time and time again, revisited in every character and episode of our journey. Experience shows that archetypes are often non-specific; we connect with those aspects that resonate at an individual soul level.

Fearing abandonment Distressing dreams usually carry a significant message and often mirror unconscious anxieties. One woman reported that she dreamt the walls of her house were filling up with liquid and shrinking, as she heard the silent weeping of an old woman. Was she this elderly person, expressing her fear of abandonment? If you fail to listen and ignore the dreams and desires that your house cries out to share, its longings will only get louder and find some other way of getting your attention.

Frightened child In a London apartment, the original windows with wooden frames were stripped out and replaced with modern double-glazed units. This provided for better thermal insulation as well as acting as a sound buffer from the incessant traffic noise. Although making the apartment more physically secure, after the work was completed the owner commented:

"The flat feels like a frightened child."

Making this significant change to the eyes of the building not only required a period of adjustment, but brought clarity to an aspect of her own soul. The unexpected result was perhaps a reflection of childhood vulnerability needing to be drawn to her attention for the purpose of illuminating whatever needed resolution.

Seeking the inner dream My eldest daughter asked me to assess the suitability of an empty property in Spain that she was drawn to and thinking of buying. Excited at the prospect of moving from England to a warmer climate, it was clear to me that Spain suited her temperament and would potentially support her creative dreams with more ease and flow. However, when I ran a *House Whispering* check on this cosy, protective but dilapidated town house, I found it to be holding a very heavy, stagnant energy, making it difficult to breathe. The entire place felt like a trap that lured you in, enticing the next person to conform to the lives of those who lived there before.

As we explored the reasons why the house attracted her, she understood how certain aspects related to her own life experiences. Its characteristic urban quaintness and scattered, withered rooftops appealed to the artisan lifestyle she dreamt of pursuing. This ratifies the concept that a person is drawn to a property by how it feels rather than purely its physical characteristics or rational reasons for moving. Having appreciated what the house ignited within her, this helped her to recognise that choosing to live there would begin to unravel subconscious personal patterns that matched those held in the memory of the house. Once these were awakened, she would have little choice but be forced to work through them. To resist doing so would lead to her becoming out of sync with the house, when further problems could then arise, especially health issues.

Although she was prepared for the personal unfolding that the house would potentially activate, she chose not to buy a property that did not support her expansive dream and would keep her trapped in a small world. There were also unsupportive energetic and Feng Shui aspects to its location, beyond being hemmed in by its surroundings. The front door faced a tall building, blocking any outward vision of life. Had there been a high building, a 'mountain' support behind the house, it would in Feng Shui terms have been highly beneficial (Whisper 7). Although this house had sung to her soul the moment she first saw it and sparked her vision of a bohemian town life, my daughter recognised that in order to realise her full authentic potential she really needed a more rural location. So the process she went through in exploring its purchase was of great value in clarifying what she truly wanted to fulfil her vision of a nourishing, joyful and expansive life, a true artist wanting to paint on a bigger canvas.

This is a good example of how we can indeed get co-dependant houses seeking an owner as well as people seeking a house. Just as we project our inner reality onto a personal partner, we do the same with a house; this acts as the catalyst towards understanding and rec-onciling certain life stories. The consciousness of a building, moulded and shaped by the lives of previous occupants, might also be seeking some degree of soul resolution. It will likewise draw in its next owner so that specific issues can play out for this purpose. The skill is to recognise what is going on and to discern whether you will benefit from moving to a particular property. Even a house you might dream of can bring unexpected surprises, as in the following situations:

Dreaming your home into existence For twenty years, this lady had daydreamed about the house behind the hill that she frequently drove past and had fallen in love with. She felt her soul would be at peace there, so was compelled to buy her dream home when it came onto the market. However, her eventual purchase precipitated many years of decline in various aspects of the lives of her entire family. Soon after moving in, the children complained that their hair was being played with and their legs pulled during the night. There were certain matters that most definitely needed to be dealt with.

Another lady contacted me when she and her husband were both experiencing the same dream of their new home, and within days found the actual property. The moment they first walked in they knew this was the house they had pictured in their dreams. After buying it and moving in, they were told that the house was built on a Native American burial ground and wondered if they had been there before. Was their dream the unrequited desires from long ago, incu-bating over centuries from countless activities on the land, reviving buried memories of ancestral or past life connections? Nonetheless, problems of a paranormal nature soon began to activate, and some very strange events and life stories started to unfold.

Going home Some people do not feel that for them 'home' is planet Earth, and yearn to find the star system of their true belonging.

Whilst teaching at a workshop in Portland, Oregon, as I stood in the centre of a magnificent labyrinth created by the host in her gar-den, I felt an incredibly powerful vortex spin as if directed upwards somewhere very specific. I had a strong sense that this structure was a vehicle or etheric ship of some kind. The host then confirmed my intuition that she had in fact unconsciously designed and created an energetic transportation 'vehicle' to take her back home to a distant galaxy. As Plato clearly states, sacred geometry creates portals into other dimensions (Whisper 7), in this case embedded in the labyrinth.

Precognition The understanding of the themes we perpetuate frequently comes to us as a sense of precognition. We may dream of something about to occur in our own life or related to the personal story of someone else, maybe to both. In moments of crisis, many of us find that we know things about which our normal sense of cognition is unaware: perhaps the whereabouts of someone or something required urgently. In such instances of accessing our higher consciousness, we tap into the Akashic memory field of resonance, piercing the veil of knowledge that connects all things.

In the world of *The House Whisperer*, a dream envisioned at night or random thoughts during the day, will often provide an insight as to what may be about to unfold, as the following story illustrates:

The Girl in the Bath

In the misty light of night, I find myself wandering, lost and confused through a thatched English country cottage, opening and closing creaking doors as I tread the uneven floorboards. Something is not quite right with the strange mix of architectural rhetoric here. The 18th century timber framing is familiar, although the hallway is larger than it should be and the windows are of Georgian style.

Why am I looking for my younger daughter? In near panic, my heart beats faster as I move more quickly now along the narrow corridors in an eerie silence, ducking the low beams as I pace from room to room. My body breaking into sweat, as I reach the bathroom my eyes are drawn to an old fashioned roll-top bath. In disbelief, I find her lying motionless under the water. Leaning over the edge, I plunge my arms into the lukewarm water in an attempt to lift her out, her body still faintly warm.

This rapid sequence of events again flashes before my eyes and jolts my whole being. I awaken to find myself sitting bolt upright in bed, my heart still racing, but where is my daughter? I try to make sense of what may have caused her death, searching my soul to understand any part that I may have played during her childhood. I even get up and check my bathroom just in case she might actually be in there. Then I remember she doesn't live with me but feel compelled to telephone her to make sure she is safe. The feelings and sensations of a moment ago continue to pulsate and shudder through every cell of my body. The air begins to settle as my sense of reality begins to normalise, whatever that might be?

Country house replay The next morning, on our journey to a country house in Wiltshire to assist the lady owner with its sale, I tell Sandy of my dream. I mention my bemusement at the absurdity of the cottage with those strange incongruous windows, and tell her of my panic to call my daughter. We both sense that it could be an omen of what the day holds in store, perhaps related to the house we are about to visit. Recounting more of my nightmare, there is recognition in her eyes. Being someone who understands the deeper psychology of people, she knows which wounds are playing out. Is Sandy enacting my feminine side, speaking softly into my ear from another dimension, guiding me to listen to my own inner *whisperings*?

Arriving at the estate, we pass the gatehouse and continue for about a mile along the woodland approach, enjoying the shimmering sunlight dancing on the leaves of the tall trees. As we get closer, the house now in sight, my heart pounds in anticipation. Feeling the fear and tension surrounding the property, a sense of loss and confusion overlays the emotional ravages of countless owners throughout aeons of time.

We pull up around the circular parking area, an old French-style fountain echoing a worn sense of grandeur. Standing in majestic splendour is a stately house with the very same Georgian windows envisioned in my dream. As I turn to look at Sandy, we exchange knowing glances. I mention that when someone is having trouble selling a property, it can hold them prisoner until they have fulfilled their soul purpose as to why they were drawn there in the first place; but she knows that anyway.

Entering the house, ominous odours of stale cigar smoke and dank wood permeate the air. The heavy wooden staircase winds around the open hall, the wailing sounds of sailors emanating from the cracked lacquer of reclaimed ships' timbers. Walking through the many rooms with the lady owner, we feel the energies of the various spaces and become aware of a sense of vigorous masculine control, a prevalent feeling of sheer abandonment and emotional wounding of the feminine. Mentioning the laced smell of alcohol in the air, the owner shares the history of various women of the house having furtive access to a well-stocked wine cellar.

We enter a small single bedroom, where I freeze for an instant with a sudden flashback to my dream of the girl in the bath. My awareness flips back and forth through simultaneous time zones. Although my eyes see a bed, my inner perception sees a bath. Sharing my insight with the owner, she reveals that the bed *is* in the actual position of where there was once a bath:

"This is the only room I converted from a bathroom into a bedroom."

Sandy sensed very clearly that the young wife of a family who once lived here was extremely unhappy in a male dominated household, typical of the country estate lifestyle of the period. Left alone, virtually abandoned by a husband who worked away for long periods of time, she was heard to say in great distress:

"I had no choice, I could bear it no longer..."

Feeling there was no other way to find peaceful sanctuary but to take her own life, she committed suicide in the bath. I was deeply aware that this was the girl I had construed as my daughter in the dream. In releasing the spirit of the young wife, it seemed that she had taken on the archetypal plight of the feminine burden of her generation. This was just one of the many story lines embedded within the house.

There was, however, something rather odd affecting its ability to sell. Over the coming weeks, whatever we attempted from various perspectives of personal and spatial resolution did not result in a buyer coming forward. The owner commented:

"It was as if the house was playing tricks."

As we sat around the dining room table one day, considering the next steps, it was clear that the owner was not blocking her own sale as can so often happen. Then it suddenly dawned on me that there was definitely someone else holding back the sale, connected in some way to this gracious country house, so who was it? Upon checking through a list of known people associated with the house, using dowsing for *yes/no* answers, it turned out to be a man who loved his work in maintaining the house and grounds. After exchanging a few words with him, the final hold on the property was released and the house soon found a new owner.

Buying a Nightmare House

Believing we are moving to a place that we feel is 'right' for us, why is it that things can go so wrong, shattering the reality of living in our new dream home? When we move house or circumstances around us change, our sense of loss of what is familiar and secure can be reinforced by a natural fear of the unknown. The shock of sudden change in our framework is fed back into our original blueprint pattern, creating trauma in our personal energy fields. This is when we hear:

"Nothing has gone right since we moved!"

Psychologists tell us that the three most stressful things in life are death, divorce and moving house. For some people, moving house is worse than divorce. This is simply because the framework of a house incorporates all nine areas of life (Whisper 7), which are all shaken up simultaneously when we move, whereas in a divorce only the relationship box is initially shattered. Repercussions then follow with finances, children, career, and in other areas to varying degrees.

Patterns of disaster   What we think and feel gets projected into our home spaces and will linger. The same applies to those with whom we share our spaces; our spouses, partners or family members will perpetuate an emotional atmosphere, making us feel comfortable or ill at ease. The effect of being out of alignment with our homes can result in the outcry:

"Why are disasters always happening to me since we moved here?"

Arguments or minor accidents can take place in certain parts of the home:

"We always argue when we go into a particular room."

Following their move, one mother reported that while the rest of the family felt reasonably settled:

"My daughter of sixteen hates our house and has major issues here."

It is often when our outer supporting structure changes that we learn by experience the importance of our alignment to whatever 'home' means on a personal level, and recognise the need for harmonic resonance around us. The feeling of being out of sync with the world, adrift with no anchor, brings pain internally and makes us unhappy. As the house feels our distress and interacts with our psyche, this can be reflected in broken dreams. With no supporting structure, we encounter problems with our health:

"There's a dark heavy feeling in my stomach... I've been really sick since I moved here."

Resonant health issues In agreeing to take on the legal contract for a property, we also take on its energetic blueprint. As with predecessor patterns, a person may choose to live in a property that holds the resonant pattern of their health issues. I once encountered an individual with early stage dementia who feared losing their job, yet was attracted to move into a house where the previous occupant had similarly suffered. In contrast, as we shall see shortly, a person can be affected by the illness of those who occupied the same house and/or worked the land before them.

When the unconscious mind recognises a threat from the building it has chosen to occupy, the energy fields of the body contract and compromise the immune system, creating a disposition towards illness. It is not necessarily only the design aspects of a building such as room shapes and beams, together with toxic materials used, which lead to an energetic fragmentation of space. More significantly, a person who is already unwell or has a propensity towards a particular illness or life pattern, may be drawn through resonance to a place with inherent problems which can exacerbate any pre-existing health condition, sometimes causing unusual symptoms they have never experienced before. This woman experienced a whole spectrum of disasters and health issues after moving house:

> *"Since I moved into this house, my life has turned a bit upside down. In the beginning I had really bad headaches, especially during the night, which led me to vomit, something I never do. Small accidents also tend to happen, and there was once a small fire that started in the kitchen in a most stupid and strange way... I also feel that this house is sucking up my energy like it's feeding itself from me."*

To bring about change means breaking the cycle of why certain forms of illness happen in one's life. Why does a person perpetuate a temperamental bias or disposition by seeking an environment that does not allow their subconscious patterns to be released?

Emotional distress In universal law, negative thoughts, especially fear and anxiety, are likely to bring challenges or difficulties into our lives. In situations of mental or physical abuse, consider the possibility that a person might in some way have a part to play in choosing that experience. We are all aware that health issues are frequently caused through stress. Anything that helps to release this build-up is worthwhile making a regular practice. Simply going for a walk in the park can reconnect you with the fractal quality of nature and help to re-adjust any fragmented energies that you may be carrying. It is worth being mindful of the vicious cycle created by subconsciously hiding from the world and not facing up to any pertinent issues through feeling unwell or just not wanting to deal with them. When a person tells me it took them years to get over something, I will ask her or him to consider why they might have chosen to hold onto the emotional distress. The reply is very often that no one could possibly have any idea of the magnitude of the problems they've been through.

Unable to enter the house One couple bought a house that the wife was initially attracted to. However, on the day of moving in, her husband went to turn the key to open the front door and froze; he simply could not physically walk in. He sensed that something felt very wrong, different to when he first saw the house. Perturbed by this, he immediately wanted to sell the place. They decided to stay in a hotel and it took several days before they could return and move in:

"Ever since then I've never really felt comfortable in the place."

When I was asked to *whisper* to the house some twelve years later, the reason why he was repelled at the front door and had felt disdain for the property ever since, became apparent. Several spirit presences lodged in the house were hovering in the entrance, including one of a murdered woman. His wife at first felt comfortable with the house because its past history had a resonance to aspects of her own life, yet something was challenging her health. Although her husband still disliked the house, he had no connection to the significance of the main stories embedded in its memory. His concern was the need to look after his wife.

A degree of resolution was achieved following a space-clearing and realignment of the active earth energies, which released the lingering spirit energies. With the house liberated from numerous overlays, clearly contributing to the fragmentation of space, it felt much calmer and the couple were much more at ease in an enhanced atmosphere. They were then able to renew their relationship with the true essence of the house, and resume their personal healing journeys without the underlying destructive influences impeding them.

Purchased with conditional money When we buy a property with money given to us or inherited, perhaps from parents, relatives or friends, there can often be conditions or a controlling influence that comes with the gift. The problem is that the energy signature of the money (which is after all a form of energy) may be tainted, as it retains a live link to the attitudes and expectations of the benefactor.

On several occasions, people have told me they feel as though they are being kept as children, unable to grow up in a property purchased with parents' money. As a result of subconsciously trying to escape 'the grip', they are unable to truly settle and make it their home. They may even move out, but often tend to get drawn back!

Poverty consciousness   Just as a property can hold blueprint patterns of disaster, patterns of poverty consciousness can also exist. On some occasions, I visit homes where people are living in unbelievable squalor, yet still expect to be successful.

A couple living in the south of France just could not make ends meet. Their finances were at rock bottom and they could not sell their house even though it was in a very desirable location. It transpired that the previous owners had been running a poverty belief programme that still echoed in the house. Having energetically reset this atmospheric imprint, it created a clear space for the current owners to look at their own belief systems around lack of money and self-worth. The important link here is that they chose a house carrying a poverty syndrome, which would perpetuate until they addressed their deep-seated issues and could dispel the established programme.

To alter these blueprint patterns, we need to connect with the healing potential of our spaces and realign them with our own personal energy signature. This must take place on all levels, encompassing the physical, mental and spiritual aspects of our being. We can draw an analogy to a CD, DVD or Blu-Ray disk that holds audio and visual content, but we need to press 'play' to activate the encoded information in order to experience it and bring the harmonic patterns into manifestation in our lives (Whisper 7). I will continue to work with people until they reach this point of clarity and potential transformation should they so wish. In helping to release unhelpful personal patterns, this also gives a property the best chance of selling.

Karmic Attraction

As we may now appreciate, our own stories and patterns, including what influences us to choose a specific house, could link back to a previous incarnation. The laws of karma determine that any unfinished business from past lives call us in this lifetime to return for resolution. We may encounter family ancestors or people with whom we have past life connections, and even be drawn back to the same property or area. This usually relates to healing either a personal situation or one of locality, town or even country. Whatever decisions we make today not only impact on our daily lives, but any further issues created that remain unresolved will then contribute to our karma of tomorrow.

On several occasions, I have come across people who quite categorically say they recognised the house they ended up buying when they first saw it, that it felt familiar. This recognition may just be a resonance to a familiar aspect of another house they once lived in. Other people claim to have very clear memories of having lived in the actual property itself in another lifetime. So the question is, have we been here before?

Role reversal In a previous lifetime, the owner of a country house in the north of England lived in the gatehouse and worked for the Lord of the Manor. In this lifetime, they had swapped roles, with a whole spectrum of issues of a very complex nature to resolve.

For the current worker at the gatehouse, the undercurrents of wanting aspects of what he had in the past rumbled just below the surface, affecting life for the current owners of the main house. Whilst he remained superficially respectful, constant undertones of subterfuge infused communications on a daily basis. A consultation was arranged as the patterns had to be broken, along with many other life issues needing to be addressed. In unravelling the complex dynamics between various groups of people from the past, many intriguing stories came to light. The extraordinary thing was, by illuminating the central themes of the situation, the current owners were able to remember some of those past events that were quite divisive and even violent at times. Moreover, within their current circle of friends, they recognised relationships with people from their past lives with whom they were still interacting on a regular basis. Opportunities arose for making amends for any wrongdoings that had taken place some centuries ago, indicating that the matter of karmic responsibility transcends time and space.

Ancestral home Although he did not know it when he bought Mottisfont House in Hampshire in 1934, Gilbert Russell discovered himself to be a descendant of William Briwere, the man who founded Mottisfont Priory in 1201. The arrival of Maud and Gilbert Russell made Mottisfont a fashionable place for entertaining artists and writers including Rex Whistler, whose Gothic revival architecture can be seen in a room dedicated to him today. The House and its wonderfully landscaped grounds, including a magnificent rose garden, are now under the care of the National Trust. Curiously, many of the Trust's properties have interesting ancestral histories that extend beyond traditional family inheritance.

Hotel pub landlord Whilst having a drink in the local bar of a small hotel in Wiltshire, I noticed a man with a rather odd demeanour sitting with his jug of ale in the corner. Intrigued by his character, I sat down next to him and began chatting. It turned out that he was the landlord. He began complaining to me about his staff as well as expressing distaste towards his customers. As he spoke, I watched him visually transform: clothes, features and all, into a landlord of a previous generation. My sense was of his same demeaning attitude in that lifetime. Needless to say, business was not good.

Restaurant in old court building In an outer district of Vienna, many businesses were going bankrupt. Visiting a restaurant with a history as a law court building, I could sense that bad and corrupt judgements had been handed out. A local woman told me that in the olden days they would throw donkeys off the church bell tower for fun. Not so surprisingly, I felt that the current owner was that judge in a past life, and he too recognised this. I guided him in a meditation to visualise and feel his previous decrees and actions, offering him the opportunity to make appropriate amends and put right the hurt he had inflicted on the people. He pondered deeply at this point. Upon my departure, I was unsure what he would do. Whilst we cannot alter what actually happened, with the right intent we can heal the events of the past by changing our emotional response in current time. When I revisited the restaurant some five years later, it was good to see his business doing very well, a reflection of his conscious commitment following the impact of our original meeting.

Moving to an ancestral 'cancer house'   Visiting a couple living in a picturesque house in the depths of rural Suffolk, I learnt they discovered ten years after moving to the property that the husband's great-uncle had lived in the same house, many years before. The owner was suffering from the same form of cancer that had caused the death of his elderly relative. The fascinating aspect to this situation is how he was drawn to this particular house, apparently by mere chance as they did not plan to view it when house searching.

There was a clear recognition of the link between the two events spanning some seventy years of time; how he was manifesting a similar pattern of repeating the same illness, the memory held in the genetic matrix continuing to play out in the same house. As he relaxed in an armchair by the living room fire, I could plainly see him as a hologram of his great-uncle, with an identical posture and sense of resignation. Located on a strong earth geopathic line, the position where he sat was in itself enough to cause serious illness (Whisper 6). During the *House Whispering* consultation, the owner decided that he did not need to follow this same pattern and made a conscious commitment there and then to work towards healing the cancer. This led to a very positive outcome:

"A small miracle has taken place in my overall condition and you played no small part in this. ...After a subsequent ultra-sound bone scan, the results came back with signs that the cancer was actually regressing and was at the stage where it no longer posed a major problem. ...I am continuing with treatment and have regular check-ups, but as far as I am concerned I am well on the way to being cured. The pain is much less, although I must wait for my bones to regain their strength. However, by far the most important change in my life was the healing that you and Sandy offered. It was a life-changing moment as I think we all realised. ...I felt something shift in the physical body and realised that I did not have to suffer this cancer. It seems there is light at the end of the tunnel and it's not an oncoming train!"

This human story illustrates that it is entirely possible to change the ancestral lineage patterning and not necessarily fulfil a similar destiny. As there is no actual time and space in truth, it may also be possible to help his uncle in a future incarnation. It is said that true healing can affect seven generations back in time as well as seven generations forwards. Through the healing of himself in current time, the resonant pattern of his late great-uncle could also be healed, thus changing the blueprint of any ongoing hereditary legacy.

Problems Selling Your Property

When wanting to move house, what prevents or makes it difficult to sell a property? Quite apart from whether we think we chose the house we live in or that it chose us, I find one of the key reasons is that we have not completed our soul contract with the house – the purpose of why we were originally drawn there in the first place.

People intuitively know that selling their home will create shifts in their lives and bring up unresolved matters that may be weighing them down. Subconscious issues they may be reluctant to recognise will inevitably need to be dealt with before a person can be released from their house and reach closure. To find a way of leaving without this resolution means they will simply be attracted to move to another property which carries the same familiar pattern. As we take our blueprint with us wherever we go, after a few weeks or months these old patterns will re-establish themselves in the context of the new house, resulting in the person being compelled to repeat the same cycle they thought they had left behind.

Confusion of issues and purpose surrounding a potential move will also cloud the essential path of release. The message we send out into the world to attract a buyer needs to be clear and focused, otherwise we will attract a confused buyer and may end up with a messy sale or one that falls through at the last minute to the frustration of all involved. One lady was so concerned about where she was going to move to that with a prospective job change, her daughter's wedding and more going on, she created a very confused atmosphere. As how a house feels is a key element influencing why people choose a property, in such circumstances what will a potential buyer relate to?

Various techniques and meditations can change inner patterns of coded programming, which in turn will create a shift in attitude and help to release an individual's hold on a house:

"When you suggested I might consider having no home temporarily and being at peace with that, it placed me in a new way of considering, thinking and just being okay with everything."

Another significant reason why people find it difficult to sell a property, or a sale falls through for seemingly no apparent reason, is because of the energetic and psychological patterns within the house itself. The framework for these patterns originates at the outset from the earth energy grids at that location, combined with the energy signature of the building when conceived. This becomes further modified by the human interaction that has gone on in the property over time. Yet to reveal and overcome these deeply buried subconscious patterns requires the key to unlock the energetic code keeping you and your home in lock-down position. Until the connection is released we often hear:

"I just can't sell my house. I loved it with a passion, but not now."

Fear of the unknown, together with finding somewhere suitable to move on to, can keep you rooted where you are. My experience shows that however hard we adopt the usual conventional methods, the following essential reasons indicate why a property may have problems selling:

Stuck energies When a person tells me their life is not going anywhere, that they feel stuck, this is likely to be reflected in the energies of the property. If a previous owner is still living there in spirit, any ghostly activity or dark, heavy energies can deter people from viewing, let alone wanting to buy the house. Nevertheless, it can be the case that if a potential buyer has a matching story that resonates with the atmosphere of the house, they may well be attracted to want to live there. The clearer a space, the wider will be the market visibility, giving the best chance of a faster sale at the best price.

Emotional attachment following trauma Another reason for a property not selling is the degree of emotional attachment of the seller. They may be desperate to sell but can harbour a subconscious hesitancy to let the house go. They may, however, have no choice owing to reasons of finance, divorce, death of a loved one, or they simply may not want to leave the area:

"Moving after 37 years is rather daunting though."

"My brother died in this house…"

"My son is buried in the cemetery nearby and I can't leave him."

Flat or apartment conversions   A further reason that can hold back a sale is when a house is converted into flats or apartments; the soul of the original building becomes fragmented and chaos soon follows (Whisper 5). To give each apartment a soul of its own, and reconnect it with the mother-soul of the building, is a positive step towards reconciling the detrimental effects of insensitive conversions.

Success in helping people to sell or rent out a property that simply isn't budging can generally be achieved by illuminating these core issues. True release of a house, enabling potential new purchasers to come along is very much down to the current owner recognising and dealing with whatever is holding things back. The shifting of these fundamental blocks can change the feel of a property, which invariably leads to attracting a wider spectrum of the market to view. The following stories illustrate some of the scenarios encountered in *The House Whisperer's* world of helping people to sell a property:

Presence at the door   A flat in Barcelona had great difficulty in selling owing to a heavy presence lurking by the front door, preventing anyone who managed to arrive for a viewing from entering. When I had words with this 'doorman', he departed and his sinister energy evaporated almost instantly. The owner was surprised and delighted to receive a phone call from a property agent that evening:

"I am not sure how I even got your number, but I believe you have an apartment for sale and I have a buyer."

Heavy energies   A desirable house in Chelsea had been on the market for six months, to rent or for sale at three million pounds. The lady owner had spent one million on renovation. After working to clear the fragmented energies and rebalance the space, we left to work on the flat where she lived. On the way there, she received a call from the property agent to say that people who viewed the house some months ago now wanted it immediately.

Romans lingering This enquiry concerned a couple trying for the past year to sell an old house in Italy. The building was 11th century with Roman foundations. Over the centuries it had been used for a number of different purposes, including as a convent and military hospital. The lady recommending my assistance described it as:

> *"A fabulous house on for three million euros, renovated with no expense spared. One of the rooms I couldn't go into, full of very masculine soldier energy… and stuff."*

Until the needs of the many generations of spirit beings residing in the house are understood, they will continue with their own agendas regarding sharing the space with others. The imprint of its long, complex history would continue to be felt, leaving the house unsold until a new owner comes along who holds a similar resonance.

Local gallows A psychotherapist who treated people from her home clinic was having problems selling the family home. It was a far from peaceful environment, beset with paranormal activity. I became aware of the constant passage of spirit people walking through the house from the front door towards the garden, causing unrest and turmoil in the family's lives. When I mentioned this to the owner, she paused for a moment before telling me that the house was built on land that was once the pathway to the local gallows, located in what is now the back garden. A major contributory obstacle to the sale was clearly the memory imprint of doom and gloom echoing throughout the house, as the 'criminals' of the past headed towards Heaven or Hell. Having acknowledged them and felt their plight, a shift was finally made.

Returning from school that day, the daughter walked in and said in a quite matter of fact way, *"They've gone."* The next day, her father was delighted to report:

"The place now feels clear like a mountain breeze, I danced around like a two-year old."

During the consultation day, three different property agents telephoned to see if the owners were now ready to market the house again. It sold very soon afterwards.

Murder prevents sale A house in Ireland was taken off the market after a year, which is not uncommon when a property gets very few viewings or receives low offers. But this was no ordinary house, as a murder had taken place in living memory in the property. Just the feel of the place was enough to repel potential buyers. There is, however, always the attractor factor, whereby someone with homicidal tendencies may be drawn to a property that resonates with their psyche and may even end up purchasing it.

Owner in spirit blocks sale A once elegant stately house in Lisbon, Portugal, sits rotting away, wrecked and sad. After the owner passed away some thirty years ago, his daughter put the house on the market. Overnight, a huge tree in the garden came crashing down. During that same week, the entire house was vandalised to such an extent it was no longer saleable. Walking around the rooms, it was clear to me that the deceased owner did not want the house to be sold and lead to the break-up of the family. In its heyday, it was a great party house that brought the family close on many occasions. The owner's intention from the 'other side' was to keep everyone together in harmonious relationship, perhaps in control himself. Could he have made any clearer statement than somehow activating the fallen tree and vandalism? The saga continues to influence the lives of the family until the next stage of resolution can be reached.

Childhood memories Something was clearly blocking the sale of this flat in Surrey, where the owner's sister had lived as a child. As the consultation unfolded, the sister remembered sensitive issues from her early childhood years and was able to come to peace with some of these memories. The extent of her release was sufficient to enable a sale to go ahead whilst maintaining her subtle but deep desire to hold onto the comfort of her nostalgia.

Unable to release spirit of a loved one   For a man whose house lay empty, we went through the process of releasing the spirit of his late wife, who had lived and died there. But even this did not help the sale. His deep love for her held their home as a memorial in his heart, preventing him from truly releasing it onto the open market.

Fear of claim by ex-wife blocks sale   A desirable house on the south coast of England was getting few viewings, let alone a sale. After deep soul searching, the owner admitted fearing that his ex-wife would make a financial claim once the house was sold, even though all matters relating to their divorce were supposedly settled. Whether or not this was a realistic possibility is not the issue; his fear was enough to block his own sale. After taking him through various therapeutic processes over several months to overcome his anxiety, he was able to release his fear. The house sold soon afterwards.

Blocked emotions create water problems   An artist working from home in Scotland was unable to sell his house. Many problems of water damage continued to abound, in spite of several attempts at mending the roof, fixing the plumbing and unblocking drains. He was getting his paintings out to art galleries but they somehow remained unseen, which was affecting his financial flow:

> *"I still feel stuck about where to go with my art, yet work is flowing very well. There is something blocking my flow of money, perhaps an old pattern still in me. I'm up and down emotionally like a yo-yo."*

Water challenges are typical of inner emotional disturbance, often reflected in some way in the physical structure of the building, as with the lady who constantly experienced flooding (Whisper 1). Just as the past-life herbal healer was struggling to get her business image across (Whisper 2), this man was sending out a dual message. He wanted to be known through his art, but at the same time was subconsciously hiding from the world. His veil of reticence meant that his art could not be truly seen. After helping him to connect with his emotional vulnerability and distress over certain matters, he reached a deeper level of resolve about projecting himself out into the world. He later reported:

"Things have shifted here, the house has sold and I'm getting my act together with my art. You came along at the perfect time, hey the universe is perfect!"

Unfinished business   A house in Italy needed some assistance in the sale process. It came to light that the husband had a past life connection with the area. Although a substantial amount of clearing and resolution took place during the consultation day, a further piece of the jigsaw needed to fall into place before a sale was possible. Once this final shift had been made, the house sold shortly afterwards for a reasonable price in a faltering economy.

Flying postman   A couple living on a fairly modern development in Berlin wanted to sell their house. After guiding them through various processes of self-questioning and tuning-in to the spirit of the house and the land, the wife remembered a previous lifetime as a male pilot, wearing a light brown uniform. In the passenger seat of the small aircraft was the 'flying postman', her husband in this lifetime. On that fateful day, her disastrous landing killed them both. The location of the airstrip where they crashed became the housing estate where she and her husband ended up living in this lifetime. Sometimes just recalling the related memory, in this instance seeing the past events in such detail, is enough to clear old patterns and free any blockages to allow things to move forward with greater ease. This eventually released the house to a suitable buyer.

Previous Owners Hanging On to Your House

People often say they do not feel they truly own their property, or that it even feels like their home:

"I don't feel like it's my home, it's as if someone else is living here."

When you have eventually moved into a new home, perhaps your dream home, why might it not feel like it belongs to you? The reason often lies with the fact that the previous owners are still attached to the house and have not let go of it in their minds. They have sold it to you and taken your money, but have not truly handed over the house in its entirety. They may still be hanging onto an aspect of the soul of their previous home, which they just cannot fully release:

"I dream of the house I used to own as I so loved it there. I put so much love into rebuilding it. I still wonder if it was not somehow possible to have kept it even though my divorce forced the sale."

When you are living with the energetic imprint of those who have moved out and are now living elsewhere, their feelings, emotions and desires may continue to overlay your home. When the previous owners still love and cherish their old home, prolonged emotional ties or any unfinished business can mentally impinge upon the lives of new owners, who are unable to fully settle and enjoy a property they have legally purchased or rented. As with the lady above who so loved her former home, they may have been forced out reluctantly through financial problems or divorce, and are bitter or sad about having to leave; even the house itself may harbour resentment.

Did your life circumstances change after moving? It is useful to enquire if the previous occupants were healthy, wealthy and happy, as this can throw light on what is likely to affect your life when you move in. Past energies lingering in your new home will impinge on your thoughts, actions and behaviours. To avoid following in the footsteps of others (Whisper 1), it is crucial that we learn to differentiate between consciously living our own lives and the influence of those who previously occupied our home. Knowing its history can help to determine if the situation needs to be rectified. This is why it is important when we move from a property to fully bring to closure the part of our soul journey relating to that particular place, and to leave a clean and fresh space for future occupants.

Cutting the cords For a person in Hampshire who experienced the previous owners mentally impinging on *her* space months after moving out, the bonds they were still holding needed to be broken. This was achieved at a metaphysical level using cord-cutting techniques. Whilst it would be ideal to encourage previous occupants to resolve their issues in connection with letting go of a house, this is rarely possible unless they are willing to engage in the process.

Thought-forms in the bedroom   When a bitter old man was hanging around the memory fields of the house that he still occupied in his mind, the intensity of his anger created a thought-form, a kind of amorphous 'mush' in one of the bedrooms. His wife had apparently left him for another man and his anger became directed towards women, in this case the current owner. When his mental hold on his former home was dispersed, releasing his unpleasant toxic attitude, the lives of this couple in Herefordshire changed for the better.

Abusive male energy lingering   In a New York apartment, a lady did not sleep well and always felt uncomfortable in the bedroom. My sense of an abusive male energy in the air was verified when she said that the previous occupant was a nasty man who treated his women badly. This intense memory imprint was reactivated by her feminine presence, explaining why any potential partner she invited back never seemed to work out. After neutralising his energy from the bedroom, her relationships and life in general changed for the better.

Releasing the spirits of pets   Just as we may need to release the energetic patterns of previous occupants, we may find the need to do the same for any pets that lived in our homes before. As one friend told me:

"I moved to a house where a parrot used to live, and kept hearing 'hello' for the first few weeks until all traces of it had been removed!"

Does Your House Want to be Sold?

When a house does not sell, we often assume the reasons are price, location, kerb appeal and marketing. Rarely do we consider that maybe the house itself does not want to be sold. It may not want to detach from the interlocking emotional patterns that have created a bond with its current owner. What is for sure is that it will not release a person until they have fulfilled the purpose that led them to be attracted there in the first place, and have since been playing out as part of their soul contract. It is worth remembering that we express our every dream and desire through our home as a metaphor of life.

Do we own our property or does it own us? Perhaps the invisible world of buildings runs the show! A journey of psychological unravelling of our past can involve tapping into previous lifetimes, and often includes loved ones or others in spirit. When a retired couple were desperate to move, the deceased previous owner was unwilling for them to leave, although they thought the house was the issue:

"The house does not seem to want to let us go."

Daughters hold back sale   These homeowners were ready to sell and had fully released any attachment to their homes, but why did so few people come to view, let alone make an offer? One lady did all she could to clean and tidy up every possible space, and from her understanding of Feng Shui placed a money plant in the wealth area. The property agent advised minimising items of furniture and rugs, but that simply made the house feel sterile and empty, not a good feeling for a potential buyer:

"I have done everything I can think of to prepare the house for sale, clearing, cleaning, de-cluttering, sometimes to extreme degrees… but nothing is happening, no one is coming to view my beloved house, I just don't understand."

It emerged that although she was not living there, her daughter had an emotional hold on the house. Even her clothes were still hanging in the wardrobe of her former bedroom, so I suggested they were removed. After going through a process on behalf of the daughter to release her emotional attachment to the house, we were bemused when the telephone began to ring constantly during the consultation. Various appointed property agents now wanted to arrange viewings. Within a week, the owner reported the success of a sale at last.

When another family were committed to emigrate to Australia, the daughter did not want to leave her school friends in Suffolk. Although her parents had truly let go and released their connection to the house, it just would not sell. In the same way as the man who loved working in the grounds of the country estate in the earlier story, it only takes the emotional attachment of one person to hold back the process, in this instance their daughter.

Italian Lamb Roasters Scupper House Sale

This couple had never felt that their stone-built house, overlooking a spectacular Italian rural landscape, was truly theirs. Yet their hearts were at home in the area. The wife was aware of people from another dimension living with them, and felt like she was trespassing on *their* domain. She really wanted to throw herself totally into the home, breathe through the walls and enjoy the space, but could never make it her own, so wanted to move from the property. She explained:

> *"After we bought the house, from the first night we stayed here we knew we were not alone… When I closed my eyes I could see people and although they were not bad, they were not friendly and I was not comfortable with the energy, a little hostile. They made it clear that they had prior claim to the house and did not want to live with us!"*

At around six o'clock every evening, the couple could both smell the cooking of roast lamb, but with nobody else around, where was it coming from? They traced the smell to the front room on the first floor, the original kitchen with an open range fire. The husband loved the smell of roast lamb but as a vegetarian, his wife said she found it quite offensive. The cooking aroma was confirmation as if to say:

> *"We were here before you."*

Alongside the hostile energy, she intuited:

> *"Every time we go back to England and leave the house empty, we get a sense that this ancient family fully take over the whole property, and when we return, they fade a little into the background. Neither then nor now do we want to live with an extended family from another dimension… There was hostility to the feminine, a very male chauvinistic attitude, the culture here is male oriented and I could sense the old man in spirit saying, 'Who do you think you are, you should go back and do your cooking.'"*

I became aware that an elderly couple once lived in the house with two granddaughters but there were no parents. They continued to inhabit this beautiful spot on the landscape, lodged in the memory matrix of the past. Looking deeper through the portals of time into the world of this family from long ago, I could see that life was far from harmonious. The young girls seemed to be orphans and I sensed an indication of physical abuse. Then in one horrific scene, I saw one of the girls running away from the house up onto the main road, where she was run over and killed by a passing vehicle.

The odd atmosphere was putting people off from buying the house, despite many viewers to this idyllic rural setting. The solution was to help free the group of spirit people trapped in time, so they could move on to their rightful place. As this scenario unfolded and was processed by the owners, deep soul searching was required to illuminate any similar parallels to events in their own lives. Releasing the distress would create a clearer space for a potential purchaser to come along. After my visit, the wife reported:

> *"About an hour after the House Whispering session, the space felt really clear and empty, to the point that it echoed. There was no sense of any intrusion at any level and it felt like our house for the first time! The next morning the house felt bigger, like it had expanded. I thought, this is nice, now we can own the house and go from here and know that the right buyer will come along."*

She made further contact after the sale:

> *"The house in Italy has finally sold. I cried buckets that day, but it is really for the best. Now we're here in our new house in the UK, I can see the difference between the energy of the two houses, we never felt welcomed there; the house never wanted us. Strangely, after we sold, I walked around the empty house, no ghosts or snakes... I checked. My intuitive gardener friend said the same, 'they've gone!' Is that because they got rid of us?"*

Etheric Gateways and Boundaries

More recognisable as city walls and town boundaries, gateways are delineated in our countryside by old marker stones, field boundaries, physical gates or track crossings. At some point in the past, evidence of many of these boundaries and gateways have disappeared through natural transition or demolition.

In many traditions, the act of beating the bounds was the custom of walking the physical village or parish boundaries, reinforcing a mental imprint of protecting their territory in the minds of the local people. With its roots in Terminalia, the festival of the Roman god Terminus took place in May, during the fertile season of Beltane. The tradition of residents and their families thrashing local landmarks and boundary hedges with sticks and tree branches, associated with places once recognised as a royal borough, is still practiced today in many parts of the country and some university towns. It was believed that the people and their animals would gain protection and blessings for the forthcoming harvest. In medieval times, this tradition was considered to be especially important in ensuring that tenants paid tithes to the monarch. Vestiges of the pagan sacred marriage of the king to the goddess of the land ensured that the earth itself would not degenerate as a wasteland. This act retained in the landscape and strengthened by human activity and memory became imprinted in the etheric matrix.

A metaphysical counterpart exists of any original structure that was once in physical three-dimensional form. Often still in place like an invisible double, these etheric boundaries and gateways continue to resonate an energetic presence that actively influence people. Some geographical areas seem to have an unspoken way of keeping people stuck in the same locality, so they find it difficult to leave and move to another neighbourhood. If an implicit pre-programmed sense of entrapment is associated with properties in a particular area, some-times just a street of houses in villages or towns, it can take far more effort to escape 'the grip'.

Our physical senses likewise have an etheric counterpart. The etheric guardians of the doorways are coded constructs essentially created by the human mind or otherworldly thought-forms. Others may have consciously programmed the invisible boundaries of our homes for specific reasons of controlling ownership. When working with buildings through harmonics, I am often 'given' the code to lock or unlock a gateway or protective structure surrounding a building or person (Whisper 7).

Prisoner in your own home In circumstances where you feel trapped in your own home, the property is likely to remain unsold. People often say they feel held prisoner, as if being controlled by some kind of outside force. The sense of feeling trapped or caged in can be a reflection of distorted geometries in the energy field matrix. This often requires a deep understanding of previous restrictive patterns needing release before occupants are set free to move house.

Through our own intentions and repetitive thoughts over long periods of time, we can unconsciously establish our own boundaries and effectively become prisoners of our own making. As our living space is a mirror image reflection of our inner psyche, our circumstances will change only when we have determined and worked through those aspects that initially attracted us to the property. As previously discussed, until we gain clarity and have fulfilled our soul contract with the house, our reciprocal relationship cannot reach ultimate resolution and come to closure. This complex weave of connection can require the unravelling of many factors, with emotional concerns at the heart of the matter.

Just as with the *Prisoner in the priory* (Whisper 2), a homeowner in Surrey feared never being able to leave, that she would end up spending the rest of her days trapped in her house:

"I don't want to die in this house."

Stranglehold inflicted by ex-partner The unseen psychological pressures that overlay a house after a partner has moved out can be quite devastating for the remaining occupant. In one situation, a woman had separated from her husband who still referred to the property as his house, even though he was no longer living there. Although she was now in a new relationship, she never felt that her ex-husband had truly left. Indeed, this created the dynamic of a relationship triangle with tensions all round, clearly affecting the quality of her interaction with her new partner. These energetic links held in the house itself were dissolved through a *House Whispering* process, leaving the space clear of previous expectations, pain and anger. No longer supported and bolstered by these old ingrained emotional patterns, all concerned then had a better opportunity to get on with their lives and reach the next stage of resolution.

Hoarding and Self-Sabotage

It may not always be the house that sabotages lives but also acts of self-sabotage, as reflected in clutter and hoarding. This is where *The House Whispering* approach can help to facilitate an understanding towards releasing symptomatic patterns that show up in our homes. Choosing to limit one's living space by filling it up with 'stuff', no matter how big or small our home, is indicative of subconsciously restricting life choices on many levels, as this woman realises:

> *"I live in such a small place in New York, completely out of balance with my psyche and yet am unable to do much about it for all the usual psychological reasons including hoarding and financially I am limited. If you have any suggestions as to what I can do to shift the energies, I'm in a big change state and would be grateful."*

Our conditioned responses from childhood are also relevant; patterns acquired from parents, siblings, teachers and others that so often affect our self-esteem, lead to internal critical behaviour and even self-sabotage. I have come across people who had very little nurturing and few possessions, perhaps brought up in children's homes. As adults they may excessively hoard material items referred to as their 'collections'. Belongings then take the place of emotional nourishment to the detriment of overall wellbeing. Once the layers of negative overlay that usually concern loving oneself are identified, they can be addressed and steps taken towards resolution. Conditioned patterns are learned patterns and *can* therefore be unlearnt, however difficult it may seem to make the choice to want to change.

Unable to move One woman took excessive hoarding to such extreme following her relationship breakdown that she was no longer able to walk. This is an example of where emotional loss needs to be discharged before clutter can be released at a physical level. Only then would her body be energetically freed-up to move around.

Blocked energies This lady openly recognises she is violating her own space, and connects her health challenges to blocked energies, reflected in physical clutter. She describes this painful process:

"I have developed a strange habit of buying lots of stuff since living here. Before, I have never been a hoarder and it feels like I am being held here, by literally getting blocked in with all the stuff I am accumulating... right now I just want to find out how I can heal or pacify this place, which really does not seem to like anybody living in it. I am also looking at my backyard, which is full of old boxes and junk, and the thought of anybody, especially you, pointing out the obvious to me, is a bit painful.

"There are many things I need to get moving energetically, and I am fully aware of them. This is not how I usually live and a succession of injuries have made me put some of the difficult jobs on a waiting-list, which is now becoming a way of life. ...I can see that this may just be part of the pattern and that my uneasiness to proceed may all be tied in with it, like some ball of string that got mangled by a kitten... I will need a bit more time, until I don't have that dread feeling when I think about tackling my house issues."

Skip collectors   In one home in Surrey, the house, garage and outbuildings were packed to the brim with old furniture and miscellaneous items collected by the owners from various skips. Of little monetary or practical value to most people's way of thinking, the excess of items served to keep them prisoner in a world that ensured they had no space to look at their emotionally dysfunctional lives. The extraordinary thing was that they had arranged a consultation expecting me to sort out their mess using principles of Feng Shui and space-clearing, and seemed surprised when I suggested they clear some of their clutter before I could begin. Even my dowsing rods went on strike!

My work was actually to help them to identify the reasons for subconsciously creating the blockages that prevented their real issues from being addressed. Suggesting an extensive clear-out in one go would not have been the solution, as this can create shock and trauma to the system, akin to a major surgical operation taking place. In the weeks that followed, slow progress was made by gradually returning items of furniture back to the skips from whence they came. An ongoing concerted effort was necessary in order for deeper inner issues to come to the surface and be recognised, before other more delicate matters could be resolved.

Clutter preventing house sale   After a remote consultation for a couple having difficulty in selling their London flat, when resolution was reached about releasing clutter, a viewing was arranged within a matter of days:

> *"It truly was a wonderful experience working with you last week and very thought provoking. We received a call from our estate agent a few days later. The viewing went well. We both sense the energy has dramatically changed here and definitely feel that the apartment has sold. Last night in meditation, as I reached our front door, all I could see was the sun, the kitchen filled with the energy of the ocean. My husband has finished rearranging the furniture and there is less clutter ...you can work your magic on our next house!"*

Embracing opportunities   This client from Sussex realised that clearing-out is not just about releasing 'stuff' and creating physical space, but about bringing enough space into your life to allow for opportunities at other levels:

> *"We are having a massive house clear out, all due I'm sure to the catalyst of the work with you, as well as doing some deep trauma work, which is proving very healing. Not sure yet whether we are preparing to leave here, or just clearing ourselves enough space to see what happens next. I remain profoundly grateful to you for setting us off on this journey."*

Encouraging a Sale

So just what gets a property sold? There is a magic ingredient that the housing market rarely taps into, that very few property agents or landlords seem to know about. This is the energy matrix holding the memory of all that has gone before and the potential of what is to come. Before a house is ready to be released and move on, the atmosphere needs to be free of feelings and emotions, hopes and fears, including from any unwanted spirit guests still lingering. Anything that can help people to release emotions from the past and attachment to their homes in the present has to be a positive step.

During difficult economic times when the property market is uncertain or when the financial cycle hits a low, it becomes more important than ever to ensure a clear path leading towards to a sale, especially when owners are desperate to move. There are a number of common misconceptions about selling property that are quite easily remedied. With a little knowledge, we can optimise our homes and maximise their potential to attract a buyer, improving the chances of selling way beyond that achieved by property agents. What many people do not realise is that the *house* actually sells itself!

Home staging   Generally speaking this is what it says, 'staged' in order to look appealing. Moving furniture around, getting rid of stuff and doing a cosmetic makeover has merits of visual appeal, allowing the viewer to get an idea of space and purpose which they may not be able to envision. But this may often not be enough as it can lack the personal touch and emotional warmth that emanates from the heart and soul of the owner who deeply loves their house. In my view, to facilitate engaging with the true feeling of 'home' cannot come from the impersonal attention of a designer or property agent. Staging can often result in a sterile atmosphere and can never be a substitute for that essential feeling a potential buyer needs to sense in imagining themselves living there, before being sufficiently attracted to put in an offer on the property.

Visibility   Another factor to consider is the visibility of a house in terms of its vibrational frequency. Aligning the original blueprint of a property to match the location brings awareness and prominence, increasing visibility for prospective purchasers (Whisper 5). When seeking a new home, we usually have a sense of what we are looking for, a specific range of desires and dreams of our perfect space. Like tuning-in to a radio station, we choose the frequency by turning the dial until we hear something we like. The attractor factor is not so much the physical bricks and mortar, but at the subtle level of what is felt rather than seen, the energetic code that resonates in tune with an individual's own frequency.

One penthouse conversion in Salisbury, Wiltshire, held an energetic frequency of a very high vibration, but was located in an urban area where the general level of vibration was a notch lower. The apartment was therefore out of sync with the locality and could not readily be 'seen' by those people searching with an expectation of the type of design normally found in that area. The solution to bring the apartment into alignment with its location was to lower the frequency, thus changing the overall feeling of the space to a more grounded earth vibration. This was achieved by physically using grounding reddish colours and some heavy rocks strategically placed at specific locations. More importantly, a further level of adjustment and alignment in the metaphysical world was embedded into the structure of the building. Almost instantly, the apartment became more visible and a buyer appeared within a week.

Right timing *The House Whispering* process certainly increases the opportunity for a property to be sold. There are however, occasions when little appears to happen following a consultation, even when everything is in place and all hidden factors have been dealt with to enable a clear path for full and final release. Although much can be achieved by working with subtle energies, the somewhat random factor of timing also needs to be taken into account.

The principle of 'right action' must always come first. There is little point in attempting to bend or manipulate fate to your personal whims and desires unless the energetic path is clear to start with. If all aspects relating to your life and the property are in right alignment, then encouraging the process is of value. Right timing comes from boarding the boat on the best tide, when the appropriate energy will join the phase harmonic and flow with it, just as a surfer merges into the peaks and troughs of a multiple wave sequence. The energy then enters the spin cycle; if you miss the auspicious gateway timing, all you can do is wait for the next opportunity, the next tide or natural gateway opening. This is often described as the Feng Shui of Time. Whilst this cycle is astrologically calculable and intuitively discernible, it is not always so predictable in its effect.

It is possible that even though fully aligned to the heart and soul of your home, the 'right' buyer may be out of sync with timing and not yet ready to move to their ideal property. If they are *meant* to move into your home, this will make your house or apartment hold back as it too wants the right potential new owner to love and cherish it as you may have done. Likewise, if you have treated your house badly, a 'bad' buyer will be waiting in the wings to come along and continue to trash it. There can actually be conscious communication between houses! Then there is the question, is your next home ready and available for *you* to move into? If not, this can hold back the release of your current property.

Speed of sale I have seen extraordinary results working with people trying to sell their home, where property agents have called as fast as one hour after owners have reached their Aha moment of epiphany, with the realisation of what has been holding back the sale. A buyer will usually appear within a period of 28 days. On the rare occasion when nothing appears to have happened after one month, I will work further with the owner to establish if any residual issues are still hampering the all-important release process. Inevitably, I will find deeper, more significant layers of personal concerns or matters that need to be illuminated and addressed, which would not have been possible during the initial consultation. It can sometimes be too demanding for the client to deal with and release everything all at once, especially if they are not fully prepared for the depth of the process involved. In deeply entrenched or long-standing situations, they may not even have been aware of the significance of what comes to light. Therefore, full resolution cannot always be achieved in a single session. A house move will always encompass and reflect the next stage of life's journey.

Reducing the price is unnecessary One way to encourage more interest in a property is to reduce the price, although in many cases I find this unnecessary. With all types of properties that I have helped in selling, the speed of a buyer appearing and making an offer usually follows on fairly soon from the seller's Aha moment. What is most significant is the subsequent resolution by the owner of what has been blocking things from moving forward in the first place. To fully release their hold on the property is a crucial part of enabling a successful sale to reach completion.

Sold for more money To identify and remedy the real reason behind what is holding back a sale will bring much greater all-round benefit at personal and financial levels. Following space-clearing, realigning and charging-up the energies of a house (Whisper 5), most properties should achieve the original asking price and sometimes a much higher figure. To raise the vibrational frequency will always improve the overall feel of a property and make it more desirable. This also has a dramatic effect on visibility to a wider spectrum of the market. You then have a very potent house that will just sell itself:

"We had so many people looking at the house after your clearing."

Renting a Property

When renting rather than buying a home, apart from the financial investment involved, all that has been said concerning finding a property to purchase is equally relevant. We are ultimately likely to be seeking a nourishing place to live that resonates at a soul level. The important consideration is that a property actually feels like a home. When the soul of a house is brought into alignment with the heart and soul of the owner(s) (Whisper 5), it is usual to hear they are much happier and have a sense of truly feeling 'at home'.

Renting out a property When wanting to rent out a property that you own, the same principles apply as when selling. The reasons a house or apartment will just not rent out are usually energetic. The responsibility as landlord is to hold the seed core of the building as grounded owner. When difficulty is encountered in finding suitable tenants, a visualisation process can help to attract the right people. One way is to see in your mind the whole of the property inside and out, and to visualise the nature of a person or family you would like to live there. This enables a clear intention to be transmitted to attract tenants with a similar vibration, who then appear as if by magic!

The lady owner of a flat in a desirable location in Surrey was having problems renting it out. She was reluctant to let it go, even though she was not living there. Further to this, the current tenants had no intention of leaving, so their emotional links had to be broken before they would release the ties and leave as requested. Once the owner had dealt with the reasons for her attachment and fully let go of her connection, a new tenant appeared within a matter of days.

Abusive tenants   When a building retains the memory of abusive actions inflicted by past occupants, deep psychological wounds can linger in its heart and soul. This predominant emotion is likely to affect its attitude towards future occupants.

A lady owner wanted to rent out her Chelsea house, but had received very few viewings over the six months prior to my visit. As I listened to the *whispers* of the soul of the house, I could hear it pleading to be released from the ravages inflicted by previously abusive tenants. The heart of the home was hurting, so it did not want to be rented out again. After guiding the owner to find the seed point location and to connect with the heart and soul of her house (Whisper 5), she was able to understand the core issue and could truly feel its pain. She promised to ensure that any new tenants would be chosen with care, and only if they really loved the house. Within an hour after her Aha moment and affirmation, two different people from the same property agency called quite independently to arrange separate viewings. The house was rented out to one of those people that same afternoon, much to her relief and amused surprise.

Current tenants block rental or sale   Another consideration when wanting to rent out a property is that a tenant still living there may have no wish to move out. Even when their rental agreement is coming to an end, the landlord can find it difficult to get another tenant quite apart from the difficulty of persuading the current occupant to leave. Where several flats or apartments occupy the same building, I have known of situations where the landlord has experienced trouble renting other units to prospective tenants owing to the behaviour or attitude of one particular individual.

When a tenant remains in occupancy of a property that is up for sale, regardless of whether they are happy living there or complacent in their attitude towards a property that does not belong to them, the thought-forms they exude into the atmosphere can prevent viewings or deter potential buyers. In one instance, a flat in Surrey that the owner wanted to sell was not getting any viewings as the tenants loved being there, the rent was reasonable and they could not afford to move, so were subconsciously blocking the sale.

Although a landlord is likely to want to continue receiving a rental income, it can sometimes be more cost-effective to leave a property empty, free of any intrusive influence of a tenant, *House Whispered* and charged-up ready for a speedy sale!

Releasing Your Connection

When a property is sold or when you move out of a rented property, many people consider they can just walk away and leave their old home behind. This, however, is not always the end of the story.

A significant stage is reached at Exchange of Contracts, indicating the finality of your soul contract with the property. Following this legal agreement, it is paramount that you release the ties to allow a smooth path towards Completion, the final contract phase. When the time comes and you actually move out of the property, you should ensure that your energetic links are cleared from the memory of your home, so all can be free. What happens if you do not fully release individual or family patterns and let go of the house?

When people hang on to their memories without accomplishing resolution, we have seen that these links can pull you back into the lives of the new occupants who will feel impinged upon by your energetic presence in what is now *their* space. This will also drain your energy, as in a sense you will be living in two places at once: physically in the new home and emotionally in the previous one. We can still love the memories of our previous homes and hold our experiences of living there close to our hearts, but there should be no lock-in or emotional attachment to the actual physical building as such. As we may now realise, our leftover patterns remain embedded in the physical and etheric structure of a building, so the spiral of energetic interchange can continue to affect all those involved.

It is important to say goodbye to your house and give thanks for its security and protection, for the blessings of experience it gave you whilst you lived there. Even if you did not enjoy or perhaps hated your home, to let it go is a matter of personal responsibility. Either way, its lessons are truly a gift. Thus, closure is most important.

Releasing personal attachment This homeowner had been renting out her flat for a while but now wished to sell. She was aware of not wanting to lose the connection with her father who had died four years previously, but first needed to relinquish her attachment to his association with her flat. His energy was very present since he had helped her to decorate. This is not about erasing memories of loved ones from your life, but about releasing the ties in connection with a particular property. She describes freeing things up for her flat to welcome new occupants:

> *"The day after your visit a couple came to view, but so far no offer. ... I also did a meditation and my dad came and sat on the sofa and we talked and then he walked out... I wonder if part of the flat not selling was me not wanting to lose a connection with my dad. I have also taken anything out that was sentimental to me. It is as though we have all said our goodbyes. I really like the feel of the flat now and I've done everything possible to cut ties, so really hoping it will sell."*

Another issue inhibiting the sale was the reluctance of the current tenants to move for personal reasons. There may very well have been a level of projected influence onto them from the owner, at a time when she was not yet fully ready to release her own personal connection. This may also have subconsciously held them back from moving out, resulting in the tenants taking much longer to leave than she had hoped for. Once her resolution gained clarity, following much inner soul searching and her commitment in letting go, a buyer eventually appeared and the property finally sold.

Packing away artefacts Given that the energetic atmosphere of a home will help or hinder the sale of a property, then consider the significance of artefacts and especially any art on the walls. If you turn pictures around or take them down, you will sense a change in the feeling of a room and thus in your own emotions. You put them there for a reason, subconscious perhaps, as you were originally attracted because you loved them or they reminded you of something or someone. Either way, they hold an emotional quality. Part of the final release in letting go of your home is to pack up your ornaments and artefacts and take down your pictures, with love and gratitude for the pleasure and comfort they gave you whilst you lived there.

Some property agents and even energy practitioners advise a dismantling process in order to sell a house. I consider this to be a harsh approach. To pack away too many belongings not only creates an impersonal environment but can also trigger an emotional roller coaster. Destroying the atmosphere that created your original heart connection with your home is a backward step that a potential buyer will subconsciously feel. It can also result in ending up living in a decommissioned home with a diffused sense of identity in relation to your space, with perhaps a very long wait for a buyer.

No trouble selling If you have experienced few problems in selling previous homes and feel that selling houses is easy, then reflect on any potential hitches that might have occurred along the way. A buyer may come along and everything seemingly falls into place, but combining this with finding a new home, perhaps under pressure, can become problematic. I have encountered many instances where the flow of communication between property agents, solicitors, surveyors and other professionals is most troublesome, and at times seems frustratingly slow. Misunderstandings and inefficiencies can appear to block your path to moving out and moving on. An awareness of consciously working with the flow of energies towards fully releasing your connection with a property will allow for a smoother transition on all levels.

Selling or finding a home is a fascinating process, always inextricably connected with our own journey in life and offering some kind of valuable opportunity for personal transformation. It is the resonance of our heart in relationship to the heart of a property that draws us to the right place at the right time. Ultimately, the quintessence of finding or selling a home relates to one essential ingredient. The sense of feeling 'at home' is the pure expression of Love. When love flows freely and in abundance, house moving can be a positive experience, bringing with it the nourishing potential for fulfilment in all areas of our lives.

Whisper 5

THE PATTERNING OF SPACES

The power of enhancing and destructive places

Fragmentation of Space and Heart Coherence

Our home is an important part of ourselves. It has the potential to reflect wholeness, allowing us to feel complete and totally at peace, knowing who we truly are at all levels. This feeling is, however, compromised when the physical layout of our living space is fragmented. This will affect the energy of that space with a direct negative impact on the lives of residents. Just as I find that a confused house will attract confused people, a house that is fragmented, out of alignment or chaotic will attract people with a similar disposition. Fragmented homes make for destructive, fragmented living.

As a result of ignorance or lack of care by an architect, designer or builder, rather than direct intention, certain design aspects and forms of construction can be especially damaging to health and wellbeing, sometimes leading to disastrous consequences. I have come across many new developments around the world where the residents experienced serious illnesses soon after moving in. In one extreme case in a house on a Mediterranean island, a person actually died from the effects generated by fragmentation of the energy fields.

Houses become fragmented for many reasons. At the physical level there are three main causes: incongruous design and harmful building materials; the disjointed relationship and juxtaposition of the building to the land; and when a dwelling has been insensitively altered, extended or divided into separate living spaces.

The effects of 'cutting chi' where angles, corners and beams predominate, will create fragmentation in the matrix of space and create subtle disturbances to the energy fields of those sleeping or spending time in close proximity. From a metaphysical perspective, the way people have lived their lives in a particular building generates an energetic residue of emotional traumas and troubles.

The world of number, associated with music and harmonics, is relevant to the quality of the space around us. A building can resonate to a musical mode or mood by its mathematical and geometrical design. It is either in tune and harmonious, or out of tune and discordant (Whisper 7). Any disturbance in these energy fields through negative thinking or traumatic events will, as time goes on, result in the geometries in the invisible etheric world getting crumpled. This creates fragmentation in the metaphysical world of space, causing collapse of the heart-coherent waves and thus affects health.

When energy fields become fragmented, this can create portals into other dimensions, allowing spirit activity or other negative energies to enter. These manifest as thought-forms, ghosts, entities and rogue visitors that can infiltrate and get caught up in the energy fields of geopathic stress, where they interact and multiply in the matrix. In the physical dimension, we feel these imbalanced energies in the atmosphere of a building, making the space an uncomfortable place to spend time. Unless this fragmentation is addressed, the subtle influences that pervade our homes and workspaces will impact on our physical bodies, the life choices we make and our overall direction in life. For a well-balanced environment, the metaphysical geometries need to be in right alignment to be in perfect harmony (Whisper 7).

To recalibrate a sick building and dispel the effects of fragmentation, a coherent energetic pattern is fundamental. The energetic qualities of the building materials used are an important contributory factor in the coherence of a space, helping to create a synchronised heart-wave resonance between people and the building as a whole (Whisper 6). If the negative energies are cleared and re-aligned and the space is resonating to a healthy vibration of the golden mean harmonic (Whisper 7), then nothing can get entangled in the matrix. Any personal issues will find it difficult to linger in the darkest corners of the web of denial. In other words, once illuminated they will stare you in the face until dealt with.

All that goes on is just a reflection of our own being, as our home is a mirror of our soul!

Proud but sad house   In an affluent city suburb, an empty family house sits patiently awaiting its fate, dependent on the decision as to when and how it will be renovated. Previous occupants had insensitively extended what was a once modest but elegant building, leaving it with a sad demeanour. The soul of the house did not readily accept such extensive alterations that diminished its pride and prominence. Today, its past history continues to play a part in the bigger picture, with the owners weaving aspects of their own complex lives into the backdrop of this theatrical playhouse. The final scene has yet to be played out.

Fragmented relationship   At a home in Mexico, the client's ex-husband had ownership of the main house that fronted the road, while she now owned and lived in the garden studio apartment. In trying to resolve certain issues between them, it became apparent that the two buildings represented the dynamics of the masculine and feminine counterparts of their relationship. The property was totally reflective of their mixed communications that needed to be taken to a deeper level for resolution of their personal problems. Following the remote consultation, the client reassuringly reported that she seemed to feel more settled, was integrating the experience of the session and noticing how the house situation opened up so many stories in her.

Attic conversions   Living or working in attic conversions is a very common occurrence these days, with many people wishing to maximise space. It is rarely recognised that sloping ceilings with exposed beams that follow a pitched roofline create 'cutting chi' energies, a form of fragmentation that can have a destructive effect on the human energy field. Moreover, where people have moved into a loft conversion, the energies of a previously 'dead' roof-space still linger in the atmosphere, often to the detriment of health, wealth and relationships. The energetic weight of working and/or sleeping under these angled structures can compromise mental health and lead to illness: *"I feel depressed in the attic."*

The hyper-modern design of one London loft apartment, with sloping ceilings and angled spaces, had a devastating effect on the couple living there. Similarly, in a North London house, the lady owner who slept under angled beams was suffering from cancer.

Suicide jump When I received a voicemail from a woman saying that her son had jumped out of a top floor window, I wondered if their newly renovated attic where he slept was genuinely to blame for this young man's attempted suicide. The design of the cut-up space had several low beams with sharp angles, creating a fragmented geometry in both the physical and energetic matrix. This opened up etheric gateways, which unleashed destructive paranormal energies that were able to infiltrate the darker recesses of his psyche. The influence of the full moon that night exacerbated his past patterns of psychosis, so that he heard voices in his head telling him to jump from the attic window, which he did. He survived to tell the tale.

Basements and orb energies In the subterranean depths of a building, the basement ponders what the other rooms in the house are doing, thinking and feeling. Damp basements, abandoned rooms and derelict buildings, little used and left empty for many years, tend to accumulate a concentration of dense energies owing to minimal or no human interaction. Any neglected space that results in a lack of chi movement allows dark paranormal energies to creep in, which then create their own blueprint matrix, held in another time zone.

As the veils between the worlds of physical and metaphysical dimensions are becoming more permeable, we are gaining greater awareness of unseen energies. Their interaction with human consciousness plays a large part in the manner of how their presence is revealed. The images of orb energies captured on film and digital photographs show evidence that they are more than willing to interact, and confirm the tingling sensations or heavy feelings that many experience in these spaces. As with people and spirit presences, the world of orbs comes with a myriad of qualities and intentions, from the spiritual realms of the angelic and helpful, to the lower astral dark and demonic, or sometimes just simply mischievous.

Underground ghosts I was told of the time when underground bunkers on the Dorset coast were being converted into holiday homes and that the builders began to experience migraine headaches. One of them kept seeing maps in his mind's eye. It turned out that these particular bunkers were used as 'secret' locations by the army to plan certain strategies of World War II. Not until one man was so unwell, unable to turn up for work, did the project leader take photographs of the complex. Astoundingly, not only were there many orbs but also an amorphous white blob positioned as if bending over a desk. The next morning, the builders' wheelbarrow had been upturned at the entrance as if to say, *"Leave us alone!"* These men, who claimed not to believe in the paranormal, were rather perturbed to realise that they were working alongside underground ghosts.

Flats, apartments and tower blocks In purpose built apartment blocks or buildings converted into flats, close neighbours and condensed thinking patterns can all cause greater unrest than physical noise or disturbance alone. Whatever goes on in one apartment will influence the lives of all others in close proximity within the same building, for good or bad. Constant mental chatter from living in shared or confined spaces can intrude upon and interfere with the emotions and attitudes of individuals and families. Are you really dreaming your own dreams, thinking your own thoughts and sensing your own feelings, or are you experiencing the intrusions of others in the belief they are your own? This can result in failure to notice what is really going on in your own life, especially in relationships. At worse, trying to ignore an accumulative energy depleting situation can lead to neglect, which is sadly all too evident in media reports of children brought up in apartment blocks.

Location within an apartment block An important factor influencing our experience of any particular floor level has to do with the position relative to the height of the building as well as the location within the overall floor plan. Imagine an entire building set into a transparent three-dimensional egg-shaped geometric matrix. Certain points will have a higher electrical energy charge with a vibrant chi life force, making it a more beneficial place to live. Inherent in nature and found in various fruits, vegetables, plants and especially eggs, are nourishing energetic zones. This same framework of high and low energy points gives occupants of the same building an entirely different experience.

Ground or lower floors have the energetic weight of other levels on top of you: *"I can't breathe."* Not everyone is physically and emotionally comfortable with the subliminal awareness of lives above them, which can also lead to depression. In contrast, the apex represents the fire element, as in 'pyra' of pyramid, and can feel unstable. I often come across the effects that living at the top of a building can have on occupants, who can sometimes become a little head crazy: *"I feel ungrounded."* Depending upon the design, living in attic spaces generally has a similarly unstable effect.

Much depends on an individual's energetic balance of the five elements: water, wood, fire, earth and metal, as described in Chinese metaphysics and used in Feng Shui. One person may need the fire element to balance their temperament and be happy living at the top of a building. Another may feel better on the ground floor where they receive more grounded earth vibrations. To consider this for a person searching for a new home is of value, matching and balancing their element bias to a prospective property. When in tune with our own bodies, we will naturally find the most propitious space to be nourished, to flourish and prosper. However, if we are in sabotage mode, we are likely to choose the most detrimental space.

There is merit in having a degree of connection to the natural Earth vibration. The further away from the ground, the less effective and nourishing the natural fractal energy becomes. If a person chooses to live high up because it suits their energy balance, ego or inspiration, certain energetic systems can be put into place to draw up and increase the grounding earth energy connection, thus getting the best of both worlds. A beneficial, well-balanced position in the height of a building is the golden mean point, a position of just over half way: 0.618... to be precise. So, in a building of say ten floors, the most propitious living space would be floors six or seven. In architecture as in nature, the golden mean harmonic is the place of harmonious fractal balance, quite different from and more dynamic than the concept of equal balance. From this position, a sense of stillness, peace and nourishment within our true centre can be found.

Balancing the elements In a spacious rooftop apartment, the fire element was flaring high and needed tempering. In the Eastern five-element system, each feeds another in the nourishing cycle, or diminishes another in the destructive or controlling cycle. So making fire feed earth will moderate the fire energy. This was achieved by adding earth colours of browns and yellows, including terracotta pots and geometric symbols of all things square. In a basement location with a grounded closed-in earth vibration, it may be appropriate to add living plants in order to expand the feeling of space.

Farmhouse Fragments Owners' Lives

When a couple moved out of London and bought a farmhouse in the West Country with several acres of land, their planned change of life-style did not work out quite as they had envisaged, so they now wanted to sell the property. I was called in after it had been on the market for six months, having had little interest and no offers.

The main farmhouse had been added to over several centuries, with numerous renovations in many different architectural styles. Exploring this rambling property, the transparent worlds of lingering occupants were immediately perceptible. Like a dolls house open at the front for all to see, a weird and wonderful range of jumbled individuals in period costume portrayed the distinctly different eras when various parts were built. Past events began to unfold visually in my mind; numerous plays enacted simultaneously on otherworldly stages, each with their own attitudes and postures. The different scenes just looped round in a time warp, the people in spirit unaware of the existence of each other, yet all influencing the atmosphere.

I became aware of spirit energies lingering in the hallways and in some of the rooms and outbuildings. The effect of this interwoven disparity, the house fragmented with entities thrown into the mix, created confusion for both house and occupants. Having bought into a dream of the good life, the couple's lives were soon impinged upon by a multitude of colourful deceased characters, the result being that they ended up living in a theatrical wonderland.

The farmhouse was imposing and well oriented, the surrounding gardens lush and full of astoundingly beautiful plants. On the surface it seemed unlikely that it would not sell, but the house felt isolated and a sense of something not quite right was holding things back. It was as if happenings in the past had dishonoured the land and the spirit elementals living in this magical garden, creating a bewildered relationship for the occupants. Walking around the outer perimeter of the house, I became aware of some kind of energetic grip encircling the external walls, preventing the nourishing earth energies from infusing into the building. The prominent image in my mind was of the house being strapped by an iron rack. Its identity felt sublimated, the occupants imprisoned, and in spite of lush greenery and water around me, I was feeling a sense of compression in my body.

The solution was an energetic one, involving a process of tuning into the various time zones causing fragmentation in the energy fields of space-time, and identifying with the occupants of their respective eras. We then set to work space-clearing and realigning the house to reconnect it with the nourishing energies of the garden. The elemental beings first needed to be placated and honoured to allow them to discharge the hold they had established. Once free to inhabit their natural environment without the confusing energies of the past, they released the peripheral iron barriers, which simply dissolved away. As each room merged with each other and with the original soul of the building, this allowed the house to integrate. With the farmhouse and land finally brought together, much vital earth energy could flow and permeate the house with the richness it deserved, and the nature spirits and elementals could come out to play.

Within the next few weeks the property sold for more than the original asking price, a success story for any consultant or property agent. The owner sent this exciting news:

"Moving is close to completion... you'd said that you had a clear sense that the house would sell for a particular sum, higher than the original market price we were asking. Well we got that higher sum. How wonderfully peculiar!"

Extensions and Conversions

As a student architect, I would be asked to prepare drawings of extensions for couples often living in large houses. This did not really make sense, as they already had plenty of physical space. Intrigued, I began to ask myself the question, why do they want more space, what is it they are really seeking? After a while, listening to the subtext of the occupants and to the silent *whispers* of their homes, I began to gain a deeper understanding of people's dreams for change.

Building extensions are like personal relationships, where the underlying reasons for wanting change are often not what people expect or even consciously want to acknowledge. Eventually, I came to realise that believing they wanted an extension or renovation seemed to be more about how people saw their lives as a metaphor for change, usually from some aspect of themselves and sometimes from a partner. It dawned on me on many occasions that what some couples needed was not a building extension but a divorce!

Apart from needing more physical space as life expands with a growing family and circumstances change, in wanting to modify our homes we are at some level expressing dissatisfaction with certain aspects of our lives, or desire to modify the expression of our soul; perhaps they are one and the same thing. For many of us, this can only be conveyed through our external environment, the outer expression of our inner self in the form of our domestic living spaces. Essentially, in developing or expanding our physical home, we are expanding and developing certain aspects of our own inner being, an ongoing progression in the constantly changing flux of life.

Extension or integration A major consideration when planning an extension is that it should integrate both physically and energetic-ally with the original soul of the building. For this reason, I prefer to call it an 'integration' rather than an 'extension' which implies a com-ponent separate from the original soul of the property. It is rare for homeowners to consider asking permission of the main house for an-other building to be added on. Why should we expect the new part to want to relate to the existing building, or the original soul to accept a new addition? In most cases, owing to disparate materials used, lack of sensitivity in the design and to its identity as a whole, it does not.

Thus, expansion through renovation and extension can frequently result in non-integration, leading to fragmentation of the physical building, which is reflected in the etheric energy fields. The mix of architectural styles and belief systems, with the time lapse between different building periods totally out of sync, compound the difficul-ties that one or more of these disproportionate aspects can cause. Disharmony can then result in problems that range from unexplain-able atmospheres to more serious paranormal disturbance, with occupants experiencing restlessness, irritability and even anger.

New additions Visiting a 19th century house in Oxfordshire, something about the more recent section, built some fifty years after the main house, did not seem quite right. Despite being a hundred years old, it felt as if this newer part had not been fully accepted by the original building, like an unwanted child not truly received into the family. The interesting connection here was that the owner recognised a similar emotion of rejection from her own childhood. Walking through the threshold, the dowsing rods crossed at the junction of the old and new parts of the property, reflecting a compression of energy owing to disparity between the two souls of the building. Just as we find at ancient sites, even though a section of wall has been removed, the rods will still register the presence of an invisible etheric wall, which usually feels like an electrical tingling sensation when walking through the crossing. Once integrated, the house and owner both felt a sense of belonging and were much more settled. She said:

"I had no idea houses had souls and energies and that they can be fragmented, but it does make sense to me now."

Flat and apartment conversions When initially conceived, the identity and soul of a house are integral. To divide up a house into apartments is a severing and fragmentation of its original soul and unique blueprint. As noted in Whisper 1, this can destroy aspects of the character held in the energy signature, potentially creating all kinds of problems. Spirit activity is common where spaces have been energetically shattered as a result of insensitive renovation or conversion, which can create a schism and open-up portals into other dimensions. Confusion in the energy fields then creates disturbance in the lives of present occupants.

Unsettled soul In a former large house in Brighton, now divided into separate dwellings, the spirit of a woman was often reportedly seen wandering between apartments. Her unsettled soul continued to meander throughout the entire building, which of course she was free to do during her lifetime. Whilst tuning-in to the lower ground floor apartment, I found myself humming a particular Christmas carol. A song or piece of music is always significant and usually carries a message relating to the issues prevalent in the building, providing a clue as to why a deceased person may be trapped in spirit (Whisper 7). This became clear when I saw her silhouette, wearing a long black dress trimmed with white lace, of late Victorian style. She poignantly told me that it was her last Christmas with her children as she was suffering from an incurable illness. The strength of emotional grief felt by this dying lady was so intense that it fragmented her heart. Unable to pass over peacefully, this caused her spirit to get trapped in 'ghost land'. As I conveyed her message to all those present, tears flowed from us all at such heart-breaking emotion. Our acknowledgment and connection in deeply feeling her pain was enough to allow her spirit to release and move on.

Integrated additions   Extending a property works very well when the design is embedded with sacred geometry and harmonics (Whisper 7). At my own house, I designed an integrated extension using the golden mean ratio combined with various other sacred geometry proportions. This included the room height, proportions of the windows, water pool and decking. All were in resonance and merged with the original soul of the house.

In Canada's British Columbia, a house extension was built with the sacred geometry centred on the heart of the original house. The new integrated building wrapped around the paddock in harmony with the land, as the owner loved to wake up and see her horses.

Hospitals, asylums and workhouses   Where any kind of trauma has taken place in old buildings such as hospitals, asylums and workhouses, which today we often find undergoing conversion into modern apartments, they can often be uncomfortable places to live. These types of homes can attract people who have a need to play out a darker side of their psyche. A well-respected crime writer lives in the tower apartment of a former Victorian asylum, the perfect environment to 'feed off the walls' for the characters in her novels.

One couple could not settle and never felt right in their flat, the sense of injured patients lying in beds was profuse. It transpired that the original large house had been requisitioned as a wartime hospital.

Living in these kinds of environments can result in repeating the life patterns of a predecessor. This can manifest as compulsive behaviour, such as constantly checking that the oven is off, a door is locked, obsessive cleaning habits and so forth. At worst, psychotic tendencies and delusional behaviour can lead to an inability to distinguish illusion from reality.

New homes on old hospital site New structures built on a site where a previous building once stood will accumulate energies from past events that took place at that location. Even though the physical structure is no longer there, the lingering imprint of its etheric double remains in the invisible matrix of space. These overlays will compound in intensity over the years until recognised and dissolved.

A lady was having disturbing dreams of airplane crashes. It turned out that her house was built on the former site of a military hospital where wartime pilots had been patients. Whatever had activated caused her to tune into the dormant memories of the injured personnel lingering in etheric space. Her dreams re-enacted their experiences, bringing them into current dimensions of space-time.

The occupants of a flat in a new London apartment block were experiencing some strange phenomena, particularly in the master bedroom. My sense was of acute pain and palpable distress in the air. Upon viewing the past history of the space, I could visibly see a profusion of blood and guts with shadowy people handling machine equipment of various kinds. Mentioning this to the couple living there, with an Aha moment expression on their faces, they explained that the building was constructed on an old hospital site. Researching further, they were aghast to discover the floor level of their bedroom was positioned at the same distance above ground and in the same location as the former operating theatre. An 'operation' by *The House Whisperer* was indeed called for to release those invasive memory imprints in the space which were affecting their lives.

Battle Sites, Murders and Sacred Land Abuse

Much of our land is permeated with the history of our ancestors, who left the residual emotions of their thoughts and actions imprinted where they once lived or spent time. Just as a residual imprint creates an overlay to the soul of a building, every landscape has its own soul overlay. This can be described as 'memory in the fields', held in the crystalline structure of the geology and in the etheric matrix. The existing patterns that persist in the memory of the land and in the psyche of people have no time limit, no expiry date. They can continue to activate indefinitely, repeatedly playing out the same themes that affect individuals and communities throughout the generations.

Time does not forgive The far-reaching consequences of the taking of land by one nation of another over many generations, and traumatic events such as war, battle, murder, plague and famine, all linger and leave scars deep in the psyche of the land as well as within human memory. The detrimental effects this can have may be visible with poor harvests and conflict amongst communities.

We are now beginning to see some degree of resolution with the healing of entire countries once battling for supremacy, the concentration camps of northern Europe being a poignant example. The devastating impact of global disasters resulting in the deaths of thousands of people, affect thousands more in numerous different ways. Many are dispossessed of their homes, may have lost limbs and experienced other forms of physical, emotional and psychological suffering, including post-traumatic shock. Experience tells us that even though a building, town or city may have been raised to the ground, the memory vibrations of places that have been bombed or trauma damaged remain in the etheric matrix of space.

Any site held in an atmosphere of negativity or distress is of greater consequence for future generations than we might appreciate. Until these energies of trauma and extreme emotional distress are cleared, the ripple effects will continue to reverberate around the cosmos. The ingrained memory of shock impact can activate and bring about similar disasters as history has a tendency to repeat itself.

In towns in England where cannon balls can be seen embedded in buildings from the time of the Civil War, the atmosphere is almost tangible. This is why groups such as *Fountain International* began to meditate and send healing to towns and cities. Their first meetings took place at a fountain in Brighton, initially to help combat local vandalism. By activating the consciousness of water, this carries and radiates the message of positive intent as well as realigning any negative imprint of memory in the fields. In healing the residual activities of places, people in current time are also being helped.

Even if no building has occupied a site, echoes of what has happened on the land will filter through the generations and influence lives. We often feel compelled to move towards something not quite knowing why. When a specific interface activates, unconscious patterns begin to awaken. We then have the choice to keep them buried and perhaps escape by trying to sell our house, or take the opportunity to look at the issues revealed with the view to resolution. In doing so, our own personal energy patterns that may have been restricted, perhaps for many years, can be liberated.

Aerial view   To get an overall perspective, I will sometimes mentally elevate myself above a property. On one occasion, when looking down from above the house I was working on, I could see soldiers wearing red and black army uniforms in battle on the land where the house was later built. Going back in time, like watching a movie of an event that once took place, sometimes long ago, it is possible to gain insight into the significant factors contributing to unrest in a home. My work at a metaphysical level in bringing forward the past allows the active energy still playing out in current time to be recognised, acknowledged and brought to rest. This changes the blueprint in the present, giving the potential for resolution and long-term peace.

There are no better examples of the soul overlay of a region continuing to be felt than at former sites of warfare:

Massacre of tribal village   At the *Equinisity Retreat Centre* in British Columbia, many natives suffered and died in the massacre of an indigenous village, over two hundred years ago. Evident on this large acreage, rich in numerous crystal beds, injustices of long ago could not be forgotten (Whisper 2). Walking the land, people imprint their thought patterns and emotions into the ground. The Earth absorbs and reflects the energies and actions of the past, which resonate deep within its core. As crystals hold an energy charge, acting as both receivers and transmitters, they can be programmed for any purpose, either intentionally or through casual actions and thoughts. Out of control crystalline land can therefore create chaos.

Whilst driving along the one-mile track from the main house towards the gatehouse, I felt an uncomfortable, angry male presence jump into the back of the truck. The owner told me that on many occasions, she too had experienced the same thing at exactly the same place on the road. Searching the area nearby the next day, we found substantial boulders on either side of what appeared to have once been the entrance to the village. Becoming aware of and connecting with an elderly man in spirit who the landowner recognised as her father in a past life, we realised that he was guarding the entrance gateway. He had been anxiously waiting, desperately trying to get her attention to obtain some degree of resolution of past events.

It is our awareness and conscious witnessing of a person or event that brings a situation out of its locked state, allowing the narrative of history to unfold. In this instance, the devastation and emotions of pain and anguish of the massacre were brought to the surface. In acknowledging and honouring her father and the natives of the tribal village, this allowed hundreds of traumatised trapped souls to release to the light, eventually bringing the land and her people to peace.

Flashback to village massacre   When I met with a couple living in an idyllic location in the south of England, the husband visualised some strange flashbacks from another century. He recalled being part of a group rampaging through the same village, leaving death and destruction in their wake. Visualising events where he was unable to hold his own power, he regretted allowing himself to be influenced by others. His wife had sensed an unsafe feeling around him; in a strange way, his past pattern was repeating in this lifetime to the detriment of his family. By seeing and feeling this vivid experience, he was able to make the necessary changes to improve his life and relationships with his loved ones.

Family at war   When I was contacted by an anxious woman in New Jersey, USA, she was constantly fighting with her sister:

"We are at each other's throats; one of us will die if nothing is done about it!"

It came as no surprise to learn that the house was built on a former battle site between the indigenous Lenni-Lenape Indians and white American settlers, some two hundred years ago. The sisters were clearly carrying the genetic imprint of the respective sides, sub-consciously seeking revenge of the warring factions. Whilst exploring the house with the family, the sister carrying the native Indian mantle visualised the following scene:

"I crouched in fear as I felt the last moments of my life approaching."

At that moment the large garage electric double-door began to open slowly by itself and stopped half-way. The door strangely began to close again after she said:

"I see my soul flying out, I am now free..."

Our work was to re-enact this memory imprint in order to ac-knowledge and witness the unfolding of emotional scars from the massacre. By connecting with the disturbed energies embedded in the land, centred in one of the bedrooms, the trauma was slowly released through drumming and voice work. As we went from room to room, the distressing sounds grew less and less horrendous as these frag-mented events began to reconnect with each other. Within a matter of hours, events from over two centuries ago were able to come to peace through the conscious connection of those who carried the memory strands of the original warring factions. As a result, the whole family were able to feel a sense of relief and closure.

Sleepy Hollow   The town of Sleepy Hollow, New York State, was the domain of the local Weckquaesgeck Indian tribe. They lived in relative harmony with Dutch settlers until war ensued in 1643, their lands taken over with countless deaths. The deep emotions of hate, fear and envy continue to simmer, waiting to be reactivated by events in contemporary life, as dramatised in many media films.

When I was called to work on the house of a family living on this land, a foreboding sense of dark and unfinished business from the appalling deeds of the past was inimitable. Heading up to the first floor where I felt the epicentre of darkness to be found, at an ill-omened moment I paused on the landing to be literally spun around by invisible forces, but managed to grab hold of the banister rail just in time to avoid being thrown down the stairs. The intense venom in the air was compounded by the neighbours' grudge towards the current owners ever since they failed to buy the house for themselves.

Following some hours of dealing with the sinister energies in the house, whilst setting up the dining room table to hold a ceremony on the ground floor, a loud 'knock knock' was heard from the room above – clearly another level of work to be done! The malevolent energies resented any efforts that would result in dispersing them to create a lighter atmosphere. Once the space was fully cleared and purified, the neighbours would no longer resonate with the property or be able to make a connection to continue their malicious barrage. Eventually, all was released and the house and its owners were able to settle in peace.

Land abuse matches owner's life This woman loved her house, located on a beautiful Pacific island with ocean views and mountains to the rear, but there were issues. It was built on indigenous land, taken away from local natives by invaders some generations ago. This large plot had more recently been purchased at low cost by developers, perhaps not exchanging its rightful value. Their act of self-interest perpetuated the historic abuse of the taking and raping of the land that in truth belonged to the locals.

This scenario was reflected in the deeply personal trauma of the owner, who for several years had been attempting to deal with psychological, emotional and spiritual issues resulting from childhood incest abuse. It felt as if the house, built on ravaged land, mirrored her abusive childhood hidden deep within her psyche until more recently brought to the surface. In unconsciously seeking resolution, her distress would have been a strong factor initially attracting her to buy the house.

Localised traumatic events or violent actions that cause individual or family suffering, as opposed to warfare affecting large numbers, can be equally devastating and continue to play out in people's lives. For a victim whose energy fields have already become distorted, living in the same environment can exacerbate emotional distress:

Violent attack In a London terraced house, the devastating and traumatic events of a rape were visceral. The atmospheric memory was so strong that as I walked into the kitchen, my body reeled in reaction to the event. No matter how hard the female victim tried to block out the experience, the dynamic replay in the space constantly reinforced the trauma in her energy fields. Some deep energetic space-clearing and healing was crucial to help her break the memory cycle. Erasing the active imprint in the house was the first step towards giving her the opportunity to process the next level of release of her pain and distress.

House built on murder site When a house was built on the site of a murdered soldier, members of an entire family suffered with cancer and other illnesses, yet were generally healthy before moving in. The young daughter died of cancer and even the dog had to be put down after being diagnosed with a rare form of tumour. In addition to all the emotional and physical stress, fragmentation of the energy fields led to constant arguments and conflict within the family.

Murder in the woods The opportunity arose for a couple living in a remote village to buy some woodland next to their house. When the homeowner agreed the deal unbeknown to his wife, she immediately began to feel sick and suffer from intense migraines. His agreement to take on the legal contract for the land connected him to the negative energetic effect of an event some years earlier, when a woman was tragically murdered in the woods. This afflicted the feminine aspect of his life, his wife. To dispel the destructive energies still resonating and disconnect her from the event, I had to work remotely to neutralise the memory imprint of the murder on the land. This resulted in her symptoms fading away within a matter of hours.

Land that Does Not Want a House Built

To serve the land and honour the ancestors, it is wise to ask what it wants and needs (Whisper 7). Some sites are totally inappropriate for houses, both from a physical and metaphysical perspective and may simply just not want a house at all: *"Get that house off my back!"* More often than architects would like to admit, houses should not have been built in certain locations, as these examples illustrate:

A house that should not have been built Approaching a modern property in an Oxfordshire village, I could hear the *whispers* of the house saying, *"I should not have been built here."* Located over an earth energy vortex carrying a very high vibration as well as being a portal into other dimensions, this made the land unsuitable for residential purposes. Consequently, some serious paranormal activity was coming through the vortex, causing chaos in the house. Looking back in time, I could see at this same location an old barn that was once used as a local meeting place. Ghostly energies were not only rooted into the earth and active in the house, but were also attached to the owner herself. Although I did not fully divulge to the client what transpired during the space-clearing session, it was far more than the usual spirit release; what actually took place was a gentle exorcism.

Cosmic meteor shards At one house in Middlesex, toxic atmospheric energy was creating havoc in the owners' lives. I could see huge shards of glass penetrating and fragmenting the auric field of the house. Similarly, in a house in Wiltshire, meteorite shards remaining in the etheric matrix appeared to protrude from the ground, filling the entire house to its centre. Not surprisingly, this caused disruption to the energy fields of both the house and its occupants.

Sacred sites Many sacred sites, especially stone circles, usually connected to planetary bodies and star systems, have a strong vortex spin emanating from the earth. These energy trajectories are like vertical ley lines that activate at certain times of the year, notably at the solstices and equinoxes. The natural earth energies and cosmic forces were harnessed to amplify the power of intention, and used for activating specific purpose through ceremony or ritual.

In the centre of the circular henge at Knowlton, East Dorset, stands a derelict Norman church. The 12th century architects knowingly located their prominent church within a late Neolithic earthwork to harness the powerful vortex of earth energies. Over the years, this sacred site, frequented by dowsers, psychics and metaphysical energy workers, has also been used for nefarious purposes; ghostly apparitions of spirit presences are commonly reported.

Avebury is possibly the largest stone circle in the world, located on Wiltshire's Marlborough Downs. A group of houses exist between the inner and outer circles of the giant henge. They should not have been built on a site with such high frequencies, more appropriate for ceremonial and other ritual purposes. For many people, these energy vibrations are too intense for normal domestic living. Working with the owner of one of these houses, I found extremely powerful energies swirling high above the roof. These needed harnessing so as not to cause any further disturbance to her life.

Another woman found her life turned upside-down after living on an extremely powerful earth energy line. She told me that what at first she felt to be a magical home, had to be sold. While initially their lives were enhanced, right from the start they experienced strange phenomena. In spite of considerably reducing the asking price, nearly two years later, the house remained unsold. Believing she understood the spiritual aspects of this problem, she remained perplexed and felt that the house had its own agenda.

Old roads We often hear of houses being demolished to make way for new roads. On occasions, I encounter a house that has been built on the site of an old road. These old roads may have once been drovers' roads used to herd cattle and geese to market, old Roman roads where chariots hastened in convoy, or even spirit roads used to convey the dead to the local burial ground. Many became our modern roads, which later evolved as dual carriageways and motorways. Like any site, unless the activity of the original function has been brought to rest, it will continue to behave in the way it was originally designed and used – why would it change of its own accord?

A family in Surrey called me in because they couldn't understand why their lives were in chaos. During the consultation, I sensed a rushing of energy through the house, as if on a main road. The owners then shed light on the problem, explaining that the house *had* actually been built on the site of a previous road. The speed and momentum of the cars continued to race through the space, allowing for no peace and quiet. The solution was to bring the busy energy to rest by tuning-in to the consciousness and activity imprint of the original road, and telling it that its function had ceased some time ago. As a result, the house became much calmer and its owners were visibly more relaxed. The energetics of a house is like a piece of computer software; sometimes you need to press the 'reset' button!

The Seed Point at the Heart of a Building

In my early days as an architect, I had many opportunities to stand in an empty building, often those that I had been appointed to design as restaurants. I found that by holding the intention in my awareness of the potential use of the space and allowing it to *whisper* to me, the actual design would visually arise in front of my eyes as if from nowhere. I came to realise that the essence of design, the needs of the physical building, were somehow held at this seed core point awaiting activation of an intention before it could manifest.

In Sanskrit, the word 'spota' means seed form. The seed point contains a coded programme, which explodes into creation through being activated by sound and vibration. It holds the harmonic code of a potential design, waiting at an energetic level to morph into physical manifestation. A building is thereby brought into being through the intention of the patron's vision held at this conception point, before being expressed through the skills of the architect and the construction team.

Taking a cube as an example, as the code explodes from the centre outwards, the radii emanate at specific angles and come to rest at defined distances ending at the eight corners. These end points of a geometric shape in the invisible world of geometry are the harmonic nodes, which hold a micro-resonance of the central seed code. The sides of the cube, like the walls of a room or house, are the illusion of creation in three-dimensional form.

For a building to manifest into physical reality, the harmonic vibrations of sound need to work with the underlying energy grid matrix. The harmonic code *is* the seed point that forms the structure of a house. The geometry of the design determines how a building will be moulded and influenced by the location, earth energy lines, vortex spots and leys. This powerful earth energy is what charges up the house and gives it a unique energy signature. Thus, the etheric grids of architecture contain the original code programme or blueprint of the actual physical structure. An important function of the dimensional matrix is to hold the coded essence of the soul consciousness of a building, or any object for that matter.

The unique energy signature and identity of a building, determined by the patron's intended purpose, is embedded at the time of conception. It is also imprinted by the energies of the planetary alignments at the time the roof is completed, thereby creating the astrological chart of the property (Whisper 7). Its intrinsic character relates to and is further shaped by the consciousness of the land on which it stands, being its 'parents' or 'ancestors'; the 'children' are those who reside or pass through the space held by its walls. Within the genetic make-up of a building, the experiences that happen along the way generate layers of emotion, all contributing to various aspects of its evolving character. Unless a live genetic code has been set up to establish its reason for existence, with programmes operating in the energy fields of space, the building will naturally degenerate and end up feeling like a very sad, dead space.

Everything that has happened within a building and on the land itself leave coded memory imprints. Harmonic imprints are recorded in both the molecular structure of the physical materials *and* in the metaphysical energy matrix of space. Overlaid onto the original soul code of a building are these additional layers of reality. These soul fragments can span lifetimes owing to a multitude of emotions and impressions that over time can either enhance the level of harmony or create a build-up of negativity and distort unity consciousness. It is therefore important to recognise and resolve any issues creating fragmentation, giving the soul resonance of a building the potential to be a truly holistic and heart-coherent home.

Locating the seed point   To resolve any problem in life and bring about change, it is essential to get to the heart of the coding that is holding the narrative. From the generative nature of the 'sweet spot', the quintessential resting place for the soul, fundamental change is possible. The skill required to locate the seed point is to know from where the heart truly resonates; conscious connection is then possible. All can be achieved from this energetic power point at the energetic centre of the property. This *is* the heart of the home, the core essence that holds the code allowing for potential change.

The heart of a house is not necessarily located at the physical centre of a building. Many people believe it is to be found in the kitchen, but that is not my experience. Analytical systems such as Feng Shui and Vaastu generally consider only a two-dimensional plan, with emphasis on the physical centre. It is more accurate to perceive a building as a three-dimensional structure in the form of a cube or sphere, although few houses are actually designed in an exact geometric shape. The true esoteric centre will gravitate somewhere between the actual physical and energetic centres of a property. The outside or garden space can also influence the location of the heart centre, which may even have additional sub-centre resonance points.

It is possible to change the energetic code of a building from this heart centre. Working from this small but most significant point in space, activating the harmonic resonance for an entire building can be accomplished. In itself fractal and self-referencing, with all areas connected and coherent within it, when a change is made at the true heart of the building, all spaces have the potential to respond. This requires that all the connecting threads in the energy field matrix have been purified and link back to the heart centre. Thus, true and powerful transformation is possible in the etheric world of the invisible geometry of a building.

Whatever message is sent out from the heart centre will radiate throughout the entire consciousness of the building, so there is no need to walk through every room to modify a house at an energetic level. As well as from this central point, the activation process can be carried out from certain 'hot-spot' locations or sub-resonance heart centre chambers. In one hotel, these sub-points were located in the library and in a small conference room, the catalysts for clearing and bringing resonance throughout the entire building.

Activating the heart centre of a house A house in Surrey had a sense of emptiness and felt neglected, yet was immaculately kept. The problem was an overshadowing dense energy preventing the owners from fully connecting and feeling its heart centre. When, for whatever reason, we become disconnected from the original soul of a building, it will eventually shut down, making it difficult for a house to feel like a home. Having undergone the *House Whispering* process and created a clear and vibrant space, the next step was to connect the owners to the heart of their home. By guiding them to search and call to the heart of the house, they were able to locate the heart centre in the spacious entrance hall. This allowed the couple to ultimately merge with their home space, when a sense of tranquillity became tangible. The following day, the lady owner said:

"Today I have a feeling of peace and tranquillity here. It was such an interesting day yesterday. You certainly left us with lots to think about in terms of how to move on."

Zero point The absolute centre, the place of stillness, of no movement, no yin or yang, just 'being', *is* the zero point. I find that by connecting to this seed point of a building and allowing myself to experience a deep stillness, the heart of the house will then come and find me. Ultimately, both hearts are united as one. By recalling who 'I Am', my sacred geometric fields connect to Source and can then resonate and spin in alignment with universal consciousness. Through the law of resonance, the geometries of the building will respond and follow suit. This approach from stillness is the ultimate in space-clearing and realignment, allowing full connection to the genetic code of a building or person. This brings the opportunity to re-tune the cellular structure of the human body, which in itself is designed to various geometries, primarily the golden mean ratio (Whisper 7).

The energetic suspension seed point is expressed through the torus, the tornado spin for DNA activation. This is the place of 'do or die', the moment of conception and full potential, awaiting activation through sound so it can unfold into creation in whatever way is needed. As one person experienced during a sacred sound workshop:

"I feel I'm at zero point – ready for blast-off!"

Zero point contains no values other than mathematical. Does that mean there can be no moral judgement, integrity or subjectivity? And if not, where do such philosophical enquiries come from? Perhaps in our quest to find who we truly are and understand our true purpose for being here on Earth, these values are simply human constructs.

All is perfect Our lives may be likened to an iridescent pearl oyster nourished by its outer protective shell. To use the analogy of an onion, we can peel away the multiple layers to reveal and examine parts of our life story, or we can cut right through and take a look into the heart of the matter. Whichever approach we take, unless we are distracted along the way or lose our sense of direction in finding our destination, we will eventually reach our core being at the centre.

The soul *is* absolute and perfect if you believe it to be so. Yet human beings have so many overlays of attitudes and conditioned beliefs that obscure our true nature, we can spend our entire lives peeling back the layers in search for Self. The paradox is that we are already fully realised, but we just do not realise it! So, unless you perceive your past as perfect and your future is about to unfold exactly as your soul intended, the life experiences you encounter may be out of alignment with your karmic blueprint. You can, if you choose, realign the energetic matrix and project your future dreams to attain your soul's purpose. We may ask, how can something that is already perfect be transformed? In the powerful evocative opening words of the ancient Sanskrit Vedic scriptures, the *Isha Upanishad*:

> *"That is perfect, this is perfect, perfect comes from perfect, take perfect from perfect the remainder is perfect. May peace and peace and peace be everywhere..."*

Psychotherapeutic Regression

To communicate with a building we need to know that a harmonic code is embedded within the soul of the house at conception, giving it a unique energy signature. To get to the root of any matter, it is essential to get back to this zero point. In some instances, after reading the energetic blueprint of a space to identify the issues towards finding resolution for the occupants, I use a technique that I term 'psychotherapeutic regression of a building'.

This area of *House Whispering* developed from my understanding of how people create a subconscious relationship with their homes. It is about the fusion of past and present purpose within the realm of energetically regressing a fragmented building. This ancient form of sacred geometric energy web-weaving brings the original purpose embedded in the blueprint of a building into current time.

Given the appropriate knowledge, an architect or energy worker can influence and change the blueprint of an out of tune or fragmented building by taking it back through space-time to inception point. This is the place before any negative or destructive patterns began to form and overlay the original blueprint. At this conception seed point, the function of a building can be re-programmed and changed, or its original purpose reinstated. This regression technique has powerful, deep rooted and lasting effects in changing the energy and function of a building. For those living or working there, this can only be dealt with at a deep subconscious level.

As with the land, a building also has a pulse, a heartbeat. When working in a property, I become aware of when the pulse rate is higher or slower than it should be, which can indicate a building under stress when its health is compromised. Should a property casually change use over time or be forced to change without specific consent from the soul of the building, confusion and fragmentation can arise. Accumulation of soul overlays then create disturbance in people's lives. As the energetic atmosphere of a building is determined by the vibrational qualities of those who interact within that space, especially with the heart centre or seed core, it is also possible they may have created or contributed to an imbalance in the first place.

One aspect of this work involves unravelling and reading the programmes, the hidden codes that people are driven by. Below the surface of the stories playing out, something else is usually going on. I find the complexity of the code will vary, depending on an individual's level of awareness and motivation.

The nature of a building works in much in the same way as our own complex psychology: its character remains for life, yet has the ability to adapt and change to new circumstances. Just as our personal energy signature is integral to our soul, a building also relates to spiritual and spatial awareness. When a building is violated and forced to conform to human whims and desires, rather than treated with love and respect, its core becomes traumatised and fragmented. As with people, these soul fragments can be gathered together within the realms of etheric space.

Because a building can change consciousness and electrical field resonance, it has the potential to be regressed back to its original seed point. This is where all old overlays of energetic patterns embedded within its history can be cleared, realigned and reconnected to the original source coding. By illuminating the inimitable soul or blueprint and re-establishing its core identity, a building can remember its intrinsic purpose. When realigning the harmonic code, if the golden mean is spinning in the geometry of the matrix (Whisper 7), there is less chance of any negative energy getting entangled and impinging on people's lives in the form of paranormal activity.

Whether a new building or one that has existed for hundreds of years, when the cause of any disharmony has been dealt with and the vibrations adjusted, the building then has the opportunity for its frequencies to match those of the occupants. It is then possible for the occupants to come into heart resonance with their property, bringing the potential for a house to become a home (Whisper 1).

Rebalancing and clearing the energy fields also makes possible a fresh start, for a new code to be set up and create a new function, if that is what is needed. The crucial question to consider is: *"Does the building want to change?"* (Whisper 6). With a respectful and right approach, it will usually accept a new intended purpose. Connecting with the consciousness of a building is a powerful way to enable full realisation of its true potential in the present moment. Only then can a house support an individual or family, or commercial buildings serve humanity in whatever way is required. It is at this stage that a building can be re-programmed in harmonic alignment to your own relationship, to effectively collaborate in re-writing your own script.

In this complex process, it may be necessary to access other dimensions for information about the original seed form coding or energy signature, which remains at the heart of the building. This is the beacon of light that can be focused upon to bring balance and assist in creating change. How can you change something unless you know its integral code in the first place? It is a bit like when someone goes to the doctor with a cough, unsure how his or her symptoms relate to the overall problem, or even what the problem actually is.

Regressing a building back to early infancy or beyond, to the point of conception originating within the mind of the patron before the structure was built, can be of enormous benefit in healing past and present patterns. To empower a building, we must reach back to the absolute core of the energy grids and understand the karmic story of its relationship with the ancestral land. Different buildings and situations will require varying approaches and techniques to bring about the desired outcome. As the energy grids are changing all the time, to connect with all knowledge held in the memory fields of the Akashic Records (Whisper 1) will illuminate what is *really* happening at any particular time and place here on Earth.

Old programmes confuse and stress building An office building in New Jersey, USA, had a stressful atmosphere. When I tuned into the invisible energy matrix, it was clear that the original owners had placed an etheric programme in the foundations, codified to physical artefacts. This tradition of many societies is what gives the consciousness of a building its purpose and power. In this instance, although appropriate at the time, it seemed that no one had decommissioned the original codes, which subsequently created confusion in the energy fields. As the building was currently being used for a different function to its original purpose, it was operating in trauma mode. The solution was to tune into the original programme and bring it to rest. By fully engaging with the codes to understand their purpose, and then deconstructing them using a metaphysical process, the building was neutralised back to zero point. It could then be re-programmed for current use and embrace its present day reality in harmony with the current business.

A professional psychotherapist, commenting on a complex client issue that I was working with, referred to the process of psychotherapeutic regression of houses in terms of personal development:

"It seems to me that whatever process we undertake for our own development, we are undertaking it from the seed core of those patterns. Thus we have control, which means we can also sabotage issues that compromise the effectiveness of this work. Even under the guidance of an experienced therapist we can still manipulate how much we are prepared to share, to allow in and to change. The House Whisperer's part to play in the whole process is in allowing us to tune into parts that may present themselves for our own journey and understanding. It's all about patterns, which often repeat, that often we just can't see. So getting to the seed point of this scenario would be invaluable. If people can find the seed point of their own hidden issues in the process, it can be liberating to the point of new beginnings..." (Beverly Martin)

What this therapist is saying about getting to the seed point of our own journey is exemplified by the problems faced by this homeless mum of a ten-year old boy in Cyprus, who feels she is stuck on all levels, unaware of what her problems really are. In seeking help, she acknowledges that among other things, she has issues with the places where she ends up living:

> "...no matter what I do, I can't fix things with my mind or my efforts. I understand that everything lies within. I've always known that. But how can I fix something if I don't know what it is?"

Changing the Function of a Victorian Chemist

This prime example of psychotherapeutic regression of a building was to prepare it for a new purpose. The intention was to change the function of a building that was originally a Victorian town pharmacy in Kingston upon Thames around 1880, to become the home of a spiritual centre. I was approached by the owner, concerned that the building should be in true harmony for her intended purpose of creating a sacred space for use as a spiritual temple.

Substantial residential and commercial development was taking place around her building, with much scaffolding erected surrounding the concrete structures. One of the windows at the side of her building was for some reason deliberately blocked by the developers, further diminishing the internal energy flow. Worse still, the aggressive manner in which the adjacent construction work was being carried out conveyed a sense of total disrespect and dishonouring of the existing Victorian buildings. My perception was that the soul of the building was in trauma, with a heartbeat pulsating faster than is normal or healthy for a residential building. It also felt trapped in the past, unable to function properly in current time.

The *House Whispering* process is firstly to ask the building if a change of use is acceptable. In order to pose the question and receive an answer, it is necessary to reach the seed core blueprint by energetically regressing the building. In this instance, this took the form of visualising a geometric purifying grid with spirals spinning through time and space, taking it right back to conception point, which highlighted all the life events that had become stuck over many layers of time. As a result, what I saw were the many activities that had taken place. The main scene was of people dressed in Victorian attire, busy stirring pans and pouring liquid into jars in a large first floor kitchen. The owner then told me that this space had originally been used for preparing and making medicines, which were sold in the pharmacy on the ground floor.

As the core seed point was reached, the original conception point where the soul of the building was embedded, I asked what its purpose was. The reply, *"To serve the residents of Kingston."* So I asked if the building would be happy to continue serving the residents with a new use as a spiritual centre. The answer was a most definite *"yes"*. Its heartbeat gradually calmed to a slower and more natural healthy rhythm, enabling it to maintain and nurture those people who would use the space. The building was then able to come into current time, fully open and ready to fulfil the owner's intended wish to open a spiritual centre. She felt the sacred geometrical structure that I had envisioned constructing itself within the energy weave of space, like the petals of a lotus flower unfolding across the site. This beautiful image then connected into the town of Kingston upon Thames before spreading across the rest of the Earth.

The Spin of the Waves

We have been handed down extraordinary symbolic texts such as the Vedic *The Mahabharata*, various Tibetan Buddhist writings and Plato's *Timaeus* discourse on the creation of the universe. All refer to creation emanating from the single point of universal Source. These works describe the construct of the cosmos as embodying an energy matrix field that holds resonance and memory, where no distance or separation exist in the quantum world of time and space.

The general view of the physical world of matter has been of random disconnected particles and waves, with no apparent order. With a greater understanding that energy is eternal and never lost, only transformed by means of what physics refers to as the first law of thermodynamics, we discover that the universe is composed of quantum waves in a state of transcendent potential. We are told that 99% of space is 'empty', yet this empty space is actually a multi-dimensional grid matrix of harmonic vibrations, linking all souls together; the souls of buildings are part of this matrix. Thus, we are all connected to a reverberating cosmic matrix of atomic particles that order space within a unified field. The structure of these particles is geometric and can be described as holding the masculine energy, whilst the space itself equates to the inner feminine counterpart (Whispers 2 and 7).

All are connected *The Jewelled Net of Indra*, the supreme of the thirty-three Gods of Manu in the *Rig Veda*, is a text attributed to an ancient Buddhist (Tu-Shun, 557-640 BCE). At each juncture of Indra's vast net is located a jewel, each representing an individual life form, atom, cell or unit of consciousness. Each jewel is intrinsically connected to all the other jewels in the cosmic matrix; a change in one gem is reflected in all. This is the essence of resonance: seeing the Self in all things, and in all things seeing the Self.

The shifting dynamics of quantum space mirrors our own reality. As all are connected, whatever action we take will have an effect on another person, place or thing. We are not separate and do not exist in isolation. A linear perspective is simply an illusion that restricts the possibility of change in our lives. If we accept that the random factor is actually one which consciousness can connect to and morph and change, then magic can happen around us. To expand our being into quantum consciousness makes it possible to harness the energy field matrix grids. In the etheric world there is no time and space in truth. It is therefore possible to connect energetically with another part of the globe from a distance, as if physically being there. The concept of using our thoughts to change the nature of space in another part of a house, town, city and even other dimensions, then becomes a realistic prospect – armchair space-clearing!

Remote space-clearing Little did I realise the impact and shift that this particular home consultation would have in initiating the development of my current framework of working remotely. During the journey to Yorkshire, I became aware in the car of a strong odour of sulphur, bad eggs. Upon arrival at the house, when the owner greeted me at the door I was repelled by a stench not dissimilar to that on the journey, and more than a little disturbed to find she had forty four cats all running free and using the house as a toilet. Bravely entering the house, as the front door shut behind me, my body trembled in panic. Although a cat lover, I made a hasty retreat from this suffocating experience, awkwardly shaking my right foot to expel some toilet tissue I had trodden on in my venture. Even more astonishing was that the woman had called me in to advise on the best colours to paint the walls to help her house sale. Stepping back from the doorstep, I politely but firmly told her that her house needed serious fumigating, not colour co-ordination; brown was the only colour that came to mind! Moreover, I explained that I would work on her house from the embankment across the road.

This day was a nemesis point, from when I gradually developed and honed a set of metaphysical skills in projecting mental awareness and etheric feelers into a space, allowing me to work with people and their homes at a distance. If we accept there is no time and space in the quantum world of matter, it is easier to grasp that we are not actually viewing anything at a distance at all, but right here and now in the present moment. All external change arises from the subtle realm of thought and is a reflection of inner shifts, which take place energetically before becoming physically manifest. This is understood more easily when we appreciate that an illness can be seen in the distortion of our aura long before becoming apparent in the physical body. To focus on being present and fully grounded when working remotely is of vital importance to prevent becoming fragmented and shattering our own energy fields whilst in etheric travel mode. Thus, human consciousness acts as mediator between Heaven and Earth.

Materials and spatial phase-lock Although a building is static at a physical level, its spirit and emotional bodies are spinning in dynamic motion. The pattern of movement depends on its function and purpose. Given that all kinds of physical materials from every part of the globe come together to collectively create a building, the potential for disparity is enormous. Why should any material have a sense of connection with another? When two materials and surfaces meet, unless they embrace each other in common resonance, disparity results in fragmentation of the energy fields. The same applies to both the shapes of building structures in relation to each other and to the geometric space around them in their relationship to the land. This again can lead to disturbance in the building and consequent health issues for both people and animals.

Where the interlocking interfaces of geometric patterns meet is the potential for a natural merge of resonance and harmony. An example of interlocking shapes can be seen in Sintra, Portugal, where the zigzag patterns of the stonework crenulations are mirrored by the spaces in between. Like jigsaw pieces turned upside-down, the shapes interlock perfectly into the empty spaces. As most buildings are not designed with this principle in mind, I have developed a metaphysical merging process for the purpose of allowing the common elements of the geometries as well as the incongruent geometric shapes within the molecular structure of the materials themselves, to come together in common frequency and resonance.

When two sets of surfaces meet in harmony, they interact and effectively speak the same language. In the physics of acoustics, this phase-locking of the harmonic interplay of waves enables them to morph and merge from chaos into harmony. The fusion of harmonic resonance allows our reality to synchronise with the heavenly layers above and the core layers of the Earth below. This awakens a deeper consciousness, opening up energetic portals into other dimensions. We can connect with the universal energy matrix and gain access to information of a more profound nature, including all that is held in the Akashic field of resonance.

Featuring strongly in the dynamics of buildings throughout many cultures is the number 432, integral to the Solfeggio harmonic scale and based on the number 9 (divisible by the number 3). The numerical frequency of 432 Hz allows total phase-locking of the entire range of frequencies, whether expressed in music or reflected in the harmonics within the geometry of architectural design. These and other harmonic tunings are made visible when certain musical notes are played to a dish of sand; the vibrating grains arrange themselves into perfect regular geometrical patterns.

The international standard concert pitch based on the note A (above middle C) was 432 Hz before being changed to 440 Hz in 1938. This shift at a significant period in world history resulted in a numerical frequency not wholly divisible by 3, with the effect of fragmenting the natural resonance of harmony.

Frequency shift In the physical dimension, fractal design goes beyond a pattern repeating itself in progressively smaller or larger scales. Fractal energy is the golden mean harmonic, a logarithmic spiral geometry that produces non-regular shapes, quite different from the rational classical geometries of squares and rectangles. When a building is energetically fractal, the natural energy flowing through it will spin the resonance of the golden mean harmonic throughout all areas. This has the distinct advantage of keeping the space defragmented and will create a self-perpetuating energy cleansing 'machine' (Whisper 7).

Changing the inherent resonance of any physical material by means of its etheric phase patterning can make it softer and more malleable. This explains in simplistic terms how in the resonant field of buildings, quantum space-clearing can bring your home into alignment with current time, or whatever time zone reality you might choose for it to inhabit. It may then become out of phase with its neighbours, still in their own time warp. If a house is living out a theatrical narrative from a past era, the residents will have chosen to perform as actors in a play, perhaps living in a dreamland as in the earlier story of the farmhouse. Conversely, when homes in the same street occupy different time zones, they may no longer be neighbourly towards each other.

By aligning our heart harmonics, wavelengths and resonant frequencies with that of the place we wish to engage, we synchronise. This phase-locking makes us invisible or transparent as we unite with whatever we choose to merge with. We can then interlock our bodies with the cosmos and breeze through, just as horses may line up and canter off together in a field, or flocks of birds move in unison as if guided by a single consciousness. It is the biological component in combination with the laws of physics that allows consciousness to morph and replicate in the natural world.

The interaction of these energetic frequencies can highlight anything that is out of alignment, and illuminate if we are out of place with our own personal life situation. As we have seen, it is possible to change the energy signature of a building and thereby its purpose and function by re-programming the coded blueprint, using the practice of psychotherapeutic regression if and when appropriate. Nothing can stay static or out of alignment with the spin of the waves!

It is also possible to diminish the toxicity of harmful materials or transmute their form into other substances in order to lessen their impact on current out of phase vibrations. Metaphysical alchemical means can also be used to regulate geopathic stress (Whisper 6), and patterns of disaster and abuse modified to bring about a more balanced lifestyle (Whisper 4). To realign the human body through harmonic resonance is a powerful mode of natural healing (Whisper 7), transcending far beyond any system that attempts to force change.

Warning It is imperative that any exploration of dimensions of space and time should always be for the highest good. It is certainly not advisable to deliberately play around with these inter-dimensional realities, or attempt to reach altered states of consciousness without the appropriate knowledge, protection and guidance, no matter how curious one might be. Scant knowledge of metaphysical realities can open up dimensional portals and allow through out of place beings that can cause trauma to the land and buildings, not to mention unwelcome personal side effects. How this ability is used, as with any aspect of energy work, comes down to personal intention and integrity, which always has karmic implications. I most definitely suggest proceeding with caution!

Clearing and Realignment of Spaces

"Sages do not have a fixed mind. They share their minds with others. They improve what is good, and also improve what is not good." (Tao Te Ching)

My reasoned approach to the concept of space-clearing in this book should already have become clear, as misunderstandings commonly arise with this term. For me as *The House Whisperer*, space-clearing is *not* about clearing what is there so that it disappears forever. This is impossible from the perspective that energy cannot be destroyed, only transmuted through the etheric energy grid matrix.

My work is about rebalancing and realigning energies, transforming bad space into good space. The concept of 'bad' space is simply an energetic environment that does not serve and support its present purpose, so needs re-balancing to be brought into supportive and nourishing alignment.

Purifying a home space will facilitate a clearer vision of what is reflected from within the people living there. As the externalised mirror of the home changes, previously held personal attitudes and behaviours can no longer continue to build up and compound. The house will then act as a clearer mirror, reflecting the underlying life-patterns needing to be dealt with by the occupants, giving them the opportunity to consider making any necessary changes to their lives.

In today's world, the nearest many of us come to purification of our spaces is to sprinkle salt in the corners of each room when we move house, or to practice smudging with sage sticks to disperse an energy that feels stuck or uncomfortable. Therapists and practitioners frequently clear their rooms or spaces of the residual energies of a person or odour, although I have consulted for many healers and practitioners who fail to do this. Who wants another's gunky aura or attachment hovering over the next person's heart space! People attending any kind of therapy session, whether hands-on or trans-personal, may bring unwanted visitors or disturbances with them. Having shed any attachments they might have been carrying, the client then goes away feeling lighter and empowered. Anything left behind in that space can consequently create havoc for the therapist, as well as for the building and the clients who follow.

As I became aware of a heavy presence in the therapy room of a once successful Surrey clinic, it came as no surprise to hear that the practitioners felt uncomfortable and unusually tired when working there. After dealing with and releasing the mischievous spirit that was sucking the life force out of everyone, the room returned to clearer space and the business profited from improved financial flow.

Total space-clearing This is more complex than just clearing negative energies, which can be likened to dusting the surface rather than deep cleaning. In the physical dimension the concept of linear time is calculable, whereas in the etheric world time can be past, present and projected future simultaneously; all is accessible and interchangeable. This explains, in simplistic terms, how events can be modified towards co-creating what some people believe to be a pre-determined future, although much evidence supports the contrary.

Whether I am working on-site or remotely, total space-clearing and realignment needs 'cooking time' for the adjusted patterns in the etheric grid matrix to reconfigure and merge with the molecular structure of the bricks and mortar. As with food, timing is of the essence, but there is no predetermined recipe: all can happen in an instant or it can take a few hours. The latter is more usual as the people involved need time to adapt, morph and change concurrently with the building. During this process, I see and feel the state of the space and materials and make adjustments at metaphysical levels in real-time, as required. People often need to adjust slowly and gently with changes that take place at a very deep level, reaching the core of the issues in what is essentially a psychotherapeutic process. The resonant stories held by the building and the occupants affect emotions and subsequent behaviour. The typical response afterwards is:

"The air is cleaner, I can breathe more easily… I feel taller… lighter and warmer… sounds are sharper... I can see clearly now, colours are brighter, like the clouds have lifted… I feel more at home now."

Chi-charging A space that has been cleared and realigned will have undergone quite a shake-up, so needs recharging with powerful and refined sound harmonics. This is carried out at a physical level using sacred musical instruments such as Tibetan bells, bowls and cymbals. Any instrument should embody the purest consciousness, and not be overlaid with any pre-programmed intention by its maker. At a metaphysical level, part of my practice is to draw down pure geometric harmonics from the ether to enhance the molecular structure of space (Whisper 7). This then settles into alignment for that particular place, augmented by programming a self-cleansing geometric 'machine' in the etheric matrix.

Charging-up any space will create an electrical tingling that can be likened to the invisible 'hairs' of the building standing on end. The sharpness in the atmosphere brings alertness, enabling us to come into conscious presence in that space at that moment. At this point, all is pure energy, holding optimum potential for the next unfolding.

Reaching resolution I would *never* attempt to clear a space before unravelling the inherent stories and gaining an understanding of what sits at the heart of the problem. Any negativity has value in helping to show us what message is being illuminated, bringing up things to be looked at in the process of resolution. Clearing spaces is about appreciating and analysing the repeating patterns within our own being. In order to change our external environment, we must be prepared to alter our inner reality. Firstly, by recognising that change is needed, then asking for help in the process of externalising:

"I need a remote house clearing of all previous energies in order to improve my health and wealth."

To clear the physical without reaching emotional resolution can create further trauma. It is a process that cannot be forced. In cases of extreme clutter and hoarding, we might suggest hiring a van to clear everything, as with the *Skip collectors* and other stories (Whisper 4), but that will not resolve the underlying emotional issues which usually need gradual and gentle release. Similarly, clearing ghosts and entities without resolving the reason for their attachment to a person, building or landscape is of little value, and can be dangerous for the stuck spirit as well as making you vulnerable to any lash-back. As previously explained, we first need to tune in and focus to get to the root cause of why a spirit or soul fragment has not moved on, and recognise our own connection to their story (Whisper 3).

Only realignment of sacred space with goals and intentions can truly allow a person to be in harmony with the space they inhabit. This in turn is a reflection of their own aspirations or endeavours – their reason for being there. Disintegrating the sticky energy web with incense is a powerful part of the loosening-up process but is not the long-term answer, as this story illustrates:

Beaten-up by ghost boxer   Whilst working with Sandy in a small house in a rural area, the owner's late father was somewhat resistant to leaving his former home. Having lit incense to loosen-up the sticky energy web, I was aware of my eyes becoming sore. This became so intense that it felt as though I was being punched in the face. When I asked the owner what his father did for a living, he said, *"a professional boxer."* Father and son were left to sort out certain matters with a view to our return at a later date. During the long taxi ride to our next destination, a black eye erupted. The driver's body language indicated that he wondered if I'd come off worse in an argument. I kept quiet as his subtle facial expressions, reflected through the rear-view mirror, offered appreciative sympathy. In any case, how could I possibly explain I'd been beaten-up by a ghost boxer!

Any undesirable activities that do not align with the highest good will be shown up during and after a *House Whispering* session. Once a space is shaken up, old patterns will find it harder to survive, as the following situations demonstrate:

Fraud exposed In Middlesex, a productive shop owner complained of working hard in her business, yet making little profit. Following our consultation session, it reportedly came to light that both the manageress and the accountant were pilfering monies, which explained her plight. The process of shaking-up the stagnant energies in the space led to the exposure of fraud, illuminating the truth of misaligned activities.

Team resignations After working with a group in London, I received a call the following week from the team leader to say that half of the twelve members had resigned. The process of space-clearing and realignment had illuminated a lack of integrity by some of the staff, no longer in a position to maintain employment. Those individuals who chose to resign had the opportunity to find more suitable jobs, and perhaps make soul-searching amends for their actions. The existing team now had the benefit of renewed purpose without the encumbrance of 'dead wood' amongst their colleagues.

Suspicion of misbehaviour Whilst working with the owner and staff of a shellfish processing factory, set in a stunning, rugged coastal region, it so happened that the former accountant team was a married couple. The husband had been fired, so went to work for the nearby competition. This, of course, caused some consternation as his wife was left running the financial side of the business of his former employer (my client), raising serious concerns over matters of confidentiality. Within a week of my carrying out a *House Whispering* process at the premises, the wife resigned of her own accord. This solved the question of any transgression, with the bonus of not having to pay her redundancy monies.

There are, however, occasions when it is more appropriate to leave things alone, at least for the time being, as these next stories show:

Ancient mariners   In one of the big sheds in a boat-yard on the south coast, the presence of sailors from times past filled the air. They seemed happy just to hang around the boats, as if supporting and advising the present-day workers in the same environment where they too were once employed.

Gentle release   I am sometimes asked to undertake a space-clearing session for an elderly parent. If they have not themselves requested this, I need to ensure they actually wish to engage in a process that could result in a significant change to their life. Whilst it is acceptable and beneficial to lightly dust the atmosphere to alleviate any thick or heavy energy for a temporary period, such as in *Care homes* (Whisper 2), I would *not* run a thorough space-clearing routine for anybody without their full permission and engagement.

When working with the consent of an elderly or sick person in their home, great care needs to be taken to prevent causing any distress. They are likely to be inextricably connected at a deep level to their existing space and belongings, especially if they have lived in the same house for much of their lives. To attempt to break these bonds, especially when a person has no wish to let go of aspects of their past, can cause serious repercussions and potential harm.

In one instance, a fragile lady of 86 years of age had lost her husband a few months previously. It was of little value to put her through the trauma of breaking away from recognisable past patterns, with much of her energy invested in years of living in a house full of loving memories. If she was to live elsewhere or perhaps a care home, then her home could be gently space-cleared to release the threads of connection. This would help her to move forward and make a new home with the belongings she treasures. The objective of gentle and sensitive release is always paramount when dealing with precious memories of a longstanding or delicate nature.

As with all aspects of *House Whispering*, my approach in bringing peace and harmony to lives is entirely about identifying and finding the most efficient solution to what the person, house or land requires. This will always be shown in the present moment whilst working.

Merging with the Heart and Soul of Your Home

Once a house has been space-cleared, realigned and the energies enhanced, the occupants will hopefully have reached their Aha moment and gained clarity of any issues and concerns. In the final stages of a consultation, I offer a visualisation meditation with the aim of giving the opportunity for merging the heart and soul of the person with the heart and soul of their living space. This phase-locking brings the breath and heart harmonics, wavelengths and frequencies into total synchronisation with the heart and soul of the property, allowing a house to feel like a home. Working together in harmony, the house supports you whilst you take care of your home.

There are occasions when the thought of merging with home brings up resistance. If 'home' has negative connotations, arising perhaps from a fearful childhood experience, a person may not trust the house to be safe. They may, through shock or trauma, be detached from their body and remain unable to truly connect with anything, even with themselves, until sufficient healing has taken place. In such circumstances, the thought of being controlled or stifled by merging with the structure of the house, representing the masculine aspect of a building, can reactivate emotional fears. Anything that emerges in a consultation can act as the catalyst to shed light on the next steps to be taken before a person can access their personal nourishing space from within. Further self-processing at a deeper level may be needed before full release and resolution of issues identified are possible.

I rarely need to revisit a property following a consultation. Should this be requested, I will check whether the person has carried out the changes in keeping with my advice following their Aha moment. If they simply need further support and guidance, I will work with them remotely. But if they just wish to go over the same issues again, perhaps to avoid facing 'the music', I remind them that they *must* take full responsibility for their actions and address the core issues affecting their life. Prior to and during a consultation, I will explain that there is little value in my attempting to fix things, tantamount to giving a pill, which rarely brings lasting change. Most people do fully embrace the opportunity, even in difficult circumstances. It is truly heart-rending to see and hear of the positive changes in people's lives, reported back very soon afterwards and sometimes years later.

Heart Coherence Visualisation

Close your eyes and feel the energies around you subside. Sense your feet on the ground and allow your centre to find itself. Allow the sounds in the room to come to you. Now gently expand your listening to reach just outside... and now to the furthest sound, and just rest in the essence of all that is. Do not focus on any one sound or judge its quality.

Keeping your feet firmly on the ground, allow your awareness to expand and sense the essence of the space around you. With every breath you take, feel the room taking the same breath. Imagine the walls and ceiling expand with your in-breath, and on your out-breath allow the room to just relax.

With each breath that follows, expand your awareness into the next room. Move across each floor and up through the building, expanding into the fullness of the house until you reach the roof-space. Again, visualise the whole of the building breathing in and out with you, the entire house flexing as if it were your own lungs.

In your mind, stretch out your hands and allow your fingertips to touch the walls of the house, back to front, side to side. Let your fingers melt into its substance as if made of marshmallows, feel the house yielding its being.

Sense your heartbeat. Now allow your awareness to wander through the rooms of the house and call for the heart of the building to come and meet you. Listen and feel its pulse. Allow the heart of the building and your own heart to gently merge, and feel the two hearts beating together as one.

Now honour the spirit of the house and know that you are at one with it, the house transformed into a true home, ready to nourish your spirit. See yourself taking care of your home, knowing it will look after you and ensure the wellbeing and happiness of all who reside within. Your home can now be a true and faithful friend!

Expand your awareness outside and connect with nature, the trees, grass and flowers, the rolling hills or the ocean, and breathe in that nourishment through the walls. Feel the energy of nature infusing into every part of your home. Hold that in-breath still for a moment, now gently exhale beyond the walls into the outside spaces, the patio and the garden, however far the land stretches, and back out to whence it came. Allow that breathing to cycle for a few minutes, settling into a peaceful rhythm of natural meditation.

Now take a long gentle deep breath in – and on the outward breath open your eyes...

Welcome Home

Whisper 6

HONOURING HEAVEN AND EARTH

How land and buildings feel and respond

The Concept of Home from Ancient Times

Our homes are part of the global consciousness network of human development. For as long as human life has existed, people have needed some kind of structure for physical refuge and protection from predators, human or animal.

Shamans, philosophers and archaeologists understand that the ancients placed value on all forms of life. They respected the spirit of the land and worked with the Earth, giving it care and attention and returning the nourishment it gave them. They honoured the realms of the gods and revered the deities that inhabited their everyday lives. In the earliest known caves of southern France, the inhabitants portrayed their understanding of the natural world in wall paintings of great beauty and simplicity, leaving us a symbolic legacy.

Many more recent discoveries indicate a high level of knowledge, intelligence and sophistication, contrary to the view of our origins in terms of progressive advancement, as we have been taught to believe. Ancient cultures at the highest levels knew the language of scholarly learning and the answers to the fundamental esoteric and spiritual questions of life. In communicating with the unseen realms, our ancestors were aware of the planetary bodies that encircle the Earth and recognised the patterns of movement of the stars. They knew that the heavens influenced consciousness and human perceptions of reality, intuitively aware that everything is in some way connected.

The early architects had much knowledge of underground water and harnessed the natural electromagnetic frequencies that emanated from the land. They assessed auspicious and vagrant energies and tapped into the power points of the earth grids, making use of the vortexes that can act as portals into other dimensions.

In comparative mythology, spiritual beliefs and desires vary only in the outer expression and cultural interpretation of their place in history, geographical location and degree of abundance. Common to many societies is the knowledge of 'placement', the act of locating individual structures in meaningful relationship to each other and in harmony with the land. To 'in-tend' means to tend to something on an inner level, a universal language of knowing, termed by Jung as of the collective unconscious. Ancient cultures recognised the specific reason and power behind an act of intent, once an inherent part of externalising personal or group values. Tribal groups, led by their chiefs or shaman priests, used ceremonial objects and tools to honour their gods and call in the ancestors. The objects in their homes and the structures themselves, where they slept with fire central to their lives, were placed and used with perceptive feeling and purpose.

Many indigenous cultures had rituals associated with moving to a new home, designing and building their houses with an understanding of geometrical and harmonic proportion. They would space-clear any unhelpful residual predecessor memory and work to ensure the health and happiness of their communities.

To consider the appropriate location and orientation of homes and commercial buildings is indeed of great value in contemporary design and town planning. Adapting these same principles to reflect the microcosm in the macrocosm is to be encouraged, offering the potential to connect people and buildings with natural harmony. This has deep rooted and lasting effects on how people feel and respond to their environment.

Ultimately, in honouring the wisdom of the ancients, we are recognising their place in our lives, acknowledging those who came before us and bestowed the gift of the land where we now survive or thrive. But for the land, there would be no place for the expression of the heart and soul of buildings, as we know them. In empowering our lives and homes on all levels, we preserve meaning and value for future generations. Our co-dependence on each other and on our buildings, towns and cities, plays a central role in our conscious evolution on planet Earth.

Geomancy and the Dynamics of the Land

Geomancy is generally understood today as reading and working with earth energies. To the ancients, geomancy was the wisdom science of auspicious placement in creating sacred space. This knowledge was not only used in choosing the sites for their stone circles, megaliths and burial chambers, but much later for many important temples, churches, sacred buildings and other structures. Their location and orientation to make use of the most nourishing earth and cosmic energies to benefit the people and the land, was once a crucial part of this process.

Probably the most important consideration of all, and one that is rarely taken into account today, is to identify the natural energies of a site and to set out an energetic map denoting the best place to build and more importantly, where to avoid. This process also identifies metaphysical imprints from previous happenings on the land, and in relation to any pre-existing buildings.

At a site visit, or from plans and photographs of a house, I will tune in and dowse for information about the state of play of the energies affecting the spaces both inside and outside, including the surrounding land. This form of geomancy also covers energy mapping around and beneath the site in question. The purpose is to recognise and analyse patterns of earth energies that disclose how the grid and vortex patterns manifest, including any geopathic stress.

Assessing the quality of the soil and the ground deeper down, known today as a Geomantic Land Survey, underpins any issues a house may be experiencing, or that might affect a new housing or commercial development. This includes identifying old mine workings or geological deposits. It should also be determined whether any new development or road building is likely to impinge on access, boundaries or view from the property. Infringement of space, privacy and natural light are common objections by residents to neighbours' planning applications. All of these significant factors create an energy signature matrix map of the area, which can then be used as a valuable blueprint template for propitious design. This will hopefully benefit people and animals in a positive way for a long time to come, depending on the degree of conscious awareness of both the residents themselves and the professional team.

Assessing how the dynamics of the land impact on occupants of a property predisposed to predecessor energies and unwanted spirit activity, requires a combination of architectural and spatial awareness. Among other disciplines, it covers psychology, geomancy, and interaction with cosmic forces. Perhaps one day we may come up with a name for this work that people can relate to – for the moment *House Whispering* will suffice.

Dowsing   We can identify what is going on in buildings and the land through dowsing, the ancient art of water divining, originally used for locating underground springs in order to establish wells. More sophisticated techniques have been developed by major petrochemical companies who use dowsing to find oil, and by enlightened surveyors to identify and map earth grids and areas of geopathic and electro-stress relevant to their projects. Dowsing is also used to locate explosives in minefields, for finding objects and even missing people.

An introduction to the art and science of dowsing involves 'feeling' the earth energies at different places in rural and urban settings. It is worthwhile taking the time to learn basic physical dowsing techniques using L-rods and pendulums, tuning-in with your own bodily senses and visually using the mind in an extra-sensory capacity. With practice, this skill becomes a powerful tool, facilitating greater sensitivity to physical and spiritual energies. Connecting with natural forms such as trees, landmarks on the horizon and sacred sites, allows us to develop a deeper relationship with the landscape and the elemental realms.

The important thing to remember is that our human body is the dowsing instrument. Metal L-rods or hazel branches, pendulums and other devices, are the tools that reflect what our energy body, guided by our Higher Self, already knows. Both are capable of indicating a response to what we are asking to be revealed, but to get the 'right' answer you need to ask the right question! Once familiar with your own personal dowsing responses, you are more likely to recognise when any questions are disingenuous or out of alignment with your intention, which at all times needs to be heart-centred.

It is crucial when dowsing to be grounded in the present moment, in the 'now'. If your thoughts are focused on the past or future, you will get a reading for that point in time, more than likely incorrect for the situation at hand. Should you wish to attune to another time zone for the purpose of gathering specific information, then take the mind to a past era or scan a time-line to focus and connect with the required knowledge needing to be revealed.

Earth acupuncture Metal rods or wooden stakes can be used as Earth acupuncture needles. In my early days of teaching Feng Shui incorporating dowsing, I had a dream the night before taking a group of students on a consultation. I was shown that if a geopathic stress line was found to be running through the house we planned to visit, I was to line up the students as if each person was an acupuncture needle. This we did with some amusement on the day, and found it worked very efficiently in transmuting the geopathic line. Intrigued by this practice, I later experimented with mentally planting etheric acupuncture needles into the Earth when physically present at a site and when working remotely. As both worked, it became clear to me that the entire process was a conscious mental restructuring of the energy grid matrix, and that no physical tools were actually needed at all.

Before engaging in the acupuncture of space, or indeed any aspect of working with buildings and the land, staying connected to one's Higher Self will usually clear personal thoughts and residual mental activity, which would otherwise get in the way; as with physical dowsing we can end up with an inaccurate reading. The effectiveness of visualising driving pins or stakes into the ground can be distorted by our own subconscious patterns, with the result that the etheric earth acupuncture needles may get implanted in the wrong place!

Distance dowsing The next step was to develop and refine my dowsing techniques beyond space-time by tapping into the Akashic field. I found that by tuning-in to the etheric energy matrix beyond the normal five senses, this gave access to the most accurate and revealing information within the etheric world. Making a connection in this way allowed knowledge in the present, as well as from the past and various potential outcomes of the projected future, to flow through the conscious mind. It was then possible to make the necessary metaphysical changes to any given situation – a most effective and powerful procedure, which I now use regularly in my work.

Power spots and vortexes Most sites have earth energy lines of various types running through the veins of the Earth, together with potent energy vortexes with life-enhancing or draining characteristics. The strength and directional rotation of a vortex spin at crossing points of the earth grids will determine whether a location is beneficial or disruptive. A building sited over a favourable vortex can make use of the natural energies in the landscape to harness its power. Houses can also be designed to specifically activate and enhance this energy. Many houses are built through lack of knowledge or sheer ignorance in locations where the strong natural flows of earth energies have become blocked or scrambled, as in the story of *A house that should not have been built* (Whisper 5). Chaos in the etheric grid matrix then causes disturbance, with devastating effects on lives.

My work includes advising professionals on the best areas of a development for locating buildings to maximise the natural earth and cosmic energies. It is especially important to identify those areas to be avoided, particularly where the conjunction of earth grid lines and vortex spins are detrimental for living or working. As the law of resonance of scale prevails, map dowsing with a pendulum is most efficient for this process. The map is a mirror image of the actual land, so it is possible to cover large areas remotely without the need to make an initial site visit or negotiate what may be rough terrain or inaccessible woodland. My findings, marked-up on drawings, can be confirmed using dowsing rods at a later site visit or by a third party already on-site. I usually find only a small percentage variation in accuracy – the wonders of dowsing!

Harnessing beneficial earth energies At a vacant commercial site in Brighton, I found an earth energy vortex of a nourishing type and recommended that the landowner did not block its natural flow by using metal reinforcing bars in the concrete foundations. My suggestion of using fibreglass reinforcement was followed-up, allowing the beneficial earth energies to flow freely into and up through the building. This power can be further harnessed and amplified by the use of metaphysical sacred geometrical structures, together with crystals and suitably programmed artefacts positioned or embedded within the structure of the building itself. This will potentially enhance the health and prosperity of all those who then use the space.

Living on a negative energy spot Unaware that her house in Portugal had been built on a negative energy vortex, little did this lady realise the detrimental effect it was having on her life. Not only was it sucking her energy down into the earth but also exacerbating spirit activity, which seems to be the least of her concerns:

"... I already knew I had a spirit in my house, and now realise I have a bigger problem which I don't know how to deal with."

Making a house transparent When a house is built on a site that interrupts the natural flow of land energies, a disturbance is created at the point of interaction, which disrupts and fragments the energy fields. The degree of disturbance will vary, depending on its strength and the personal issues of those living in the property. What is for sure is there will be challenges to health, wealth and relationships.

One solution is to make the house 'transparent' by tuning-in to the energetic Ki Signature of the house and harmonic patterns of the land. By listening, witnessing and reading the common frequency signatures of both, then adjusting and merging them through fractal waves at a metaphysical level, this can effectively make the house invisible or transparent. The natural energy flow can then continue its fluidity of movement along the landscape as if the house was not there, thus diminishing any prior disturbance.

The location of one couple's house in Herefordshire interrupted the natural flow of energy from the hills down to the valley below. After carrying out the transparency transformation process and other space-clearing alignments, the female partner reported:

"Your work has completely transformed the house. I am sleeping well, feeling settled, safe and strong, much more robust – in fact I recognise myself again. The energy between us is much softer, more respectful and loving."

Landscape chakras These swirls or vortexes of energy that some people call chakra points in the land vary in intensity, quality and direction of flow. The function of a chakra is akin to a transformer; its purpose is to transpose high vibrational energy from the etheric fields into a lower vibration, compatible with the frequencies of the Earth.

The lower harmonic energies can then nourish the physical body, while the higher frequencies activate our higher spiritual centres. Energy is of little value unless it can be harnessed within a frequency bandwidth for a specific purpose. Chakra energy thereby transposes or rearranges itself through interaction with corresponding centres of the human body. Any blockages will prevent the full nourishing cosmic power from being absorbed. This means that the Earth can gift a building an emotion, a positive spin energy charge or chakra point.

Geopathic Stress

The term 'geo' means earth, and 'pathic' from pathos (suffering) is the Greek word for disease, so geopathic literally means 'dis-ease of the earth'. Geopathic energy is a natural quality and earth dynamic, so is not a problem in itself. It is when humans construct buildings over geopathic areas that the vibrational interaction leads to fragmentation of the energy fields, giving rise to discomfort or stress. For the wellbeing of the land and her people, geopathic energies and electromagnetic fields should be considered when locating and designing buildings. Simply don't build over them!

Atomic patterns and energy forces surround us all the time in the form of a fine global geometric network, interrelated to the etheric matrix counterpart of geopathic energies inherent to the Earth. As with vortexes, various energy lines, leys and earth grids embodied in the land can be harnessed for their positive aspects or avoided owing to detrimental effects. In places where the earth grids and natural energy flows have been disturbed or become fragmented, generally through human ignorance or by activities for excess profit, control or manipulation, this again disrupts the land. The resultant interference to our electro-sensitive mental and physiological patterning, levels of perception and reasoning, then causes an overload on our systems and our brains go into scramble mode.

Does your home make you sick? When underground water flows beneath a building and electromagnetic fields from pylons or masts radiate nearby, this will exacerbate any pre-existing problems caused when an earth energy line meets an obstruction such as a house. The cells of the human body are less able to regenerate, resulting in a weakened immune system and lowered resistance to viruses, which can lead to more serious illness and disease. Medical treatments can also be compromised:

> *"Geopathic stress at my home is also causing my health to suffer. My doctor has suggested that I contact you for your advice and to arrange a House Whispering consultation."*

A 'cancer house' Having just bought their first house, a couple find they have moved into a property with a history of geopathic stress and illness. Feeling they have unknowingly bought into a nightmare, the familiar pattern of arguments began. With a growing sense of uneasiness, they discover their West Country home is known locally as a 'cancer house', and were told that in olden times nobody would live in such a place. They then learnt that the previous owner died of lung cancer and his wife had severe dementia. The neighbour was also suffering from cancer. A local dowser apparently found no less than five underground water streams crossing and intersecting underneath one room. Plaster cracking throughout the house and an apple tree in the garden covered in cankers were both indications of intense forms of geopathic stress. Desperately wanting to believe that something could be done, the young woman told me:

> *"I am beside myself as I'm sure you can imagine. In all other aspects this place could be a lovely home."*

Whilst initially attracted to the house through a deep resonance, both the house and its historic location clearly activated some inner personal issues needing to be brought to her attention for resolution.

Animals and insects Disturbed earth energies can also affect the health and wellbeing of our animals. When a friend met some farmers from Anglesey, North Wales, who took their prize cattle to the Smithfield Show in London, they explained that their forebears could once graze much more of the land. This was not only because there were fewer buildings on the island, the construction of the motorway had resulted in a significantly lower milk yield from the cows grazing on one side of the carriageway. Whilst unfamiliar with the term 'earth energies' or 'geopathic stress', these farmers fully appreciated how their animals responded when man fractured the land and disrupted the natural environment.

Ants, bees and wasps all love this juicy geopathic intensity. I was once called to a house in Austria that was plagued by swarms of ants. After metaphysically diverting their route from the garden, the ants continued to carry on their busy lives in a direction which by-passed the house. Considering that the natural earth energy was there before the house was built, do humans have a right to complain? Needing a solution, it was possible to move the geopathic line by tuning-in to its vibrational code, uniting with it for a brief moment and then directing it to move to another location. Another approach is to recalibrate the vibrational signature of the line and alter its resonance to one that the ants will not be attracted to walk on. There are no hard and fast rules; appropriate action depends on the needs of any given situation.

Along with other creatures in nature drawn to this earth energy, domestic cats naturally transmute what we consider to be negative energies and are doing their job in protecting their owners. Despite being a cat's natural predisposition and environment, if the geopathic energy is too strong and persists, it can eventually make them very ill. In some instances, bodily functions fail and lead to their death.

The brainwave frequencies of dogs and horses are, however, more aligned to those of humans. Being adversely affected by these harmful energies, they intuitively avoid geopathic stress zones. Using techniques such as dowsing to detect these negative areas, we can take precautions to avoid them. The principle of reducing the harmful effects through resonance is always my preferred approach.

Accident blackspots Certain locations are renowned for more road traffic accidents than might normally be expected. This is not just because of bad road markings, dangerous bends or poor visibility. Accidents are prevalent where geopathic energy lines or leys intersect at specific locations or when they are out of balance, notably where the energy spin creates a vortex of confusion. Predecessor energies from old roads and former tracks that may have been used to carry the dead continue to resonate in many physical places in the landscape. Whatever once took place at a particular location becomes lodged into the memory field matrix. An accumulation of energetic imprint patterns then creates the potential for repetition of similar events, leading to further collisions.

Even where a location does not have a known history of being an accident blackspot, strange happenings can occur. Outside his former home, a ghostly figure was desperately seeking this homeowner's attention, unhappy with certain changes she was making to *his* house:

> *"I wake up to yet another car crash outside my home, yet it is not designated as an accident black spot; the road is not unsafe in its layout. I just do not understand what is going on."*

This example of what I call 'psychic geopathic' is generated from a build-up of paranormal activity rather than geopathic stress, and can create a trauma zone leading to an accident blackspot. The darker energies jangle and unnerve the geometries in space and get caught up like a fly trapped in a spider's web, the food of the geo-psychic fundamental for survival. As negative human thoughts and emotions become entangled in the web, they too become food for these dark energies, as in the *Childrens' homes* (Whisper 3).

Electromagnetic Fields and Underground Water

Although the foundation of modern electrical science can be traced back to the ancient Greeks, Egyptians and beyond, it was not until 1883 that Thomas Edison re-invented the electrical transformer. It was to take another twenty years or so before the common light bulb was available in domestic homes. Until the use of modern-day building materials such as concrete and plastics, and the way electricity is harnessed, there were far fewer problems with disturbed earth energies for human beings to cope with. Neither was our diet depleted in vital minerals from the soil and water.

The complex matter of electromagnetic fields (EMFs) raises many issues of serious concern. Because our bodies inherently encompass magnetic polarities, with countless sensitive and delicate neurological pathways that are electrical in nature, we need to be mindful of the levels of electromagnetic stress we expose them to. When a house is located in the path of these frequencies that reach out and impinge on the unconscious mind, the occupants will feel under constant pressure, unable to relax in their own homes. It is well documented how living under power lines or close to pylons, electrical sub-stations and especially tetra masts, can all cause serious illness, including ME, MS and cancer.

The human body is remarkably good at adapting to things that are bad for us, commonly when they are consistently so. Generally underestimated are the effects of pulsating transients, the on-off frequencies of varying Hz levels that target our systems. These are considered more damaging than exposure to a consistent frequency, especially if we are dehydrated or lacking in the mineral magnesium.

We may not be able to see these invisible force fields, yet know they are there. Imagine a radio playing your favourite channel, other frequencies are available and blasting out elsewhere, we are just not tuned in to hear them. Similarly, devices designed to deter rodents in our gardens emit a sound frequency generally inaudible to humans, yet we see the results.

Reducing harmful effects of EMFs Further to rebalancing the harmful earth energies affecting the land, another important reason for taking a holistic approach to design is to reduce the damaging effects of electromagnetic fields that constantly bombard our lives. Most significant are transformers, which although they perform their function in changing alternating mains current to direct power for our devices, the radiating electromagnetic fields cause considerable disturbance if we find ourselves spending time close to them.

Young brains are especially vulnerable to the damaging effects of modern technology, with smartphones, laptops and wireless tablets all playing a significant part in everyday lives. The resulting techno-smog affects sleep, the ability of our cells to regenerate and leads to tiredness and poor concentration. With increasing awareness, many schools are re-assessing the merits of Wi-Fi in classrooms. Biologists confirm that even infrequent exposure to EMFs can cause our white blood lymphocytes to die off at an alarming rate. Maintaining a strong immune system is therefore of paramount importance.

The low-level radiation from certain types of fluorescent and eco-lighting has also been shown to be damaging to health and work efficiency, commonly causing depression, migraine headaches and some forms of cancer. Combined with the poor design of buildings and blocked energy chi flows, this explains why many people feel below par or irritable whilst working in open-plan offices especially, and when visiting certain large stores and supermarkets.

Cell and cordless phones Wherever we go in today's modern world, we see people running their lives from cell phones, keeping them switched-on in jacket and trouser pockets – what better way to 'zap' one's body with radiation, especially the heart and reproductive organs. Of even greater harm is leaving your cell phone by the head of your bed, waiting for its alarm call to awaken you. When talking on a cell phone whilst sitting in or driving a car, being enclosed in a metal box results in amplification of the microwave transmission waves to the physical body. Using a hands-free device is generally much safer, albeit the added factor of Bluetooth transmission waves.

Cordless house phones of the digital type also emit continuous frequency signals, found with many models to be more harmful to health than cell phones, whether in use or not. It is always good to be mindful of where you are in relation to the base station. Positioning the human body between the handset held to your ear and the base station means these signals are going right through you. They are also amplified with the use of electronic hearing aids.

A friend shared this story of a house on the Jurassic coast, located next to a field where a cell-phone mast had been sited. A child of three-years old constantly moved her pillow to the other end of the bed. When a disrupted line was dowsed to run diagonally through her bedroom, her parents understood what their young daughter had instinctively known all along – that she felt restless and had bad dreams when she laid her head where *they* had placed her pillow. She sensed an innate need for a peaceful night's rest away from the electromagnetic disturbance of the mast.

Black streams Earth is largely a water planet. The human body contains on average 70% of this natural element with its unique properties in absorbing and transmitting information. Many forms of illness are caused or exacerbated by dehydration, so drinking clean energised water is of vital importance. In pure form, healthy spring water from the ground, mountains or volcanoes, carries the nourishing fractal geometry embedded in nature, which resonates with the natural harmonics of the human body. When a spring, stream or well is contaminated, or its organic response is restricted and channelled from its natural course, water loses vital life force and can acquire some of the characteristics of the electro-grid and associated transients, carrying the strong electromagnetic fields many miles further away. It then becomes what some refer to as a 'black stream', with the effect of directly destabilising our energy fields if we live or work in close proximity.

Plants considered poisonous such as ivy and ragwort, flourish in these negative environments. Livestock and horses in fields where they proliferate will suffer if they come into contact with such poisons. In the context of earth energies, we tend to use the term 'negative' to mean harmful, but much depends on how we interact with these energies, such as building in the 'wrong' place. The term 'negative' actually refers to yin energy. Both yin and yang polarities co-exist naturally and are intrinsic within the Earth.

Through dowsing and other metaphysical techniques, we can identify black streams and unbalanced earth energy lines. When a structure is built above an underground water flow that becomes affected by electromagnetic disturbance, disruptive vibrations are set up in the building. It will no longer be in supportive resonance to the benign natural pulse of the Earth, known as the Schumann resonance of around 8 Hz, which parallels our natural brainwave patterns.

Geo-psychic energies   In her new home in Wiltshire, this woman not only had problems with water but the distorted energies caused by draining nearby lakes contributed to geo-psychic manifestation:

"There seems to be an issue with rising damp in the new property and interestingly enough massive subsidence and damp with the previous property that I lived in. The Internet is intermittent on wireless but works on cable and the engineer said that he couldn't understand it, as the strength is good. He looked at me straight in the eye and said, 'You have ghosts!' I have had experience of dealing with energies as a healer and an intuitive, but after numerous health challenges know the wisdom of not attempting to clear the house on

my own when I am run down and depleted. This house and estate was built on three reservoir lakes, two of which were drained (perhaps not successfully) and one still exists as a brickfield meadow. Despite the hot weather, we found that the kitchen had water coming through... so where is this water coming up from?"

The homeowner acknowledges that she also had problems with water in her previous property. As water relates to emotional memory, there may be underlying painful memories that she is not dealing with. Has she considered why she is drawn to living in houses where underground water is a significant contributory factor in her health challenges? The phrase, 'healer, heal thyself' is a good reminder that taking our finger off the pulse so to speak, regarding our own health and wellbeing, can lead to disastrous consequences.

Clocks creating disturbance A house in Suffolk had many loud ticking clocks, three together in one room creating an irregular combination of discordant rhythms. Clocks that refuse to tick together and are out of sync create confusion and fragmentation of the spatial energy matrix. This has its own inherent pulsating rhythm in relation to the beat of the Earth and to the house itself, and can affect our own bodily rhythms; in this case, contributing to the owner's health issues.

No need to move the bed I am frequently called to a property when a person has been told by a dowser or energy practitioner to move their bed, as it is located over a geopathic stream. In my experience, what is more significant is that the person is likely to be out of alignment with the harmonic consciousness code of the geopathic energy. It is the disparity between the two energy fields that causes fragmentation and disrupts the human immune system, resulting in illness. When people move the bed, or use a device to deter geopathic stress, this buys into the concept of duality. When we choose to come into unity, the concept of 'me' and 'whatever' is hurting me ceases to exist, thereby minimising any potential harm.

In one instance when a lady was told she had a geopathic stress line running under her bed and contributing to her illness, she moved her mattress to a different room. This felt better as the new space dowsed clear, but within a couple of days the geopathic line was back in the new bed position. She then moved the mattress to another room, with the same scenario repeating. This went on until she ran out of rooms to try! Owing to her resonance with the negative earth energy imprint, it became clear that *she* was the carrier of the geopathic matrix code, the damaging aspect exacerbated by her fear, which created even greater harm. After bringing her into heart-merge unity with the harmonics of the etheric geo-psychic fields, she found immediate benefit. She has had *no* symptoms or negative readings of geopathic stress since the *House Whispering* consultation nearly two years ago, and continues to be clear.

Harnessing the Energy Grids

There are products on the market that claim to rebalance and harmonise the damaging effects of geopathic and electro-stress. Although it is best to avoid creating problems in the first place, there is value in all approaches that suggest the intention to resolve something in life. There are, however, limitations with any mechanical tool or device. Primarily, they do not address the root cause of an issue, which is never entirely physical as there is always a psychological and energetic component. Using devices can also result in over-reliance, then being no different from taking a pill to just deal with the symptoms. Certain gadgets and even some forms of jewellery, based on natural mineral, metal and water configurations, harmonise energies by interacting with the human body, and are found by some people to be of value. These are nonetheless becoming less effective as human consciousness shifts into higher vibrational states.

As geopathic and electro-stress have a metaphysical energetic counterpart through resonance with the interactive vibration of people and their homes, an alternative solution is to use geometric structures created visually in the etheric matrix by the mind. Setting up a conscious programme is a very potent remedy, and needs knowledge and great care to be taken. An etheric machine, with the ability to morph and change consciously, can adapt to and keep pace with developing needs according to the requirements of people, the land and buildings. Any device that does not allow this flexibility may bring initial benefit, but can then have the effect of holding you in the damaging pattern it was designed to resolve in the first place. The issues that we encounter naturally change over time anyway.

Whilst it is possible to move, divert or transmute these lines, as with the ants, I would never attempt to get rid of anything that is an intrinsic part of the natural balance of the Earth, albeit distorted at that time and in that place. Working within the etheric matrix to harness the energy grids is a potent way to bring about resolution.

Essentially, I work on the principle of shifting the frequency of a space in relation to the damaging earth energy line. To acknowledge a problem recognises what needs to be dealt with, but to liberate something by fighting it merely takes a duality approach; a mentality that perpetuates further issues at many levels. Knowing that 'All is One' in any situation changes the vibrational frequency code and can render imperceptible the symptoms that people may be suffering.

One way of dealing with disruptive frequencies caused by blocked energy lines or concentration points is to rebalance and lock them back into their original grid patterns. By effectively neutralising their scrambled geometries or merging them back to earth, the damaging effects that result from subtle energies becoming locked into the grid matrix system are rebalanced. Only when these harmful energies are taken out of three-dimensional reality and resonate with higher vibrational frequencies, can our environment be cleared of vagrant forces and consequent sources of stress dispersed. When shifted into another dimension of reality, negative energy lines and earth grids do not go back to how they were, but transmute into other dimensions and become harmless here on Earth. Thus, changing our relationship to embrace unity alters our perceived reality.

By tuning-in to geopathic and electromagnetic energies, absorbing them momentarily into our cognitive experience and changing our own reality to a higher level of frequency, we align with the quantum fields beyond time and space; the invisible cross-space communicator of universal consciousness. The resulting shifts can bring extraordinary and unexpected solutions for all concerned:

"You and Sandy came to clear the geopathic stress in my home in Worthing and amazing things have happened since then. My energy was so much better the next day and I feel almost back to the way I used to be... I had put my bungalow on the market just before you

came and two weeks after your visit I had an offer of the full asking price. At the same time a friendship moved onto a different level and I had a proposal of marriage. So within a month of your visit I had an offer on my bungalow and a proposal of marriage. We are getting married in a few weeks."

Seeking Permission of the Land

As discussed previously, a basic psychotherapeutic approach is to ask the spirit of a building if it is happy with a specific proposal and wants to change. In the case of a new build or re-development, is the land giving permission for the project to go ahead? Professionals at all stages of the planning and build process rarely consider the all-important question: *"Does the land want a house or any building on it?"*

When the spirit of the land answers *"yes"*, this will assist the entire process from the design, obtaining planning consent, efficient construction through to completion, which will benefit all involved in terms of time, expediency and cost. If the land says *"no"*, then meta-physical energies can influence the project to be marred with plan-ning refusals, building delays and other obstructions, all too common in the construction industry. When we refer to consultants, the most important body to consult is the spirit of the land itself.

When asked to give advice on a building or construction issue, my approach is to examine the underlying causes of the problem. If the land does not want to be built upon, or the soul of a building does not want to be split up and fragmented, it will express itself through those who oppose the Local Authority Town Planning application. At planning proposal and permission stages, any issues of resistance or obstacles encountered can often be attributed to the angry reaction of ancestral or unseen energies in the surrounding land, particularly by what has happened there previously. Local residents can therefore influence the energies of success, either consciously or otherwise. The traditional battle-lines drawn up between applicants and neighbours, residents and local councillors, can be an indication of previous boundary issues, past life connections, battle trauma, or conflict with-in existing buildings. This is one of the reasons why *House Whispering* input in the early stages can have significant advantages. Vigilance is especially pertinent in cases of the restoration of listed or protected buildings, which are inclined to make extra demands – they know that they warrant special attention!

Seeking permission of the ancestors When asked to advise on a housing development on a Polynesian island, where various problems were threatening to prevent the project from going ahead, it was clear to me when tuning-in to the spirit of the land that no one had asked permission of the ancestors. As a result, the lives of some of the team members were being quite seriously affected. My work was to appease and negotiate the situation at a deep core level by connecting with the ancestral energy and ensuring their voices were not only heard, but also considered and incorporated into the scheme. I then marked on a map of the land the earth energy lines and vortexes, showing where the architect should avoid locating the buildings. By addressing both the physical and energetic aspects to minimise disturbance of the natural earth energies, this would help to prevent illness among future residents living above or close to any potentially damaging housing zones.

Dishonouring Mother Earth All who lived in a particular apartment block in Jordan had health and relationship issues. The builder responsible for construction had not asked permission of the spirit of the land when he cut into Mother Earth to lay the foundations. The kick-back effect of dishonouring the land was so great that when I checked the physical and metaphysical intensity levels of geopathic stress, the readings were 10/10, very high indeed. Anything over 6 indicates serious illness and potential cancer forming levels.

As the original owner and builder had passed away some time ago, it was now down to his son (the client) to make amends. He was willing to make an apology to the land for the misguided actions of his father, a conscious act that can be carried out in such circumstances on another's behalf. Whilst guiding him in a visualisation, I was aware of the powerful presence of Quan Yin, the goddess of compassion. Coming out of the meditation with tears in his eyes, he shared his experience:

"I saw this woman in shimmering light dressed in blue and white."

We had both experienced the Divine Mother, each in differing ways. Having made his peace with the spirit of the land, the son also promised to make offerings to Mother Earth in his involvement with any future building projects.

As we walked through the building to re-check the geopathic levels, the readings were astoundingly zero – totally gone, healed all within a couple of hours. I find the depth of true healing achieved in this way to be so fast and permanent, giving a profound sense of respect for buildings and the land, as well as honouring the elemental and angelic beings. Very different and far more beneficial than the get rid of approach to any perceived negative issue, including geopathic stress. By virtue of the inherent connection to universal Source, any committed personal resolution towards change brings far greater permanence, ensuring long lasting effects for future generations.

Sites Not to Be Built On

The ancients would not have considered building on land that had 'negative' energies. Whilst we now know that geopathic stress can cause or exacerbate illness, it is less commonly recognised that the effects of violent actions such as rape, murder, warfare and so forth, can attract comparable detrimental energies and bring about further events or incidents of a similar nature. Therefore, unless the trauma embedded in the land is brought to rest and the active resonating patterns are remedied and returned to their original natural state, we should *not* live or build on damaged land.

Genetic imprint of plague and pestilence Entire generations in localised regions were once wiped out by plague and epidemics such as smallpox, tuberculosis and venereal diseases, all leaving a legacy of what homoeopaths refer to as 'miasms' among their descendants. In my experience, these miasms transcend space and time. Although the physical signs of a disease may no longer be transmitted, the metaphysical imprint continues to resonate.

Why one person is susceptible to suffering a disease and another not, is analogous to being attracted to a house where individuals encounter either harmonious or destructive energies. If we have a resonance to a particular illness, then we are more likely to contract it through an empathic connection and fragility of our system, which at some level we agree to take on. Thus, building and living on energetically polluted or infected land can sustain perilous consequences.

This was exemplified when I was asked to assess the energetic value of several shops in Kensington, London. A ground floor unit that had been empty for some time had a dark, heavy feeling. I just knew there was something very wrong with this site; the overwhelming sense was one of death. Upon further investigation, it became clear that a corrosive earth energy line running through the site was coming from a plague pit, a mass burial ground located some distance away. As it would need high energetic maintenance to prevent it from going bankrupt, I advised the client not to rent the shop unit. Although it would be feasible to raise the vibration and optimise the energy charge to make the unit feel better, the main building and several shops on either side were part of the same site. The ongoing negativity in the atmosphere would spill over into the client's area unless all occupants came together for a joint site ceremony and collective energy clearing.

A business located in South London was similarly affected by its connection to a plague pit. Upon checking the earth energy lines using a pendulum to map dowse, one major geopathic line was found to come from the direction of Blackheath, a few miles away. Although there is some uncertainty over historical plague pits in the vicinity, any suspicion in conscious memory is often sufficient to create a negative vibration. The dowsing response to the question of whether there *were* plague pits on the Black Heath was a big *"yes"*. What is for sure is that a conduit of negative energy currents from that direction flowed through the client's property, affecting their health and trade.

I am often asked, *"Could you not just change the energy of an entire area?"* While I believe it is possible, without permission from those concerned to change the energies in a building or the land, this would create energetic shifts in the lives of people not necessarily seeking change. The karmic path needs to be trodden with care and respect; we all have subliminal reasons for living where we do.

Contaminated land We should not build on land that has become contaminated from toxic chemicals or nuclear waste. The site of old rubbish dumps, frequently purchased today by developers for housing estates, emanate toxic gases and low-level isotopes, making them extremely unhealthy places to live. Similarly, houses built above granite formations expose the occupants to radioactive radon gas, known to cause lung cancer. Factories left derelict or destroyed because of chemicals they once exploited that drained onto the site, should also be considered contaminated land. Not only must residential properties not be built on what is already contaminated land, we also have a responsibility to take steps to prevent this happening in the future.

On a derelict site of many acres in Glastonbury, Somerset, a sheepskin factory and tanneries once used toxic chemical processes, including sheep dip now recognised as extremely harmful to health. The neurological systems of some individuals were so badly damaged that some farmers in the region are known to have committed suicide. The local council made the well-informed decision for the land to remain dormant for many years and refused dozens of planning applications. Today, on this former blot on the landscape, buildings once doomed for demolition are now home to a community café, studios and teaching space. Perhaps these consciousness raising high vibration activities, talks and workshops, will result in a metaphysical transformation of the land – only time will tell.

Toxic chemicals We no longer allegedly allow chemicals that are hazardous to health to be used in the workplace and in our homes, or toxic waste to pollute our drains and spillages foul our seas, yet how many builders and developers consider the soil? One of the many problems facing us today in bringing greater awareness to those who farm the land is the long-term implication of spraying with harmful solutions. This not only affects the Earth and her crops, but also wild animals, dogs and their owners walking through or alongside hedges and field boundaries.

We only have to look in many homes to find cleaning products using bleach, which scientists tell us that even in miniscule amounts breaks down the ozone layer, so what does that do to our bodies? The list is endless of harmful chemical ingredients in personal care and laundry products, soft furnishings, genetically modified foodstuffs and additives. Some older mirrors carry a degree of mercury in their composition that can continue to give off toxic residue. Mercury and arsenic were also once used to treat fence posts to prevent rotting at the base, causing untold damage to the air, soil and life forms. Some eco-lamps contain mercury and need careful handling. Many aspects of modern living are unfavourable for optimum health.

Distressed buildings How a building is physically treated has the capacity to cause tension at a soul level. Materials including lead pipe-work, concrete, asbestos, various forms of air conditioning and heating installations, can all cause distress and make occupants feel extremely unwell, particularly if systems are faulty. In many respects, the house may be trying to protect its owners, whose lifestyle choices frequently add to the problem. A building *can* have an emotional cry for help, so it would be wise to listen and honour its needs.

Another very important aspect of 'sick building syndrome' is the combination of atmospheric and earth energy forces, which have a significant vibrational impact on emotional and psychological states of being. These aspects of our spaces are far more damaging when not understood and left to run out of control. A build-up of emotional toxicity in homes and offices can lead to geo-psychic phenomena, when people are likely to experience headaches, nausea, fatigue, irritability, and feelings of unrest in their own familiar environments.

We should therefore be mindful of the quality of the vibrations we encounter, as we too will begin to similarly resonate. The deeper implications are that as we attune to higher levels of frequency, we become more sensitive to lower vibrations. Where it is not possible to avoid the negative ambience of places or people, one solution is to transmute their vibration to a less disquieting frequency, whilst at the same time consciously work to bring a higher vibration to your own surroundings and personal energy fields.

For the Earth to evolve and transform, a shift in consciousness has to continue if we are to 'be the change'. It is vital that we clear and energise our environment in order that the spaces we inhabit can take the next step in evolutionary progress. As we clear physical debris from our homes and streets, we also need to dissolve the continually forming clouds of distorted energies and negative emotions from the etheric counterpart of our spaces. It only takes the personal commitment of a few to change the attitudes and behaviours of many. We all have a part to play in transmuting lower level vibrations, bringing in the light and sending it out with loving and purposeful intent.

The Architect Holding the Vision

The philosophy of the ancients was to respect natural law, with all aspects of a building from the ground up designed to be in harmony with Heaven and Earth. We have the choice to incorporate these principles into our buildings today, yet with the exception of enlightened patrons, developers and designers, very few contemporary new structures are built with this holistic approach in mind. The early architects and stonemasons were aware that the soul of a building must be able to respond and morph with changing needs. Machines and modern materials that can't breathe simply cannot do that.

Throughout the birthing and construction process, the architect holds the vision in mind from the original design concept to the finished project. This enables the etheric fields containing the memory of the completed building to maintain the highest achievable potential for success. The construction phase can then proceed right through to completion with utmost efficiency throughout every level and for every trade. In my experience it is possible to perceive the entire design in an instant, as time is not a factor in the etheric world. This makes it feasible to rest in that still core point and observe, allowing the design to come forward when ready. It is this witnessing that enables the vision to unfold from the seed point, which holds the full knowledge of all that is contained within (Whisper 5).

Designing a building is analogous to composing a musical symphony, where every part relates to the whole. Each part is found in everything and interacts with the vital energy signature code; its harmony, rhythm and melody fused together with the objective of elevating the spirit and inspiring the soul.

As the purpose and function of a building can be shaped and influenced by the architect, who may impose his or her own life patterns and emotions, the purity of thought of all involved is essential for the clarity of any building scheme. If the people designing and constructing a building are distressed, angry or mad, then they will create the same resonant emotion, affecting all those who live or work there. Miserable builders lay unhappy bricks and a disjointed work-force create fragmented buildings, leading to people becoming dis-connected from their homes, workplaces and even their colleagues. If everyone involved is happy and of positive disposition, this supports an efficient workforce and allows all parts of the project to flow in total harmony.

Communication by bees and ants In the natural world, bees and ants operate as a unified group, collectively working together as a team to support each other for the benefit of the whole. When a queen ant is separated from her colony, her subjects will continue to build fervently according to plan. Apparently, even if she is far away, the queen transmits the building plans via group consciousness. This incredible form of communication prevails as long as she is alive. However, if the queen is killed, all work in the colony stops – no ant will know what to do.

The queen bee at the centre of a hexagonal hive generates similar knowledge in harmonic resonance within the group matrix to control and influence the worker bees. Their shared characteristic is that the female holds the template that allows all to play their part. Yet the queen bee is not the boss, even though many feel she should be! She is actually the greatest servant for her community.

Building project delays In many instances, homeowners and sometimes developers begin a building project that simply doesn't get completed or is subject to constant delays, resulting in increased costs and numerous other challenges. The following scenarios show that a degree of resolution of life issues must be taken into account when developing land on any scale.

Where a new house was being built in the garden of an existing bungalow in Berkshire, nothing was going to plan. After seven years, it had still not been completed. With constant issues and disruption to schedules, something far more serious than the familiar building delays was affecting this project. Human psychological factors, with emotions erupting as a result of paranormal influences, overlaid more practical concerns and created mayhem.

Whilst tuning-in and connecting with the property, I heard the sound of a helicopter hovering overhead and felt this was significant, so I ran down to the main road to find an air ambulance landing near-by. A vehicular accident had taken place right outside the house to where the now deceased previous owners of the bungalow had moved. During the construction of my clients' new house, various tradesmen would suddenly get very angry, both verbally and some-times physically. They would then calm down and apologise saying, *"I don't know what came over me,"* a typical phrase when ghostly influences overlay a person's own sense of rationale. In the process of space-clearing the energies in and around the site, the wrath of the previous owners radiated from the immediate vicinity of their last home. The spirits of these angry people, disliked by everyone in the village, were overshadowing and affecting the builders and the current owners' new housing project, causing the long delays in com-pletion. Their blatant disapproval that anyone should profit from a development on what used to be their land, created anger and confusion in the etheric matrix. This scrambled clarity of focus on all levels and resulted in the road accident.

At another house, the spirits of previous occupants still present during conversion works were not happy, seeing the current owners as trespassers. Needless to say, the builders were obstructed and tam-pered with and nothing went smoothly, falling out with the owners when costs escalated. To maintain a good energy flow between all involved in a project is reflected in agreeable financial matters all round – money is after all an energy flow exchange.

Honouring the Earth Elementals

Most of us love and protect our animals, birds and wildlife, together with the sacred landscapes revered by our ancestors. We need to take this further and extend our care and concern to the devas, dryads and elemental beings inhabiting the etheric realms of nature. Each has its own consciousness and soul contract for evolutionary purpose, capable of interacting on a subtle level with human beings.

When we attune to the natural world and connect with the spirit of the land, it is good to recognise and *whisper* to the elementals and the natural guardians of the gateways. Share in the power and vitality of the elements by drawing into your home the fresh air, pure water, vibrant fire and expansive tree, plant and flower energies. Through breathing in these energies and sending them back out, we cycle the energies of nature's gifts. In doing so, we are feeding our soul and that of our house. We are actually soaking up the fractal energies that shape, form and nourish creation. Through their golden mean geometry and scent of high vibration, roses especially have the power to transform consciousness.

Working on our gardens requires a level of communication with the natural energies of the land, the trees in particular. Cutting down a tree without its permission has been known to cause all kinds of problems for the culprit. When I notice that a tree has been cut down and enquire when problems started for that individual, on many occasions I have heard it said:

"Life went pear-shaped after we cut down that apple tree!"

Just as you should let a tree know you need to cut it down or prune its branches, it is important that when asking the land if it is happy to be built upon, the inhabitants of the natural world are also acknowledged and consulted. If for no other reason, it is a matter of courtesy to prevent them from suffering shock when the machines arrive and disrupt their natural habitat.

The residual anguish from past traumatic happenings will overlay an intention to make change and cause damage to part or all of a site, however inadvertently. Any intention of a potential unsympathetic design about to be put into action is sufficient for the land to respond and the elemental energies to react and fight back. When the elementals are disturbed, their energetic lash-back is felt through the three-dimensional world. By virtue of a planned proposal, a level of reality exists that the build process will eventually happen. As far as the elementals are concerned, it is already as good as done.

There have been many occasions when I have been shown what I call 'ring rods' around the perimeter of a building. Similar to a metal cage, these invisible structures indicate an elemental hold on a property, denoting a fundamental disturbance of the natural earth energies at some time in the past. In the story *Farmhouse Fragments Owners' Lives* (Whisper 5), we saw that when the restrictive barriers created by upsetting the elementals were diffused, the farmhouse was then able to absorb the nourishing land energies. Having respect for the elementals and keeping the nature spirits content and happy will always benefit the design and construction process.

Tunnelling through a mountain Commercial activities such as mining, tunnelling and quarrying all create disturbance to nature's underworld, having a knock-on effect on nearby residential properties. Where a roadway was being tunnelled through a coastal mountain in southern France, the violent use of explosives was not only physically shaking the buildings sited above and shattering the soul of the Earth, but was having a significant energetic and emotional effect on the residents. To placate the ongoing trauma, I needed to connect with the spirit of the mountain to acknowledge and soothe its distress. By tuning-in to the mountain's energy signature and wavelength frequencies, I was able to recalibrate and neutralise the shock effects. To bring it fully to peace, I used a metaphysical technique of gently washing the mountain with soothing cool waters from the nearby ocean. Through this healing transformation, a more settled energy was reflected in the buildings above, with tangible benefit on the lives of the residents.

Trauma of demolition through explosives How a building is demolished will determine the impact on the surrounding land and the consequential effects for future occupants. With no coherent system in most societies of holistic care, it is rare in an economic climate of short-term gain to see sensitive and careful dismantling, allowing for the honouring of old buildings. Whilst explosives demolition is initially less expensive, the true long-term cost of residual trauma can amount to a far greater financial burden in terms of time off work and medical bills owing to ongoing health implications.

When the power station in Kingston upon Thames was demolished with explosives, an entire area of residential housing was later built on the site. In one apartment I was asked to visit, the after-shock on the occupant's life was significant. The solution was to tune into the fragmented sound waves continuing to reverberate from the painful trauma felt by the etheric body of the land, and bring all to rest using metaphysical techniques. This resulted in a much calmer space for the occupant.

Mountain desecration   When the side of a Mediterranean island mountain was cut away for a housing development, the earth elementals and the local people were seriously upset. As permission of neither the mountain nor the people had been sought, the elemental energies took to warfare with the developer through the mouthpiece of local residents' objections.

At the landowner's country house, guns were displayed on the walls in his entrance hall. Symbols of warfare, located in the area that in Feng Shui represents life path and career, did little to help his role as project developer or his relationship with the community. A ceremony was needed to offer apologies to the land, and to honour and placate the earth elementals of the mountain. This gave the opportunity for a more accommodating attitude towards him and the project.

Restricting the natural flow   On an idyllic South Pacific island, the builder of this housing development had constructed a high brick boundary wall enclosure, cutting off the vibrant energy stream from the active yang mountain to the receptive yin energy of the ocean. By impeding this natural flow, the houses and residents were prevented from receiving this natural nourishment. My approach was to carry out a gentle metaphysical process to energetically dissolve the enclosure wall, allowing the natural dragon energy from the mountain to once again flow unimpeded to the sea.

Desecrating a sacred grove   A proposed commercial building project in East Anglia was experiencing seemingly insurmountable problems. The design team were finding it difficult to move forward, with obstacles constantly placed in their path. To begin with, many people wanting to visit the site complained of not being able to actually find it. Upon my eventual arrival, I could see immediately what the trouble was. In the centre of the site, radiating exquisite natural beauty but with an overlay of trauma, was a sacred grove of trees around a pond. The intended design was to obliterate this and put a car park over it, not a sensible plan at all.

I initially walked the site to feel the earth energies and located the various zones using dowsing rods. I then prepared an energetic landmapping profile showing the propitious areas, but more importantly where not to build. Once the architect incorporated my suggestions into the scheme, things went smoothly at all levels. Not only did the local council grant planning permission, the elemental and meta-physical energies were happy too.

Guardians of the gateways The entrance gateways of our cities, towns and villages are significant locations (Whisper 4), indicating the transition points between worlds – the threshold linking where we are coming from to the space where we are going. Both sides of these gateways are protected by an access code, a consciously placed programme to ensure that our intention of entering is compatible with that of the energy signature of the space we wish to walk into.

We should enter only with permission of the guardians of the genius loci or spirit of place. This is because they will check you out to ensure that your intention and heart resonance are in alignment with the consciousness of the space they protect. If this is not the case, you are likely to be out of alignment with an aspect of your soul pur-pose and journey in life. As this can potentially lead to fragmentation of your own heart waves, your presence can then cause harm to the metaphysical inhabitants of that space.

In proceeding towards a gateway, the first step is to be clear about the reason why you wish to enter that space, and then fall still before asking permission. It is often easier to sense these gateways in rural areas when walking in nature, your feet connected to the vibrational memory of the Earth. You may simply hear the voice of the guardian of the gateway, or experience a happening in the natural world as a symbolic sign of consent. Be clear in listening to the true answer, rather than interpreting any response according to what you wish to hear. If you are not given permission, then do not attempt to enter. Look deep within your heart at your intentions. Sometimes it can simply be that you are not sufficiently focused at that moment, allowing distractive thoughts to interfere, so it may be worthwhile trying again later or on another day.

At the entrance of many temples, we find statues of animals flanking the main door. They are located specifically to smell your fear. If you choose to enter and attempt to ascend through the temple structure when your heart is not in resonance, you will be 'fried'. Thus, the customary mechanism of checking you out is for your own protection and continues to be applicable today.

Ground Breaking and Ceremony

The knowledge of astronomy and astrology, with regard to appropriate timings for carrying out ceremonies to honour and bless the land and her structures, plays a major role in all ancient cultural traditions. Ceremony and ritual are rooted in respecting and communicating with the natural world, the inhabited spaces of living and working, and the cleansing of the physical body. The indigenous peoples living close to the Earth, with religious traditions and strong family lineage, use sacred ceremony to honour all life, the soul of the land and spirit of place. Many shamanic cultures bear witness to numerous varied practices, from highly spiritual vibrations to lower earthly activities, some considered by the Western world to be very strange indeed.

For much of our planet's population living in the dislocated mayhem of concrete and steel jungles, this knowledge and practice has been lost. Prior to the commencement of any construction project, it is advisable before the foundations are dug to honour the land by carrying out a traditional ground breaking ceremony. This approach not only respects the earth elementals but also obtains the vital permission from Mother Earth to build upon her nourishment. In setting an important precedent of right approach for work to begin, gratitude is a great attitude.

We saw what can happen when permission of the land and of the elementals is not obtained before cutting into the Earth. A ceremonial laying of the foundation stone before actual construction begins, and a final handing-over ceremony of site ownership from the builder or developer, are important acknowledgments of the project itself and of the land. Today, if these ceremonies are carried out at all, they tend to take place for the sake of publicity. The real purpose behind them is seldom given emphasis and goes largely unnoticed.

It would be of great value if design and construction teams also carried out various other ceremonies throughout the build to ensure the energies are kept in balance and do not to hinder the build phase. Ensuring the best energetic alignment at all stages, and keeping the spatial energies clear of general residue, will also help to maintain optimum levels of chi to benefit the entire project.

Our forefathers would energetically 'tune up' a building within the etheric matrix at the design stage, during construction and after completion. Applicable to both new and existing property renovations, the purpose of the final tune-up is to activate the key node points of the geometric matrix. The building will then be in alignment within itself and resonate with the natural frequencies of the land. The activation process is about raising the vibration of the molecular structure of the materials to create an energetic charge and engender capacitance. This makes it possible for the building to hold and maintain an optimum charge and thereby nourish its occupants. Being in correct alignment will maximise its power and enable smoother flows of energy within both the physical and etheric configurations. It then comes alive and will resonate like a well-tuned musical instrument.

Objects representing the five elements, referred to in the Eastern traditions as water, wood, fire, earth, metal; or the four elements of air, fire, water and earth, recognised in Western systems, can be used to activate and work with these energies in our homes. Beloved items such as crystals, stones, bells, feathers, incense, water and candles, kept for the purpose of dedication and purification, can all be blessed and used for sacred ceremony. Making a mandala or medicine wheel is another powerful way of connecting with the compass directions and seasons of the year. It is good to give thanks and to honour the spirit and guardians of your home, or indeed of any building or sacred space.

Buildings with No Soul

Many houses built by developers have no real client or design input as such and therefore no true connection to anyone's heart and soul. A house designed for one site and then copied and built on another, can often look and feel out of character to its location – a 'cookie-cutter house' I tend to call it. Likewise, off the shelf house modules constructed from custom made templates often have a sterile feel. Whilst economical in terms of cost, a design devoid of a heart centre is rarely in harmony with the heart and soul of an intended location. Lack of sensitive positioning on a site, compass orientation, Feng Shui aspects and so forth, can estrange a house from the land. This then brings about fragmentation of the energy fields, leading to an unhealthy environment for the occupants:

"The building feels dead, lifeless, as if it is soul-less."

When we hear this expression, can we restore the heart and soul to a building that may never have known a true sense of identity? If a house lacks any connection to Source or resonance with the Earth, it is unlikely to radiate a sense of security or feeling of welcome, and perhaps should not have been built on that plot of land in the first place. As we shall see, there *is* something we can do about it.

Isolated properties As I drove into a suburban area of Surrey, the emotions activated within me were a reflection of the house I was about to visit. Feeling empty and bereft of any sense of belonging, I arrived at a newly built house to find it actually sited on wasteland. Meeting the lady owner, she too seemed like a lost soul, desperately searching for some meaning to her life, yet had chosen to buy this house that totally reflected her existence in the barren suburbs.

Similarly, visiting a Wiltshire manor house that felt sterile and empty, the adjoining land was isolated and desolate, unconnected to Source. The house reflected the owner's psyche; experiencing broken dreams, as though nothing belonged to anything.

Baptising a building When I visited a house in Hertfordshire that felt empty and soul-less with no sense of heart, it clearly needed some form of recognition almost as an afterthought. This is when the inspiration came to me of re-birthing a house through baptism. It may seem strange to suggest that we can use the element of water to baptise an existing building, or undertake a secular baptism on completion of a new build, yet to acknowledge that all life comes from water and initiates the soul is inherent in many sacred and secular traditions. It is therefore not so remarkable to consider revisiting the birthing process to bring back the soul of a structure into the world.

After taking the owner through a ceremony using the water element to activate and bond with her house, the sense of change was palpable. She was much happier and at last felt connected to the soul of her home, which was noticeably warmer and more comfortable.

Although I was brought up in the Greek Orthodox tradition before being introduced to world religions and philosophies, until undertaking this ceremony I had not fully appreciated the true power and significance of baptism – bringing to birth and initiating the soul through water, the primordial substance of creation. This can take place with water that carries the energetic blueprint of the land, or can be achieved metaphysically with the intention of connecting to a pure sacred water source.

Until the breath of life comes into a building, it is perhaps no more than a modest pile of bricks and timber, or whatever materials are used. A building cannot be brought into fullness of being in the vibrational world until the soul is birthed and enters the physical structure. Honouring the connection to Mother Earth and Father Sky nourishes the soul from above and below with the full range of elements in balance and harmony. Only then is a building a fully conscious programmable instrument, capable of adaptation and change. It will grow with us and respond to our every whim and desire, influenced by cosmic and earth energies and by human activities – our beliefs, fears, loves, and sometimes stupidity.

The Trauma of Bad Design

Conscious architecture means building in harmony with the land and intrinsically within the building itself. Design based on the principles of nature supporting the life force chi to raise consciousness and enhance physical nourishment has no trauma. When we live in fragmented and disharmonious spaces that fail to nourish and support us, especially when our residual memories recall a less than positive experience, the contraction of our energy fields can lead to the incubation of debilitating illness.

Our buildings reflect who and how we are. How we feel goes far beyond our response to the three-dimensional materials of construction. When we only perceive the visible material world vibrating at a physical level, complete with earth-bound energy lines, focusing on the harmful effects of geopathic and electro-stress, our reality will keep us grounded in the lower vibrations of life. When the energy in our home is blocked, stagnant or out of balance, that same imbalance will be reflected in our physiological and psychological functions. The resulting strain on all our compensating systems will disrupt our auric field and manifest as physical illness.

Frequently encountered is the same old familiar story of lack of insight and awareness by architects, surveyors and structural engineers, of working in harmony with the natural world around them. More commonly, the developers want a quick turn-around of their investment and insist on employing those less discerning to come up with a profitable scheme, in theory acceptable to the Local Authority planners. The not so peculiar aspect is that the hands-on builders themselves often have a better understanding and appreciation of the nature of the land than their office-bound bosses. Moreover, with the expediency of technology and computer aided design, there is no longer the same quality of human interaction with sheets of paper and graphite pencils, or even communication with the client.

The trauma of bad design comes about when we do not bring the soul into architecture. The building remains just a heap of physical materials put together with no coherent holding or fusing pattern at an energetic level, giving our heart-waves little prospect of resonating in the space. We saw earlier that 'accidental' design can by default create trauma in our energy fields, leading to illness and even death. There could very well be litigation in this field when more people become aware and fully acknowledge the detrimental effects of toxic design, together with the inappropriate location of many homes and businesses that impact on lives and cause serious health problems. A case in point is the young man sleeping under several beams in an attic conversion, as described in *Suicide jump* (Whisper 5).

When our environment is in balance and harmony, our general lifestyle is supported by the natural flows of energy around us – the key to optimum health. A building that is designed or rebalanced to enhance strong, positive life force will therefore support any ongoing healing process. The aim of architecture should be to design consciously and create buildings with heart and soul, to inspire and nourish the people, the land, and the buildings themselves.

It is not hard to see why architects and developers need to be responsible and perhaps even held accountable. To be educated in what space does, with full awareness of the relevant issues, draws attention to the fact that unconscious design leads to poor health. Project managers must not only ensure a productive and profitable workforce, but also put these essential principles into practice in their own offices. My view is that architects and the construction industry have a high level of responsibility for the health of those who live and work in the buildings they design and build, while doctors frequently have the challenge of curing the ills that the design and construction industry contribute towards. It would, of course, be ideal if building zones were located and structures built for the legitimate benefit of the health and wellbeing of the land and her people.

Organic Architecture and Healthy Spaces

We have considered that the true purpose of a building is to generate and hold the energy of its original blueprint. As so often happens with people, its original soul can become clouded over, obscured by the activities and stresses of everyday life. By fusing ancient principles with contemporary design and development, we *can* create vibrant, healthy new buildings and transform existing buildings to provide healthy spaces that house our physical needs *and* uplift us energetically, mentally and spiritually.

The value of ecological materials Organic architecture is about creating geometries of natural dynamic forms using a variety of ecological materials, all with different vibrational chi values. One of the main qualities of certain materials applied in correct combination with others is to maximise the energy charge. As nature designs on the principles of pure geometry holding the charge to sustain life force (Whisper 7), the same should ideally be reflected in the physical world of buildings.

Just as we minimise environmental damage by avoiding the use of toxic chemicals, we need to make informed choices concerning favourable building materials. The eco-friendly aspects of holistic design both reduces environmental damage and has a low impact on destroying life force chi and wasted kinetic energy. Natural materials hold memory of their original purpose and fractal connection to the universe. The closer they are to nature's fractal nourishing geometries, the better for our health. In helping to nourish our physical bodies, the nutritional quality of our diet and other lifestyle factors are obviously also important. How the unseen energetic qualities of certain materials and foodstuffs influence the subtle balance of our personal meridians can be demonstrated with muscle testing techniques such as kinesiology.

The use of low carbon materials wherever possible, will make the best use of the consciousness and health values of a structure. Local materials retain resonance with the land; vernacular buildings vibrate with the local landscape and relate to native tree, earth and river life. A building correctly designed and built of natural organic materials, with an energy blueprint resonating to fractal frequencies, allows the body to resonate with nature's harmonics. Buildings that can physically and energetically breathe allow people and animals to do the same, keeping our chakras spinning in healthy balance. We are then in a better position to cope with the disturbed earth energies and pollution encountered in everyday life.

To incorporate the golden mean ratio and other sacred geometries into the overall design proportions of a structure adds a metaphysical element, allowing a building to resonate to and be sustained by universal healing energies (Whisper 7). The use of ecological building materials and sacred geometry work independently, but together bring a valuable added dimension. In creating what physics calls 'shareable waves', they evoke memories in our genetic and spiritual energy bodies of our innate human resonance to the harmonics of universal law.

Interiors and finishes   The integration of various methods of chi input, including Feng Shui and Vaastu (Whisper 7), can incorporate a selection of materials, finishes and ecological paints. There are no hard and fast rules or formulas for the choice of perfect colours, bearing in mind that different vibrational qualities all influence energetic balance, and will affect outlook and overall levels of comfort. When I say to people, *"decorate your house, change your life,"* it means choosing optimum colours and making changes in keeping with their own personal energetic blueprint compatible with that of the building. This will raise the potency of that space and the energy levels of those spending time there, bringing more focus and meaning to their lives. Enhancing our environment can also help to break repetitive physical and psychological behaviour patterns.

My approach to choosing materials and colour schemes is based on the direct energetic response of an individual in accordance to his or her own chakra balance. As with kinesiology, through dowsing we can identify whether a particular material or colour will expand or contract the heart-wave spin and therefore the strength of a person's aura. A building responds in much the same way and also has a say in the matter! I will offer to the soul consciousness of the building a material or colour and test its response. The greatest degree of energetic expansion will indicate the most propitious choice for the building to reach its highest vibration. The ultimate stage is the integration and balance of the building with the people themselves, which is of great benefit and will bring joy to their lives. Sometimes a balanced compromise has to be reached, especially if several people share the same house or workplace.

Happy molecules It is good to consciously connect with the same space for a time, and allow the molecules of the unified cosmic field to build up. This changes the emotional dynamic of the materials and gives them a heart-based feeling, transforming mundane walls into happy bricks. The natural flow of atmospheric energies, when in right alignment to a site and to the energetic structure of a building, all contribute to enhancing experiential value. This will also increase the sale or letting potential and desirability of houses, newly finished or converted apartments and commercial buildings.

We do, on occasions, find a relationship between people and their homes that are not a disaster from the outset. There *are* also happy houses. Happy buildings make for happy people. The aim is to help create more of them. A happy and healthy building will serve and support you at all levels, physically, emotionally and spiritually. Buildings *whisper* to each other and communicate this important work to the souls of other buildings and their occupants.

Whisper 7

THE POWER OF DIVINE ARCHITECTURE

Finding your true purpose

Weaving the Female and Male Energies

'In the beginning *was* the word', we are told in the Bible. The original demotic Greek *en arkhai aine ho logos* translates correctly as 'in the beginning *is* the word'. This denotes that all beginnings are in the absolute present moment from the single still point of unity, the 'I Am' at the centre of all that exists. From the yin and yang harmonising opposites, come the three primordial energies, the sound of 'Om' composed of Ah, Ooh and Ma – represented by the Holy Trinity in the Christian tradition.

The concept of two harmonising opposites implies that there is an observer *and* an observed, each with experience of the other. Only when the polarities merge does duality 'disappear' and unity 'just is'. This is why 'nothing' cannot be a 'no thing'. An intrinsic prerequisite for maintaining the vital balance of yin and yang is the continual interplay of these two energies that brings about relationship between another person or place – in this instance in relation to home.

So, from chaos comes order, from the void of nothingness comes sound, the potential seed form or 'spota' in Sanskrit, the essential energy signature of all things to be created (Whisper 5). From the potential co-creation of the two polarities, the masculine and feminine in the dance of life can merge and take us back to unity, the absolute origin of Higher Self.

Whether as a man or woman, we all need to have these energies in balanced proportion. It is not so much about equal measure, but the degree of each required within our surroundings at any particular time, according to individuality and temperament. To facilitate the sacred weave, the logical, reasoning left hemisphere of the brain needs to meet the artistic, emotional aspects of the right brain. When the two polarities are out of balance, our behaviour can become either too active or aggressive, finding no rest (overly yang); or passive and submissive, not wanting to participate in life with others (too much yin). When synchronised and in perfect balance, the yin and yang forces of nature have a better chance of achieving harmony.

This is symbolised in the Vesica Piscis, the almond shape formed by the intersection of two circles, where the circumference of one meets the centre of the other. This union opens an energy portal that brings forth the birth of 'an-other', the Son or Christ Child within the Vesica geometry. We see this depicted in medieval architecture, such as over the central portal of Chartres Cathedral. The Master builders conceived and built this extraordinary cathedral on an ancient Earth Goddess site, expressed through the mysterious veil of the Black Madonna, and dedicated it to the Divine Feminine, represented by Isis, Kali, Quan Yin, the Virgin Mary and Mary Magdalene.

The principles of balance and harmony exemplified in the yin and yang, the dynamic weave of the feminine and masculine, bring nourishing support to enhance life. This is conveyed in the geometry of the pentagram and hexagram. The pentagram, the five-pointed star intrinsic to the golden mean harmonic, symbolises the feminine pro-creative power, the nourishing sanctuary within a structure. The masculine framework houses and protects the feminine space, as does the hexagonal honeycomb of a beehive. The hexagram or six-pointed star, inherent in the stable mineral world and in the crystal-line structure of water, is represented by the interlocking triangles of the masculine apex and feminine womb – the sacred marriage. This ideology is a concept beyond rhetoric, the expression of Love.

Many ancient Masters describe architecture as living books of knowledge. Its true purpose is to convey the message that we are all part of the harmonic order of the universe, with the potential to be united with a Higher Power. Our experience of walking through a sacred building or labyrinth here on Earth, designed to capture and harness the cosmic energy of Heaven above, unites the celestial and the terrestrial. Thus, our connection with buildings and the land takes place through a merging of personal experience with an intuitive feel for the rational geometry of a structure. The play of creation, with all its multifarious expressions, is to show us we can find our way back to the original source-point of unity. The ultimate aim is to recall and 're-member' the broken links of our whole selves in connection and alignment to absolute universal Oneness, the place of no beginning and no end.

Feng Shui, Vaastu and Nine Star Ki

All cultures have adapted their own way of working with a fusion of complex principles drawn from many civilisations, all with the objective of reflecting Heaven on Earth. The purpose of the exquisite architecture of Chinese and Tibetan civilisations, of the great cities in northern Asia, Egypt, ancient Greece and many South American cultures, is to remind us of our intrinsic connection to Source. This application of cosmological wisdom is about microcosmic expressions of universal law inherent in the macrocosm of space. This same expression developed as a reasoned approach into codified systems in the East.

Feng Shui is the Chinese system of eternal spiritual principles going back at least 3,000 years. Even more distant knowledge is found in ancient Egyptian and Vedic (Indian) Vaastu traditions. This exemplifies a sophisticated knowledge base, demonstrating the harmonising movement of celestial forces within all aspects of life. It is the creative impetus embedded and embodied in the energetic matrix of all creative endeavours, whether expressed through the physical and etheric structures of sacred classical architecture, art, literature, music or ceremony.

Vaastu Shastra The Vedic tradition was allegedly written down some 5,000 years ago at the beginning of the current Kali Yuga, the last of the four great ages of a creation cycle: the present Iron Age preceded by the Gold, Silver and Bronze Ages.

Knowledge of religious scriptures, astronomy, medicine, Vaastu and other subjects, was originally handed down verbally through the generations in order not to lose phonetic accuracy through written transliteration. Only with the rediscovery of ancient texts in northern

India in the 1930s, has a resurgence taken place in the West of the art of Vaastu, the science of building and architecture.

A complex life-map system is expressed through the trinity of the Hindu gods: Brahma, Vishnu and Shiva, and their associated deities. All these aspects of the creative, abiding and destructive forces of nature are in fact energies within us, which throughout human life we find ways of externalising.

Feng Shui The fundamental practice of the 'Art of Placement' – the foundation of the art of living – is based on the philosophy of combining harmonising opposites. The balance of visible and invisible flows of chi relates to the yin/yang forces in the play of creation. For anyone whose direction in life has taken them towards exploring the purpose of mankind and the nature of the universe, the journey of the human soul towards self-realisation, Feng Shui in a formal sense represents attributes of this same journey – from birth to enlightenment, beginnings to completion, duality to unity; the only difference being in the timescale and the intent behind an action.

When I was introduced to Feng Shui in the early 1990s, it immediately resonated with the principles I had intuitively been incorporating into architectural design over the previous 25 years. With this understanding and as an architect and musician, the realisation that these practical principles could be incorporated for the benefit of healing buildings and people was formative to the development of my work as *The House Whisperer*.

The full power of Feng Shui needs clarity and resolution of the energy of a space, honouring the original identity and character of a building. Indeed, a major part of my work uses the forces of nature to bring balance and harmony to the environment, in keeping with the approach of our ancestors. The fundamental thinking behind it all is that a balanced and healthy person in a happy state of mind, living and working in attractive and harmonious surroundings, can achieve fulfilment in all areas of life.

The value and full depth of a Feng Shui analysis is dependent upon what the individual practitioner takes into account. The advice given is frequently based purely on systematic and codified information, which in many instances differ owing to conflicting sources of knowledge. A true Feng Shui Master illuminates the metaphysical aspects of a home in the context of a person's life, and always has profound intuitive perception of the spirit world of the ancestors. Many practitioners and schools of learning tend to ignore or fear this all-important aspect, without which the principles remain mechanical and may not always be relevant to the client in our modern era.

The Ba-Gua   This is the inherent life-map used in Feng Shui to read, interpret and modify our lives in relation to our home spaces. Considered during a consultation are the eight (Ba) life trigrams (Gua) set around the central Tai Chi, symbolising the Higher Self. Comprised of nine sections, the Ba-Gua focuses on the nine areas of life common to all people: career, relationships, elders/ancestors, wealth/blessings, health, helpful friends, creativity/children, contemplation, and illumination/fame.

The Ba-Gua life-map is used in several cultural systems. In Classical Feng Shui, the Chinese use the compass sectors and directions to position the life-map over a plan of the house. The Tibetan Black Hat system takes the setting of the Ba-Gua from the front door irrespective of compass orientation, and also considers the layout from the door of each respective room as a micro-scale mirror of the main house. Both systems are of value in analysing and illuminating the energy flows in buildings, and can be combined in the hands of a skilful practitioner.

The term 'enlightenment' (Ming) is the conjunction of the Chinese words moon (yin) and sun (yang). Each trigram is composed of a variation of yin and yang lines reflecting the cosmological feminine and masculine weave. The basis of the I Ching divination system has 64 hexagrams, each formed of two trigrams creating six yin/yang lines, intrinsically linked to the DNA codon, the number of squares on a chessboard, sacred geometry and other esoteric philosophies. The symbolic shapes embedded in the Egyptian *Eye of Horus* each represent one of the 64 sub-divisions that comprise the whole.

Nine Star Ki   Whilst Feng Shui essentially considers space, the Japanese system of Nine Star Ki concerns the cycles of time. Both systems consider the yin/yang balance of a person. Within Feng Shui itself, disciplines such as the Four Pillars also consider the energetic time-cycles of the individual.

Based on the trigrams of the I Ching, Nine Star Ki explores the cosmic dynamics underlying human interactions by looking at our lives in 9-year, 9-month and 9-day cycles. Inherent within the nourishing and destructive cycles are the physical and subtle energies of the five elements: water, wood, fire, earth and metal. Where we are on our personal time-cycle indicates the influences likely to be encountered, which interact with our inner patterns. In some years we sow seeds for our next phase, some years are better for consolidating certain aspects of life, while others bring more opportunities for a successful outcome, leading to greater abundance.

Astrology of the house   The astrological chart of a house can be drawn up from its birth date. The moment of 'birth' is generally considered to be the time when the roof is completed, when Heaven's energy is captured into the soul of the building. One of the ways of finding a pattern match between the client and the harmonic of a building project is by looking at the movement of heavenly bodies to determine which planetary aspects offer the best time for a fortuitous outcome. By comparing the astrological chart of the house with a person's own natal chart, their synastry will highlight areas that are in resonance and harmony, and those where the influences are more challenging and possibly disruptive.

My approach as *The House Whisperer* incorporates various elements of Feng Shui to benefit home and work environments, and to assist with finding solutions to individual life situations. The system of Nine Star Ki is a valuable guidance tool that gives a long-term perspective on the cycles of life, and can complement Western or Vedic astrology. Both practices help to illuminate greater depths of understanding of the complex interweave of people, the land and houses.

How the Ancients Located and Oriented a Building

In former times, the suitability of the land was first considered before deciding upon the most propitious place to locate a building. In the Vedic tradition, the architect would carry out several tests including tasting the earth for its sweetness. The ancients deemed it essential to walk the land and feel the patterns of earth energies to determine the areas to avoid and those to venerate. Above all, the land should be happy and speak to you.

In applying these principles today, we must first ask the spirit of the site: *"Does the land wish to be built upon?"* When the answer is *"yes"* and all other factors are satisfied, this sets the foundations of a good space. The position for the house will present itself through the consciousness and spirit of the land in conjunction with the essence and purpose of the building itself. When we engage in honouring Mother Earth and the nature spirits, and listen to the esoteric signposts, nature will find ways of working with us: a bird may land or rays of sunshine illuminate the ground. That particular spot may well be the right place for the house to be built upon and beneficial for the people who will subsequently occupy it.

The next logical steps to consider are access to the site and the views from the location. The proposed building should be designed with the best compass alignment to one of 16 energy gates, being both physical entrance gateways *and* etheric portals. Function and purpose of intended use are always a consideration. A place where people will come to be nourished and socialise, such as a restaurant, will have different energetic requirements to a family home or an industry with a large workforce. These decisions were and still are made using intuitive perception, and cannot be learnt from textbooks alone.

The purpose of the design team, from conception through to completion, is to hold together these values and ensure the auspicious energies flow unimpeded throughout the project. Knowing where the gates of energy are entering, both now and in the future, helps to identify the life pattern of the buildings and of the site itself. Whilst the design may be optimum in the present, these portals may need readjusting to align with maximum earth and celestial flows as time moves on.

Landscape Form School Whilst traditional Feng Shui is fundamental to China, many other cultures have sanctified similar principles. These look at the physical formation and balance of landscape features to determine the suitability of a chosen site, specifically to identify whether they capture nourishment and support or hinder the energy of the land to be built upon.

The Landscape Form School embodies essential elements that include the 'black turtle', a protective mountain to the rear of the site. In contemporary life, this can be a hill or a building at the back of a property that supports but does not overpower it. A house standing alone on a hilltop has no support, an unstable structure liable to be blown by the wind and drained of nourishing energy.

Looking at the site with the mountain in the background, we find a yang 'green dragon' hill to the right-hand side and a lower yin 'white tiger' hill to the left, both continuing round from the mountain to create an armchair formation. This protects and supports the Feng Shui area and is the most auspicious place to build. To the front is found the 'red phoenix', a flowing stream or road along the lower part of the site, acting as a buffer against the outside world. The landscape formation is then in best alignment, providing living and working environments with a sense of security and empowerment.

One of the most powerful visual and physical examples is the temple complex at Delphi, Greece. Here the protective mountains wrap around the back of the site, a 'red phoenix' road is to the front, and in the centre are the various temple structures.

Landscape Form School principles are exemplified in the layout of ancient dynastic tombs in China. The Chinese also applied this formula in determining the location of the Emperor's Imperial Palace in Xian, the main capital of Shaanxi province called Changan, meaning 'Eternal Peace'. It was also incorporated in the construction of the Forbidden City in the capital Beijing, with the supportive artificial Coal Hill to the rear of the city.

The city of Hong Kong holds this same formation and has great financial success as a result. We find the protective mountains at the rear of the city, the 'red phoenix' ocean to the front, and in the Feng Shui central spot are the commercial buildings. A residential building constructed at Repulse Bay has a large square hole in the structure to enable the dragon energy from the mountain to continue its flow unimpeded to the ocean, and avoid bringing 'bad luck' to the residents.

Locating and working with natural flows of visible or underground 'water dragon' energy will empower a site or building. Lakes, ponds and water features are located to amplify and enhance these natural energies, and in some situations to drain negative energies away. Water reflects the essence of the soul and represents the gateway between this world and the higher realms. For these and other esoteric reasons, many water gardens are found in China's summer and winter palaces, and at major public buildings.

The Ming Tang is the open space in front of buildings, such as a garden or an open square; the area where Heaven's chi charges up the land and feeds the Feng Shui zone where the buildings are located. For this reason, an open space, garden or courtyard frontage beyond your front door is of great value and most important.

The compass orientation of a property should ideally capture the propitious energies of Heaven and Earth. In Feng Shui, the internal space considers the position of the front and back doors, placement of various areas and rooms in the house, including the best location for furniture, mirrors and artefacts in different rooms, such as a bedroom, office and elsewhere. A desk up against a wall, for example, is considered bad practice, a form of self-sabotage. Good light, heat, ventilation and sanitation are important factors that will prevent sadness and discontent. All will support or hinder the chi of a space to either be free flowing or blocked, auspicious or detrimental. These aspects can be correlated with an individual's own personal energy map, astrological and Nine Star Ki chart.

Some designers and architects have more recently adapted these principles to create excellent living and working environments in the West. Today, they are used largely as a method for reading and understanding, changing or repairing the relationship between people and buildings. For full benefit, these coherent principles need to be applied to the degree that the patron or client holds the knowledge and conviction of assured integrity in a holistic approach. To optimise the success of a project by considering all these factors can help or hinder the initial land acquisition, design, town planning process, construction and ongoing use, even the final sale or rental of the completed property or development.

Wealth and Financial Success

"Good fortune is lighter than a feather, yet no one knows how to carry it. Misfortune is heavier than the earth, yet no one knows how to avoid it." (Tao Te Ching)

Many factors contribute to our experience of financial wealth as a reflection of an energetic flow of abundance, not just at a materialistic level but also in relation to our emotional and spiritual lives. Where we live also plays an important part in determining our belief systems and choice of a favourable or destructive home, which in turn will reinforce the state of our finances. With a little discernment, we can apply common sense in looking at what makes one property and its occupants happy and financially successful and another not.

In Feng Shui, your fortune determined by your date, time and place of birth is dependent on the Three Lucks: heavenly astrology shows previous life's work; personal endeavours reflect the focus of the soul's journey in this life; Earth formation concerns location and place in shaping the environment. These combined forces epitomise individual success in relation to Heaven and Earth.

Many financial problems: *"I never seem to make ends meet!"* arise from a very basic lack of physical support, the foundation of many ancient systems. Lack of support in our lives physically and emotionally is also the reason why some individuals become unwell. In the home, the 'mountain' translates as a solid wall with no window openings; the headboard positioned up against this wall makes for a safe and supportive night's sleep.

Flushing wealth away Whilst visiting a couple in Middlesex, I noticed that in the wealth area of their house they had built two sets of toilets. This had an adverse effect on the optimum energy flow, resulting in life crashing around them both health-wise and financially. Quite literally, their resources were being flushed down the drain. A fundamental concept in Feng Shui is the importance of keeping the toilet seat down. The physical and visual energy of the home is drawn down by the flushing action, so the memory dynamic in the energetic space is always active, even between flushes.

Water flow creates wealth A building located under Richmond Bridge in Surrey, originally had its main door facing the river flowing away from it. With the intention to convert it to a café, once open for business the river would have drained its energy. We relocated the entrance and installed large glass doors to face the water flow so that it would nourish the building. Business success continues years later.

The garden support Landscape Form School principles consider enhancing and sustaining the potential for wealth. The configuration of the back garden of a house should therefore have a good solid boundary fence to the rear. It is also good to have a strong high fence on the yang right-hand side and a slightly lower fence on the yin left-hand side. If the garden drops away from the house, there can be financial issues and money loss.

Wealth shaped by the land A common cause of financial failure is the shape of the building plot. A narrowing of the rear part of a garden squeezes out the flow of wealth in both personal and business affairs. At a house in Surrey, there was no physical way of expanding the width of the far end of the garden, so I deployed a metaphysical solution of visually expanding the width using geometric resonance, then energetically setting it into a fixed holding state. This resulted in successfully expanding the owner's relationship to financial wealth.

Tweaking the money spot In one couple's house, the core money spot was found to be located in a specific area of the living room by the window. It was so responsive to being activated that any enhancement to that area brought immediate wealth in various forms. The client was very happy indeed.

Sacred Architecture

According to the Roman architect Vitruvius, there are three fundamental principles of sacred architecture that must be considered for a building to be balanced and harmonious. Firstly, the function of a building must accommodate all practical requirements for its intended purpose. Secondly, the structure or framework that supports the building must be both purposeful and beautiful. The third principle is beauty itself. Buildings need to speak to that deep part of the human psyche that responds to beauty and harmony, inherent in the laws of the cosmos and in nature. The ultimate test of good architecture is to create beauty from structure and function.

Buildings designed to these principles, incorporating sacred geometry, geomancy and other sacred time-honoured practices, can be perceived as transforming a basic three-dimensional bricks and mortar building into conscious architecture. The importance of nourishing the mind, body and spirit is rarely considered in building design these days. Whilst there are indeed enlightened architectural projects, very few modern buildings are designed with any sense of spiritual harmony at all.

Ancient Greece, as well as the medieval cathedral schools such as at Chartres in France, held the teachings of Plato and the study of the Seven Liberal Arts to be a fundamental spiritual path: the Trivium – Grammar, Rhetoric and Dialectic; and the Quadrivium – Arithmetic, Astronomy/Astrology, Music and Geometry. The classical Greek architects were trained in music and spatial resonance, sacred geometry and geomancy. The study of how these principles fed into and expressed themselves in architecture, musical harmonies and the law of octaves, as well as various healing systems, established a deeper understanding of the universal laws of nature. In accordance with the Platonic maxims of goodness, truth and beauty, our ancestors were nourishing their most valuable resource, their people.

The Italian Renaissance Masters used the principles of sacred geometry as a guiding formula. Beneath the paint on the canvases of their masterpieces, we often find hidden grid lines of geometric proportions. Using the golden mean and other sacred ratios, the artist reflects the harmonic patterns of universal law, thereby raising our spirit and connection to the Divine. In the artwork of Leonardo da Vinci, the pentagram overlaid on the human form incorporates the Vitruvian system of the rational circle and square, and the irrational golden mean proportions. Even when unacquainted with the underlying rationale, we can be moved emotionally by what resonates at a deeper level. The highest form of art is ultimately that which touches the heart and soul. A painting or piece of music imbued with feeling and inspiration from the heart of the artist or composer will likewise touch the heart of the viewer or listener.

From a young age, I was drawn to study music, philosophy, world religions and sacred geometry, a combination that in retrospect I recognised as of value to the fundamental training of architects. It soon became clear to me that the ancients designed buildings by considering the energy matrix of space and the energies that impact and affect that space, including our human intention and focus.

A healing temple, designed to the laws of sacred geometry and celestial harmony, is a building for life enhancement and transformation. A building designed consciously and built of fractal, natural ecological materials can be activated by being sung into existence. The purpose of sacred geometry in a sacred building, incorporating the world of invisible structures, is to remind us of our absolute nature and heart connection to Source. A sacred building is designed to take us in stages on an inner journey of self-discovery, from where the concept of 'architectural procession' derives. In replicating universal law and activating the microcosm within the macrocosm, we are guided back to Higher Self.

Buildings and the underlying land are said to have an etheric double. In fact it is the other way round; the reality of etheric space is actually reflected in the physical world of matter. The mathematical and geometric blueprint of a design, reflected in the unseen subtle world of the energy matrix, becomes manifest in the physical world as a mirror image of universal cosmic law: 'as above, so below'.

The Cathedral Schools The most exciting aspect of the medieval building process, which applied as much to the smallest church as to the greatest cathedral, is the identification of the exceptionally skilled Master Masons by their unique, often idiosyncratic carving styles. As the Masters changed, we recognise the distinctive characteristics of each group by their way of creating various profiles and figures, and how they arranged them into doors, windows and arches of complex, geometric proportions.

These extraordinary accomplishments resound with dynamic harmonics; many have remarkable acoustics. At Wells Cathedral, Somerset, England's first cathedral to be designed and built entirely in the new Gothic style, the unique octagonal structure of the late 13th century Chapter House with its intricate ribbed vaulting supported on a central column, has been described as 'a glorious theatre set in stone'. My experience suggests that architecture is not frozen music as some people suggest. The power of the music is both in the architecture itself and in the way the acoustics of these 'symphonies in stone' reverberate within a building.

A natural resonance occurs when a human being enters a temple, cathedral, church or any sacred site designed to universal law. Our cathedrals continue to live and breathe as they receive our conscious input. By walking in and interacting with the sacred space, alive and resonating to universal harmonics, it will respond to your presence. As you listen and tune into these magnificent structures, you may feel them 'dance' and 'sing', with the potential to bring you into alignment with your original energy signature. In creating resonance through this relationship, we can break out of the physical walls of illusion and access a natural and profound form of healing. It is then possible to hear the musical harmony of the untouched soul and enter into the magnificence of the glory of creation.

Symbolism on many levels is inherent in the sacred geometry and architectural layout of our sacred buildings. By sitting quietly or meditating beneath or close to a fractal geometric structure, such as a rose window reflecting the essence of the Divine, our energetic codes have the potential to be reset. In creating sacred space by harnessing these alchemical principles, the ancients perceived other dimensions of reality; they knew the secrets of how to transform consciousness.

House Shapes and Sacred Geometry

"Let no one ignorant of geometry enter." (Plato)

Perhaps partly what Plato infers in the inscription over the door of his Academy, is that without the knowledge of geometric codes, you have yet to be initiated into the teachings of the ancient secret language that allows transformation in the quantum field. Only then can you hold the key to access the inner world of the spaces you may wish to enter or engage with in your spiritual quest. Just as you need a key to unlock the door of your house, you will need a password, a code to be allowed by the guardian to gain entry through an etheric portal. Without the code, there is no access (Whisper 6).

On my first visit to Kings College Chapel in Cambridge, in my early twenties, I entered through a side door unaware of the interior architecture. As my eyes were drawn up to gaze at the vast open space of the vaulted ceiling, I stood rooted to the spot in awe, exhilaration quivering through my whole being. To experience this intricate forest of delicately carved stone structures was a moment of true awakening to the energetic power of sacred geometry. I was later to discover that this ecclesiastical design is based on the root-three rectangle, an irrational geometry most sacred indeed, with the ability to transport the human soul into other dimensions.

The universe is created with patterns; by replicating these mathematical patterns, we strengthen our connection to universal law. Geometrical structures include the five Platonic solids: cube, tetrahedron, octahedron, dodecahedron and icosahedron. My work with buildings includes identifying and drawing together the geometric shapes and energetic strands that are out of harmonic resonance with each other. Just as the shape of our abode moulds our physical body, our home reflects aspects of our lives that are incomplete or incoherent. By incorporating sacred geometry into our buildings, we capture the pure and potent natural energy of the universe to support and enhance every aspect of our lives.

The energetic patterns of each geometrical shape, size and layout of the three-dimensional spaces of buildings and rooms, interact with our own coding, whether we are aware of it not. Much depends on how we draw down that energy and manifest it through our inherited and conditioned patterns. The geometry of a design allows each different function to create that all-important sense of meaning, and determines whether a space feels secure or unstable. This will influence our outlook, mood and subsequent behaviour, for better or worse. If we feel disquiet in the building we are in, then it is unlikely we can fully concentrate on the activity in hand, whether at home or in a business meeting!

Our buildings today suffer from a lack of knowledge of sacred alchemy. The ancients designed buildings and the layout of entire cities with an esoteric understanding and feeling for these natural forces in their relationship to the lives of people and communities. Each room was designed with specific geometries, thereby infused with energetic patterns for the purpose of performing a particular function, be it sleeping, eating, musical performance or healing. Within each space holding the geometries, the node points provide the framework for activating the resonant frequencies (Whisper 1).

In terms of purpose and function, if a building is intended as a hospice to care for those with life-limiting illness for example, to incorporate musical harmonies into its design will create a propitious space to assist in the peaceful passage of the soul on the next phase of its journey. In ensuring the life force flows freely, we enter spaces that allow us to connect with harmonic rhythms.

Square and rectangular shapes   Most of us need stable reference points in our lives. Rectangular or square are considered the best shapes for plots of land, buildings and rooms, as they stabilise our energy and sense of direction within a structure or space. It is better for the longer rectangular sides to run north-to-south rather than west-to-east, preferably facing squarely the four cardinal directions. Vaastu considers it unacceptable to deviate off-square by more than twenty degrees either way.

Circular forms   Circular represents heavenly energy, which is why we find many stone circles, temples, and sacred buildings designed as circular structures. Circular denotes spiritual wealth and also material prosperity if aligned with right purpose and intent.

Irregular shapes   Random chaotic lines and spaces are epigenetic; the effects of non-linear shapes are unpredictable. A building or room of irregular shape represents incompleteness and instability, often leading to poor health, and in some cases even madness.

When a lady drew a plan of her house at a workshop, I asked if she had problems with her spine. Indeed, her physical body misalignment mirrored the irregular shape of her home – or had she chosen a home to reflect her distorted body?

Dividing stairs   A staircase located in the centre of any living area can create a division or separation from an aspect of your own psyche. Living with this symbolism may lead to compartmentalising certain aspects of life. We might indeed consider if this dynamic was chosen at a subconscious level, reflecting the person's temperament.

Pillars and columns   The repetition of building elements such as pillars or columns represent both the separating and unifying aspects of Heaven and Earth. The rhythmic pulse can reflect features of the energy signature of the building itself, and has the potential to come into resonance with the natural healing energies of the Earth.

Perceived size of a property A house can feel too big if it does not match the aura of your own personal energy body, as if you are rattling around in it. There may also be something out of alignment between yourself and the space you inhabit, especially if the house is physically not overly large for the number of people living there.

Equally, a house can feel too small if your personal energy fields have expanded, especially as you take on greater responsibility out in the world. It may simply be that you or your family have outgrown the space or there may be problems with the energy flow, making rooms feel claustrophobic and cramped. The resultant feeling of wanting to break out can shut down your spirit.

The Golden Mean Ratio

"There is geometry in the humming of the strings... there is music in the spacing of the spheres." (Pythagoras)

The power of Mother Nature in the design of universal order, the growth of plants and in the physical make-up of the human body, is generated and nourished by the golden mean harmonic. Indeed, the golden mean is also referred to as the Divine Proportion, to remind us of our true connection to Higher Self.

The energetic nature of the geometric matrix allows for efficient growth in all forms of life in the animal, vegetable and mineral kingdoms. The golden mean ratio is about patterns of beauty, the feminine generating life force intrinsic within the systems and frequencies of the cosmos. It is the harmonic of the golden mean spiral that organises the patterning of leaves unfurling on trees and plants in order to maximise their exposure to sunlight. Exquisite examples of the golden mean ratio are to be found in the sunflower seed head, a pine cone, the fern, a nautilus shell, feathers of a peacock, the rose, and in the dancing florets of Romanesco broccoli.

An apple is fractal and cutting it open reveals a pentagram at the core, the golden mean harmonic to which the vibration of the human heart resonates. Maybe an apple did not fall onto Newton's head whilst meditating under a tree; perhaps it was a hologram of knowledge of the golden mean harmonic that descended upon him!

All systems of measurement, from the earliest known megalithic yard, are informed by the mathematical harmonic relationships of planetary dimensions. Ancient classical architecture incorporates geometries that embody musical harmonic ratios, including the golden mean; all correlate to the proportions of the human body.

The golden mean is often inaccurately referred to as the Fibonacci series of numbers, characterised by compounding addition: 1+2+3+5+8+13+21... each progressive number being the sum of the previous two. The lower end of the sequence of numbers does *not* actually embody the golden mean ratio. In music 1:2 is an octave, 2:3 a major 5th, and so on. The golden mean ratio of 1:1.618 (Phi Φ to three decimal places) is only reached when the numbers are of very high values approaching infinity. Fibonacci originally came up with this logarithmic spiral sequence when he solved the puzzle of calculating the expansion of pairs of rabbits over the course of one year.

The golden mean is the only harmonic that has no stress at the node points, where the waves cross. It is the pure expression of fractal geometry in the physical and etheric realms, relating to our double (or multiple-strand) DNA helix. As the geometric construct of the pentagram, through its harmonics we can send any intention on its carrier waves with infinite expansion.

Because the natural earth grid holds consciousness and intelligence within the cosmic spiral galaxy, its inherent harmonic code pulsates and resonates around the globe. The golden mean by its very nature interpenetrates all substances and barriers it encounters in reaching its target, making it a powerful tool for manifesting intention and ensuring our dreams and desires come to fruition. Our latent empathic relationship to one another is through the resonant sharing of the harmonic waves of our hearts. This is how we attract others of the same frequency – the core essence is Love.

The Song of the Land

"Geometries are gateways to other dimensions." (Plato)

In the cosmology of the ancient world, the relationship of the people to Mother Earth and Father Sky was how they intrinsically related to and came into alignment with the land. Attuning to the ancestors helps us to become aware of the energetic structure of the land. Our ancestors understood the planet they inhabited as a sacred living being, with bands of telluric currents and leys that snake around the Earth's crust. In China they call them 'dragon lines', the Australian aborigines refer to them as 'song lines'.

The powerful earth energies connected to the heavens were fundamental in locating their sacred sites. They recognised that if the proportions of their stone circles and temples were not in harmony and their sites in geographical relation to each other not in correct alignment, then the music would be discordant. Discord is dissonance, conflicting sounds that are not in accord. Dissonance, however, as well as certain specific harmonics, creates gateways into other dimensions, the invisible worlds from where all is possible. Noise could therefore be considered as harmony in the making. Unravelling its chaos to form a cohesive whole implies there is intelligence – an intelligent seed within the heart of the memory matrix. Likewise, a building that is out of balance will be reflected in the discordant, out of tune harmonics, and responds by feeling the pain – just as do we.

Just as the vibrations of the natural world influence our voices, the landscape formations of hills and mountains, rivers and streams, also shape our language and character. This can be heard as one travels from one part of a country to another, as I was acutely aware when working on both coasts of Scotland. As the landscape changed from the gentle rolling hills in the east, to the more rugged mountains of the west, so did the tone and intonation of the distinctive local speech patterns.

There is value in taking any opportunity to visit places in the landscape and spend time being still and connected. You may feel a familiar resonant frequency giving you an awareness of the vibrational pattern as it correlates to your own inner sense of soul. As we sit in the fractal field and attune to the spirit of place, the soul of the land, it is possible to witness the silence in the sound, the still point at its centre. Using sound as a conduit for energy to flow through a sacred site, ancient hill fort, stone circle or temple, reactivation of the structure brings remembrance of its original purpose. The musical signatures held in the stones vibrate through the physical and etheric sound patterns. With standing stones, this is truly a standing wave.

When we attune to certain frequencies of the Earth or a building happens to ignite our own resonance, we may experience something of a gateway that transports us into other dimensions of reality. The practice of sounding our individual note and aligning our own vibration to the harmonic resonance of a space opens-up energy portals, allowing us to metaphysically travel through time and space.

We can make our structures and the land resonate with creative harmonics through sacred sound, musical instruments, the voice, poetry and art. As we play, sing and dance, a site becomes alive and we feel and share its joy. In accordance with ancient teachings and schools of learning, this celebration is all the more empowering when we gather together with others of similar intent.

All creative endeavours connect with the energy matrix of light and sound and can bring purification to our spaces. In honouring and healing the land, by feeding the spirit and nourishing the soul, we raise our own consciousness. A sacred grove can feel wonderful, but it is no longer magical if the trees are falling down. This work needs to be carried out on a continuous basis – it is an opportunity missed to reach an Aha moment and then not to fully embrace it.

Crop circle formations   My experience of crop circle formations is that they are three-dimensional geometries that translate and resonate to musical harmonics. They are seen mostly in Wiltshire, southern England, imprinted in cereal crops of wheat, maize and oil seed rape, and found worldwide in snow, ice, sand and woodland. It has been shown that wheat harvested from these formations produces stronger and more vigorous crops when the seed is next planted.

Many of these landscape temple designs contain coded information reminding us that number and geometry is a universal language of communication. These complex patterns of sacred geometrical proportions generate their own silent sounds; sonic patterns that reflect known cosmic geometries and others of a more mysterious nature. Crop formations seem to interact with the consciousness of the Earth, having the subtle power to transform our human sense of reality. The location and symbolic expression of these formations determine the various kinds of experiences that people frequently report, including a distorted sense of spatial awareness and of being transported beyond time and space.

Singing monks   When spending time in atmospheric locations, especially old ruins, churches and abbey sites, I am often aware of a more profound sense of space, far beyond romantic sentiment. When more than one person experiences a similar event at the same time and in the same place, this indicates an imprinted memory pattern embedded into the site; the consciousness of the past remains active in the timeframe of the present moment.

At Glastonbury Abbey in Somerset, the auric field of the ecclesiastical remains exude a sense of the activities that once took place on the original abbey site. The still intact 14th century Abbot's Kitchen, built to sacred geometric proportions, is renowned for its highly reverberant acoustics. On one occasion, whilst chanting with a group of people under the radiant vaulted roof, the session activated the voices of medieval monks who clearly wanted to join in, resulting in their deep, haunting tones actually being captured on a recording. As I felt the physical presence of one monk very perceptively merge into my body from behind, my voice surprisingly dropped suddenly to a deeper unfamiliar pitch.

Silent temple sounds and the power of stone   I have been filming and recording sound at sacred sites since the early 1970s. At Karnak Temple in Luxor, Egypt in 1993, I discovered a still point that was so silent, when you listened back to the 'nothingness' on the digital tape recording, the same deep stillness could be felt. It was as if the silence within the recording held an atmospheric memory that had become embedded in the etheric matrix of space. I pondered whether it was possible that this ancient stone structure could have 'recorded' its knowledge of events and emotions over the millennia.

Back in my studio editing the film footage, I asked the temple if it could play back its sound – and it did! What came through was an intelligence held within the stones and in etheric space. The result was a seven-minute video with the music composed through me, reflecting the knowledge and emotion of the structure at that time.

The building of Karnak Temple took a very long time to complete. Possibly begun around 1500 BCE, construction continued during the reigns of about thirty pharaohs. This embraces the concept that embedded in a sacred building, music as a form of imprinted memory contains the essence, diversity and complexity of entire civilisations and cultures within its blueprint. In the graphic image of a human body transposed over the Temple ground plan, there is evidence that geo-energetic lines follow corresponding human meridians and chakra points. When activated by conscious connection, these patterns of harmonic vibration and resonance have the ability to unfold through musical composition.

I have since experienced buildings and landscapes 'writing' their music in many other places on my travels. This awesome expression allows us to experience in a matter of a few minutes the essence of thousands of years of feeling the sentient emotion and wisdom.

The Harmonies of the House

Just as language forms and shapes our world, music can shape the character and design of a building. Through sound waves, a building can reflect back its sonic signature as geometries and living notes.

A building can be compared to a dynamic musical composition, with the instruments providing the harmonies, rhythms, melodic lines and counterparts to the main theme. Each event that occurs has its own unique harmonic vibration and distinctive sound quality, a sonic signature conveying the actual state and character of a building. This is further influenced by the overlays resulting from human activity and any spirit presence, together with various flavours of the natural landscape in that location. Thus, all events that have taken place influence the emotions and mood of a space.

In the early 1970s, a scientist friend helped me to connect an electronic organ to a converted television set, so the music could be displayed as visual patterns on the screen. I was fascinated to see that pure harmonic intervals created beautiful geometric patterns, whilst disharmonic sounds resulted in distorted, fragmented images. More recent technological developments demonstrate similar effects of harmonics on water molecules, both visually and in physicality. The molecules respond to discordant sound by arranging themselves into fragmented looking blobs, yet when exposed to purer vibrational frequencies, the individual crystalline structures form exquisite geometric shapes. This is very much how I perceive visually and audibly the quality of space in buildings.

The music of buildings In essence, a house is like a musical instrument and the homeowner the conductor of an orchestra. Each instrument finely tuned plays its own part in the same piece of music. The melodic line within the harmony represents the thread of life running through a building. The character of a building, even each individual room, is dependent upon its note. The musical signature of the occupants, the members of a choir, may or may not be in accord with their surroundings. When in harmony, they are in peaceful balance, supporting one another. Thus, the resonance of the land, buildings and people make music together, creating the 'symphony of life'. It is possible for *you* to change the music track – and your life.

Try sitting quietly and listening to the sounds in a building. Focus first on the room you are in and feel the quality of the silence. Then expand your awareness into other rooms, resting your attention within each space for a few minutes at a time. Notice how the sound changes in accordance with the various materials and the size and shape of the rooms. With your inner perception, sense a mixture of energies; they will either blend with your being, grate on your nerves, or a mixture of something in between. This may tell you intuitively what music is needed to harmonise yourself in that space. To suggest any particular composition is of little value. As we all have a unique 'note', the sound needs to reflect our own personal and emotional connection to the harmonics of that space.

The music we pull out of the air is already in the consciousness matrix, so depending on where we are aligned at that moment, we too can draw down information in the shapes of the appropriate harmonics. By tuning-in to your home, to the programmes that run constantly in the energy fields of space, you may hear what codes are needed to realign the resonance to bring peace and calm to your spaces. A good start is to play the heart-coherent music of composers such as Mozart and Vivaldi, as they incorporate many powerful harmonics. Implicit within the geometry of sound are the proportions of harmonic intervals, rhythm and melody. These frequencies of heart-based harmonics and resonant rhythms can transform spaces.

Ancient music used modes in their expression, such as the Gregorian chant and various Greek Ionian, Dorian and Myxolydian idioms. The relationship of harmonic intervals to the geometric proportions of architectural space is an important part of my work in composing the 'music of buildings'. The key is in being open to listening to the silent *whispers* of sounds and receiving these expressions emanating from the soul of a building. Using the faculties of mind and inner perception allows compositions to flow through me. When playing instruments, I enjoy combining and merging ancient music with modern rhythms, and just going with the flow as all unfolds.

Whilst walking around a house to sense its emotional character and past history, I will sometimes hear a piece of music or a song in my mind, reflecting the emotional patterns held in the energy matrix of the property. This gives me a clue as to the human story simmering away in the background, and will often unlock the narrative that is about to unfold. The next two examples illustrate:

Musical box tune   At a house full of mystery and intrigue in New Jersey, a young girl had died in a fire some years ago. Sitting at the piano in the same room, I began to play a composition that I came to call *Edwina's Song*. The daughter now living there had an emotive connection with the young girl in spirit and told me her name. What came through was her memory imprint, as if she was still winding her musical box that carried on repeating her favourite tune for years and years, in soulful comfort.

Christmas carol   When consulting in a flat in Brighton, I heard the gentle melody of a Christmas carol. This was the catalyst that alerted me to engage with an elderly lady in spirit from the Victorian era. She was then able to come forward and share the distressing story of her last Christmas with her children, which enabled her spirit to release from a world of trapped emotions (Whisper 5).

Unseen energies affect room acoustics   Embedded in the unseen energy matrix of our homes and workplaces are life events, emotions, thoughts, dreams and behaviours, which can all be heard as audible acoustics and change the inherent patterns of the harmonic codes. Thus, the sound quality of a space is affected by the attributes of the energies of human activities; any change in the happenings within a space will alter the sound, which in turn indicates a change in the patterning of the energetic matrix.

240

At a house in Wales, I sensed a sticky thickness in the atmosphere of the living room. The quality of the space was so congested that trying to hear voices was like listening through cotton wool. I recorded the quality of the sound of speech and piano playing both before and after space-clearing. The sound afterwards was quite sharp and crisp, so much so that when the owner walked into the room she remarked on the clarity of our speaking voices. Just as etheric debris was cleared from the *School controlled from another dimension* (Whisper 3), when audible sound becomes clearer and more vibrant, it is a good indication that the space itself is clearer, as if the cotton wool has dissolved.

The effect of audible acoustics on clear space brings balance and harmony. The purity of a space can be demonstrated by the vibrancy of the harmonics of musical instruments, especially of the ringing type such as Tibetan bells. The appropriate geometrical proportion of a room will allow the inherent harmony to vibrate and expand into full power. The natural compression and release of sound is what enables a building to play its music and to sing with joy. As space expands and contracts, the quality of the sound can make a place feel good and happy.

Abbey Road's Studio 1 is usually perceived as bigger than the other studios, owing to the power of the superb music created and recorded that still lingers in the air from the Golden Days of the 1960s. Current musicians comment that this uplifting atmosphere, where the walls hold memory of so many emotions, continues to inspire creativity for contemporary recordings.

The harmonic imprint will morph and change from day to day, even hour by hour, as new experiences influence the space and create contrasting sound vibrations. As sound fades away, it soaks into the physical walls of a building and its etheric counterpart. The resonant memory of the notes overlays and augments whatever was there before. The updated patterning of pulsating sound frequencies stay in current memory form until further activities and emotions, whether negative or positive, sad or happy, modulate the pre-existing vibrations. These further imprints overlay the core energy signature of a building and the surrounding land, all adding another flavour.

This is generally what is changed during a space-clearing and realignment session. For the deepest shift to take place, access to the vibrational software codes holding the original conception zero point, is needed (Whisper 5).

Aligning with the harmonics of a building Listening to the sonic frequencies of a structure makes it possible to tune up or re-tune the core nature and intention of a building or even the actual site. Using the sounds of Sanskrit or any other language may be appropriate, depending on the harmonic character of the space; again it is about getting a sense of what is needed to bring balance to a certain place at a particular time. So, a composition is full of potentiality, held at zero point in dormant suspended coded seed form, waiting for the right time to be activated through conscious intention. This can simply be a wish to hear a particular piece of music by choosing the right track and pressing the 'play' button.

Once we establish resonance with our personal energy signature and fine tune the harmonic code of our homes to resonate with higher vibrations, this can add another dimension to our understanding of the grid matrix. Many tools and practices can be used to achieve this, including sacred geometry, sacred sound, meditation and visualisation. Exploring the effects of the resonant acoustic frequencies of space on the molecular structure of the etheric matrix reveals that the play of light and shadow is indeed a magical form of spatial poetry.

We can encourage our buildings to come alive, to feel the pulse and rhythm of their heartbeat. Just as the wood of a beautifully made guitar or violin matures as it is exquisitely tuned and played, a well-designed and energetically clear house will mellow and respond to being treated with love, care and respect. However, just as when an instrument is neglected or played without conscious connection, a house can fall into disrepair and resemble a neglected soul with its spirit subdued. The musical harmonies will then be unable to reach their full potential and true magnitude.

To awaken a structure and bring it alive is ceremony on a continuous basis. The ancient tradition of ongoing sacred chanting of the Perpetual Choirs is still practiced as a living form of meditation in some parts of the world today. Enjoy and feel your home as an instrument that needs to be venerated and allow it to be tuned, played and sung to its full glory. By joining in with the symphony of the house and the land, you will activate the heart and soul of your home.

Vibrational Healing

"The cure of the part should not be attempted without treatment of the whole. No attempt should be made to cure the body without the soul." (Plato)

What is healing? It is a matter of recognising the perfection of the natural order of the cosmos, which holds the vibrational coding *and* blueprint of an intrinsically healthy home or person. We are attracted to the resonance of a house that reflects our own vibration to celebrate the beauty of creation so that a healing process can take place.

Healing past and current patterns that control our lives should be important to us all. Just as the human body knows how to heal itself, our buildings let us know what they need. Very often this is through their occupants, faced with challenges that act as the catalyst to prompt them to address what is going on. In healing ourselves, we must address the healing of our homes and workplaces; this cannot happen in isolation. If a building is sick, the people and animals residing within will also become sick. After all, our house is mirror of our soul, so by healing your home you are healing yourself.

Plato's statement remains as valid today as when it was written, around 2,400 years ago. Physical, emotional, psychological and spiritual factors must *all* be taken into account in the healing process. The first step towards self-help is to recognise that something needs to change. The opportunity to create change can only happen when we become fully conscious of what is *really* going on. When our repetitive patterns that created our initial problems are recognised with clarity, we can begin the process of healing our interwoven relationships on all levels. This will often bring up old hurts and wounds, a necessary part of any journey of personal transformation.

If we do not address the issues generated by and linked to our life stories at a metaphysical level, we may find that any current blueprint of illness held in the home will pull us back into old energetic patterns, making the benefits of any ongoing healing process less effective. Perhaps more people would devote time to healing the environment and addressing the harmful consequences of geopathic and electro-pollution if they realised that there is a direct correlation between environment, health and personal life path (Whisper 6).

Changing the harmonic vibration of our familiar surroundings can activate our true selves as multi-dimensional beings. It is of great value to learn more about the science behind the framework of this holistic interaction. We have the choice to take personal responsibility and deal with causative factors or go back to the doctor for allopathic remedies, which often amount to little more than a temporary fix. To reach our own solutions whenever possible is both empowering and will bring longer lasting results. Nevertheless, there is a valid place for vibrational *and* allopathic remedies as long as they help us to get to the root cause of a problem. It is actually possible to temper any negative effects of toxic medicines by employing vibrational techniques. So if we need to take them, we have the sonic tools to deal with any unhelpful side effects.

At therapy centres around the world, healing work is being accomplished with sonic scanning, light body and colour activation. Some of the most powerful ways to fine tune our physical and etheric bodies are through working with these frequencies. Many modalities inspire us to open our minds and hearts, to raise our vibrations and discover new kinds of healing techniques and practices. The following are some of my experiences with people and buildings:

Aligning with the breath At a property in the Lake District with a vibrational discrepancy in the relationship between the house and garden, the outer walls of the house needed to be 'dissolved' to allow them to merge. This was achieved consciously by using a form of prana-merging to align their common resonant frequencies. Metaphysically focussing and breathing through the walls allowed the energy of the garden to soak through and nourish the house.

In Oxfordshire, the garden of a house straddled what was once the village boundary. I could feel the invisible line that had now disappeared under the grass, clearly traceable using dowsing rods. My feeling was of the land energetically divided, which was affecting and contributing to the various energetic problems that the house and its occupants were experiencing. By using a metaphysical breathing technique and visualising the inclusion of the section of garden outside the original village boundary, both parts were able to come together in harmony with the heart of the house.

Sonic scanning We know that therapeutic tapping techniques change habitual patterns. Several systems that incorporate rhythmic pulsing can also be of great benefit in helping to uncover personal subconscious programming, and to dissolve any negative and unwanted vibrations from our energy fields.

By using the practice of sonic scanning and visualising various harmonics running up and down through the human body, any change in sound or variation in the frequency of the voice quickly identifies blockages in specific areas. This can illuminate issues that we may have been carrying around for many years, the root cause having remained buried in the depths of our subconscious.

As well as for personal healing, I use similar techniques to search for and identify any blockages within a house, loosening up the locked energetic patterns of the geometric crystalline grid. This is indeed sound therapy for buildings, working on the pulsating harmonics of the energy centres of a property in the matrix of etheric space. Any obstructions can be released using various practices such as metaphysical re-patterning of the geometries, musical instruments, chanting, and sacred sound. Most importantly, the full engagement and dialogue with the client allows a gentle unravelling so they can recognise and feel the core issues that gave rise to any blockages within themselves. Once clearly illuminated, the person is then in a better position to decide upon a course of action for change and to take responsibility for dealing with any concerns, which are usually very visibly mirrored externally in their home. The outcome is invariably one of positive transformation.

Bio-Mobility In 1990, I was trained in Bio-Mobility, a system of working on the energy flows in the muscles of the human body, which hold the memory of any earlier physical or emotional trauma. This has direct impact on other bodily systems that can become disrupted and cause pain, preventing an individual from feeling safe. By applying pressure to the insert and origin points of the muscles and then using gentle manipulation, this allows a person's memory pathways to energetically unwind back through to an original traumatic event, allowing the potential for full release. For beneficial effects to be lasting, the weakened muscles and corresponding ligaments may well require strengthening exercises. My work as *The House Whisperer*, identifying and releasing energy blockages through space-clearing and realignment of people and their homes, later turned out to be based upon similar principles.

The harmonic healing key In the fascinating world of fractal attraction, the intelligence of the human body knows its perfect design codes and has the ability to draw on them when needed for healing. Once we tune in and connect with our individual blueprint, we hold the harmonic key to modify our vibrational codes. Bringing balance to a person's vibration or aura results in adjustments to the neurological pathways; this strengthens the immune system and sanctions full activation of the body's own healing instrument.

Personal healing is more effective when there is emotional detachment from both facilitator and recipient, especially when involving a loved one. Using the harmonic key allows us to find, draw down and unlock our original DNA codes, giving access to and reminding the body of its original healthy organ blueprint. Thus, past patterns and memories held at cellular and energetic levels can be transmuted; it is even possible to discharge the most serious diseases and transform damaged cells into healthy ones.

When we become unwell, our aura or energetic body manifests an imbalance that we may be unaware of, quite some time before actual physical symptoms appear. The wonder of this activation process is that it enables true healing to take place in the metaphysical realms, prior to being felt by the physical body. It is also a deep form of counselling, which goes beyond many currently recognised forms of energy therapy.

One approach to healing, whether in person or remotely, is by visualising the past, present and projected future energies of the recipient's blueprint as being in perfect alignment with their original code. At the same time, through the etheric grid matrix we can bring balance to the physical, biological, neurological and auric systems on all levels. It is possible to release and realign all in a few moments, as time is not a factor in metaphysical reality. By learning to fly through and navigate the energy grid, we can see any issues needing attention in relation to the corresponding cellular structure. In this way, the required knowledge is accessible for self-healing the human body as well as for healing buildings and even places.

Hidden Healing Structures

"...for there is nothing either good or bad, but thinking makes it so."
(Hamlet, W Shakespeare)

Energised sacred space can be explained as the hidden spinning structures that keep the universe in motion, the music that holds the cosmos together. This resonance clears and rebalances space by restructuring negative energetic particles into positive and highly charged ones. This is reflected in the quality of the atmosphere as it resonates to our human design of material and subtle harmonics. When replicated in our homes and workplaces, greater harmony is possible in our personal and business lives.

All begins in the mind before moving into action. When we are well, our 'good vibrations' are felt by our homes, which in turn have a positive influence on the quality of our thinking. Focus and clarity of thought are important factors in allowing access to the intuitive higher mind. This is the value of working with energy, to enhance the synchronistic quality of life for people and their spaces. So, by changing your thought patterns you will change the aura or atmosphere of the places where you spend time, and even the metaphysical realms to where you travel.

Sounding the golden mean harmonic The underlying purpose of any therapeutic work is to be guided to higher levels of consciousness. This can facilitate self-discovery of immediate issues and concerns, as does bringing the dynamics of sacred geometry and harmonics into your life. Many of us have experienced the elation and value of healing sound baths, with crystal and Tibetan bowls and gongs taking us into unknown depths. The relationship between the Sanskrit chant, sacred geometry and the golden mean ratio can be experienced through sacred sound, especially voice harmonics and overtone sounding.

In workshops, I guide people to sound with the voice the ratios of the natural octave, replicating the harmonics of the cosmic order and connecting directly to the Divine matrix or 'music of the spheres'. Using this technique, when reaching the golden mean harmonic, just past the mid-point of any musical octave (0.618...), this sets a spin in the atmosphere of a space, which is felt in every part of the body like an electrical tingling that can make the hairs on your arms stand on end. This ratio reminds our physical and energetic bodies of their original natural design and absolute connection to universal Source.

I am told by those experiencing this expanding nature of space for the first time, how remarkable it is to find oneself in a room that both feels and visually appears to get bigger simply through the power of sound. One lady explained that as soon as she let go of thinking about the emotion that brought up in her, she was suddenly transported back through a portal to the primary moment of creation.

In sound healing groups, I guide people to find their own unique note as a personal healing vehicle. To unblock and release trauma lodged in a particular area, our higher intelligence needs to guide our voice to generate the missing harmonics. Finding and activating our own energy codes ignites the fire in our heart, giving us the opportunity to tap into the power of universal consciousness. This allows what we are not to fall away, revealing who we truly are. To recall the pure sacred geometries inherent in universal law can put back together our disconnected and fragmented human sense of reality. So, by discovering how to use the voice to sound and activate your inherent DNA vortex spins, you can create the vibrations needed to realign your original genetic codes. To experience the tangible vibrations of the alchemy of sound can be a real awakening.

Once the perfect frequency signature or individual note is found, by allowing those vibrations to breathe through to the blocked areas, any emotional knots will gently release. The response of the body is remarkably fast and what is revealed can be of a very deep nature, often unravelling and bringing to the surface an emotional memory related to a traumatic event or unresolved life issue that has remained deeply buried, perhaps even from another lifetime. When this is seen clearly, any physical aches and pains often relax or disappear:

"I was totally unaware I was carrying that sad trauma from the past... the pain has now gone from my heart."

As always, the choice is yours to decide to deal with anything that is illuminated. Once we discover our true Divine potential, we are in a better position to help and serve others, and miracles can happen.

Spinning light structures   The resonant vibration of the golden mean can take us into a higher state of consciousness, leading to profound realisations, as this lady attending one of my workshops vividly describes:

> *"The golden mean has no ending in expansion or depth into the cave, as that is the nature of its harmonics. I was taken to a place that I would call the alchemical red. It was so deep and vivid, right in the third eye area. Yes, the reddening fixes the substance; I know that from alchemy. Wow! And it was similar to the green hexagon in size and shape that I saw on two separate nights a while ago, lovely clear green that spun very fast. The green and the red, my goodness!"*

The spinning geometries to which she refers are a natural part of the universal sacred geometry matrix. Through visualisation, I am often given various geometries in the form of architectural light structures beyond space-time, experienced more intensely when working with people, buildings and landscapes. Spinning geometries, energy balls and healing spheres of light, travelling or dispersing through the atomic structures of the energy grid matrix, can all be used for realignment of space, creating protective shields, and for healing any part of the human body.

When recovering from surgery, soft clouds of green elixir can be visualised floating down and penetrating any areas that have been assaulted by the procedures. As a form of light medicine for houses, you can gently pulse clouds of green elixir through your home, room by room, until your entire home is full of them. With further pulses, send the elixir clouds out through the roof and up into the sky, then keep repeating until total stillness is reached.

Symbols download at Chartres   In 2002, a small group of us spent four days visiting Chartres Cathedral in France. On the first day whilst sitting quietly, cold chills were felt as we became aware of a small group of Templars in spirit checking us out. We realised that the original Master builders were still caring for the cathedral, their consciousness remaining very present. The cathedral is a living, breathing organism with significant relevance to our lives today, just as the Platonic philosophies were at the foundation of Chartres.

After a couple of days, I sat in a local café over the road, frustrated because I could not understand the secret geometries of the cathedral. On some inner level, I was aware of them vibrating in the etheric field as I had studied and analysed the structure for many years, yet something was eluding me. My friend asked, *"What's your problem,"* so I explained my dilemma. She said, *"Have you asked?"* Then it hit me, the most fundamental question that I address in my work with houses and clients, but for myself I did not ask. At that moment the floodgates opened and the knowledge of all I was seeking began streaming down through my crown chakra. My whole being knew and recognised the cascade of holographic symbols, yet my mind could not comprehend them. The speed and sheer quantity became so profuse that I had to let go of trying to understand and just drop into my heart and feel the knowing. This profound and moving experience was indeed a point of personal transformation, refocusing my relationship with the consciousness of buildings.

I then went back into the cathedral and sat looking at the mesmerising colours of the stained glass of the south rose window. It felt as though the shimmering, dancing light from the glass was being guided by a higher intelligence, activating the codes to re-programme my energy blueprint. I had the choice to resist or allow it to do its work in clearing old patterns in my personal energy fields. So I submitted to its grace with tears streaming down my face, attracting sympathetic glances transcending language from a couple of elderly French ladies.

The next day, during a meditation session sitting on the curved stone steps at the base of the Templar Towers, one of the Templars in spirit approached, reached out and handed me a golden key. This was indeed an honour. Realising that I had undergone an initiation of light through the rose window, my connection with sacred buildings and the work that I continue to do today, was truly acknowledged.

Coded Shields of Protection

The sacred space of our homes can become violated in many ways, from the physical or emotional to the extreme of paranormal interference. Intrusion of our locked doors and secure windows can be devastating, but the energetic bombardment from atmospheric energies and especially negative human thoughts, can be much more forceful and damaging. Protection from this metaphysical form of psychic attack is then required. It is, however, always advisable to try and resolve problems with those who may be directing negative thoughts and intentions towards you, assuming you can determine their identity.

Just as a harmonic code is embedded into the soul of a building at conception, giving it a unique energy signature, protective coded structures can be programmed to surround a person, building or an entire region. There are many practices to do this. Shields of protection provide a powerful and effective form of psychic self-defence. Protection is not necessarily about preparing for battle, but essentially about strengthening your own energy fields. It is important to allow the natural energy to flow, whilst at the same time preventing any unwanted energies from passing through the structure of your shield. When a person puts up emotional barriers through fear as a subconscious form of protection rather than truly coming from a place of conscious connection, they too are likely to become blocked on all levels. Thus, protection from the standpoint of fear is of little value.

My first experience of visualising a geometric protective shield was when I visited a mother in Yorkshire, whose son had leukaemia. His bedroom was close to an electrical sub-station. As I stood in front of the sub-station considering how to proceed, I could hear and feel the destructive vibrations of the transformer. I was guided to call on the spirit of Plato, a Master of sacred geometry. Unexpectedly, a lattice-frame structure suddenly appeared as if from nowhere, its geometry multiplying in complexity. Encircling the sub-station, it created a protective shielding structure preventing the harmful energies from radiating outwards. The structure penetrated the earth but was kept open to the sky so that the harmful energy could release safely upwards; to have fully contained it might have created an implosion. When I turned around to look at my assistant holding the dowsing rods, I watched in awe as they slowly released from their crossed state to an open position. This indicated that the newly created energetic barrier was active in preventing the damaging effects of the electromagnetic fields from flowing towards the house and further depleting the boy's health.

At the time, I questioned how an invisible structure could prevent electromagnetic energy from harming those in the vicinity. It was some years later that I fully understood what actually occurs when a protective shield of this kind is created. As with geopathic stress (Whisper 6), it is not about blocking or getting rid of something, but about changing the energy signature pattern of the 'damaging' activity and bringing it into phase-alignment with whatever is being harmed. The geometric shield around the sub-station did not block the electromagnetic emissions as such, but transformed the frequency wave harmonic to phase-lock with the energy signature of the house and its occupants. This effectively rendered the electromagnetic fields invisible, so they could do no harm. I have developed and continue to use variations of these intelligent shields with ever-increasing complexity of coded programmes, according to the need of any situation.

Creating a coded shield Energy protection shields must be programmed consciously in order to hold clarity and power. To create a simple coded shield, imagine a fine gold wire mesh surrounding your whole body or house in the form of a sphere, with crystals at each of the node points, the crossing points of the mesh. Sense the boundary of the golden shield that you have visualised in your imagination, and now programme the crystals with the intention that the structure can breathe to allow the natural energy to flow through. This is not a solid structure as in a warrior's shield, but a web-like lattice grid that butterflies may flutter through freely.

The essence of creating a successful coded protective shield is to expand into your eternal presence from your heart, whilst at the same time keeping physically grounded. Maintain a strong core of stable energy through all your chakras by feeling the love and Divine presence from the universe filling your aura. Releasing any residual fear from past patterns will protect any confused or fearful parts of your being from getting involved and entangled with potential forms of geo-psychic energy or attack waiting to infiltrate. Managing your own boundaries is crucial to prevent being affected by or taking on unwanted energies, or even to encounter entities that you may be challenged to contend with. To be fully in alignment with universal purpose, your invisible multi-layered energy shield embedded into the etheric matrix needs to pulsate and vibrate to the highest levels.

Programming your shield To take this one step further, whatever programme you choose to set for your coded energy shield, your visualisation will create the dimensional reality in both the physical and metaphysical realms. You may choose to use vibrational means to create geometrical structures in space, or to mould your chosen geometric shapes through sonic harmonics. A good way to reinforce your golden mesh shield is to visualise power symbols being added to the crystals, then see them replicating the coded information through resonance to the thousands of other crystals located at all the other node points. Maintain your golden shield and energise it for use whenever needed. Your empowered coded shield can also be infused with the following affirmation:

"Allow only that which serves my highest and best welfare to enter, all other energies are to remain outside."

Should you have concerns when you go away and leave your home unoccupied, even for just a few hours, you may feel it is a good idea to surround your house in a protective aura of light or golden mesh. Some people do this subconsciously; whatever your approach, it is best not done through fear as this creates a duality field, which resonates in the background and can activate in unexpected ways at a later date. The bigger picture is that whatever happens in your home is a reflection of some aspect of what may be happening within yourself or others with whom you share your living space. This concept is consistent with the message throughout this book that you and your home are inextricably linked at physical and emotional levels of your soul journey in life.

Preventing destructive energies from entering When you create your shield, any destructive energy that you seek protection from will know at some level that you are establishing boundaries. It may then attempt to re-establish the link and send its 'hooks' back into you. If you hold a power that others would like to tamper with for their own use, whether human or spirit entities and soul fragments, it is advisable to re-create your shield with a stronger coding. When you breathe to reinforce your shield, be aware that this can create a temporary gap in the etheric matrix, a way in for those who know how to try and find the gateway entrance to access your shield. So, be strong in your intentions and affirmations. The vulnerable aspect is that your light shield is there for the taking by those who are able to break the code to gain access, but it does not belong to others who seek to feed off you. You may choose to visualise a mirror to reflect the focus away from anyone who attempts to intrude on your space and disturb your peace. It is of little value to be drawn into their games or to engage in perpetuating manipulative battles.

Linguistic codes Language is a symbolic resonant set of codes that embody the laws of the universe, and can shape the quality of space. In Sanskrit, the phrase *naama rupa* means 'name and form'. The power of any language is in the spoken vowels and consonants. Each symbol or letter has a geometric shape with a corresponding sound, which activates intention and brings any thought or concept into manifestation. From this seed form, the programmed code explodes into creation as it unravels through harmonic vibration.

The oldest known languages of Sanskrit, Sumerian, Aramaic, Hebrew and Greek are closest to the language of the universal mind, and deemed the most powerful. We encounter many forms of symbol energy throughout our lives, such as Greek letters used as scientific symbols, and more recently geometric symbols in crop formations, all influencing the energy grid matrix.

Being fairly fluent in spoken Greek, I find myself thinking in the language within a matter of a few days of being in Greece or Cyprus and immersing myself in the culture. On my return to England, I realise my thoughts once again reframe in English. Those who have crossed continents regularly from a young age do this naturally; the moment they step onto familiar soil they instinctively know the silent language code of the country. A longer journey by sea seems to precipitate this sooner than arriving by air, as if the water holding cellular memory tells the child within us when it is time to switch. The resonance of a specific language pattern, held in the invisible matrix and retained in our memory, will usually align within a short space of time, as and when required. This aptitude is perhaps also related to the unconscious projection of the mind, just as we mentally project and go on ahead of ourselves when planning to travel, especially when preparing for a more distant journey.

Redundant codes I was asked to help resolve a problem with a residential building project in New Jersey, USA. Working from my studio in Kingston upon Thames, I could see etheric screens acting as shields to partition-off an area of the living room. As I focused closer, it became apparent that they not only had some kind of foreign script written on them, but had been consciously placed in order to deflect anyone from trying to see in and listen to private conversations. Tuning in to the now redundant coded shields enabled me to find a way to unravel and collapse the screens holding the programmes. By returning them to zero point, the energies that were subliminally hampering the project were rendered neutral.

Curses and manipulation On many occasions, I have encountered the intentional programming of objects placed in someone's home. This is usually to control and influence the way they think or behave, ostensibly to gain some kind of benefit. In a house in Greece, I found an object that a maid, on behalf of the wife's mother, had placed behind the headboard in the bedroom in an attempt to split up her daughter's marriage. A curse or hex is a form of programming that can be decoded in the same way as an energy shield. One needs, however, the ability to tune into the programme to perceive the active code before attempting to deconstruct it.

Evil intentions An anxious Greek woman was getting strong feelings of wanting to drown herself in her own swimming pool. Hearing her voice over the telephone from Athens, it was clear to me that her suicidal thoughts were not her own. Tuning-in more deeply, I discovered that her husband's new young lover practiced black magic and was planting these urges in her psyche. Using suggestive, manipulative thought-forms, they were trying to get her to commit suicide so they could then move into the house together. The wife desperately needed protection from this sinister plot to kill her. Her husband had even given her an icon for Christmas, programmed with evil intentions to diminish her energy. I was most concerned to come across such scheming trickery. Whilst I immediately set to work on decommissioning this malevolence and create protective shields around the wife and her home, the girlfriend was initially able to tune in and break down my coded programmed shields.

This consultation took place during my formative years of working with teachers in higher realms, reminding me of knowledge I had used in other lifetimes. Having received guidance on constructing coded shields and now been shown how to generate more complex codes to make their defence more robust, I felt confident that the shields were successful in preventing access to the house. Yet somehow the woman practicing the magic was still managing to get at my client. How could this be happening? It turned out that the wife was unknowingly wrecking the power of protection by letting her husband in through the front door. When questioned as to why she was doing this, negating the work I was doing on her behalf, she simply said. *"I still love him."* Well, love does open doors!

Emotional detachment It is a matter of personal responsibility to ensure that our intentions are clear. The power of wanting something, perhaps not in our own best interests or to the highest good, can override even the most powerful of protective shields. Any emotional involvement or desired interest in an outcome can cloud our judgement, opening-up fissures in our energy fields to allow various forms of energetic attack to get through; our Achilles heel.

In the *Bhagavad Gita*, Lord Krishna presented Arjuna with the dilemma that he would hurt his family and friends if he fought in battle. His quandary was about emotional detachment from the results of making a decision. What may be right action in one situation today is not necessarily so in another set of circumstances or perhaps even tomorrow; inaction presents the same problem. Most actions of cruelty simply play out old hurts and wounds; wanting to hurt others back is a form of revenge, often masking jealousy, anger or resentment. In desiring a preferred result to any situation, we may not be coming from a place of total integrity; our emotional reasoning will therefore perpetuate karma. The other dilemma is that in stepping aside from issues that relate to our own life story, even though we may feel it is not our problem, choosing to ignore a situation of conflict can also add to our karma.

It is good to remember that the journey of loving ourselves, our fellow beings, our homes and sacred landscapes, is ultimately one of self-responsibility. To be 'responsible' is the ability to respond, to act in the present moment in an appropriate way, according to the need at that time and in that place. We do not have to hold onto vast amounts of information in order to make the right decisions, as all knowledge is accessible in the Akashic field of memory. I find that working in this way allows for the grace of knowledge to descend, so that whatever is required in any given situation will present itself.

The Alchemical Chalice

Our home is a Golden Vessel, an alchemical chalice that holds and reflects the innermost dreams and secrets of our lives, embodied in the sacred weave of the feminine and masculine. The structure of a house can be seen as yang, the material masculine that provides strength, support and protection of the inner sanctuary, the delicate yin feminine womb-space. In this sacred substance, human consciousness can initiate birth or re-birth at its highest potential.

To recapitulate on the key message of this book, in the human co-creation of reality we are not separate from the consciousness of our homes. We may perceive a house to be an inanimate object, but exploring deeper we find much more going on below the surface. The psychology of home considers our spatial environment. This is why it is of great value to reach an understanding of the nature of the house, to recognise and identify with its being-ness, and be touched by its soul as it speaks to us on many levels. We are all facilitators in illuminating our own patterns of how we relate to our homes. Without addressing the energy grids of the cosmic matrix holding the predecessor imprint of a building, we have only part of the story.

With many years experience of working with buildings and the land, I am profoundly aware of how we are influenced by our external environment, often to the detriment of overall wellbeing. Becoming conscious of the interwoven layers of connection with our homes, not to mention a multitude of entities and disembodied spirits, can help to identify the patterns that led us there in the first place. In the quest to understand our life's purpose, we discover the reasons why a house and its occupants are drawn together at the outset. This may be to resolve certain issues concerning other people and places in our current or a previous lifetime, usually in search of peace, contentment and happiness.

My role as *The House Whisperer* may be likened to that of an alchemist, blending together all the ingredients from the unseen realms, reflected in physical terms using coded language to explain the mysterious and hidden meanings of the fragmented aspects of Self. A deeper relationship manifests when we choose to engage with a sense of our own personal resonance to the harmonic signature of our homes. To bring the inherent genetic coding of our buildings into the same resonance as the land and her people encourages all to resonate with the intrinsic vibration for which they were conceived.

In weaving ancient wisdom into modern context, bringing the heart of a person into resonance with the heart of their home embraces psychology, philosophy, geomancy and science. This is expressed, enhanced and sustained by the metaphysical elements of sacred space. To penetrate the primordial intelligence of the universe opens up the gateways in aligning the frequency of our heart harmonics to their original authentic code. Thus, as capacitors of cosmic and earth energies, the harmonic structures of our sacred buildings play a vital role in supporting the alchemical journey of the soul. Our homes can act as the catalyst in taking us to the precipice of flight in what is ultimately an ongoing transformational process. Most transpersonal and psychotherapeutic work is about this journey.

In the archetypal stages of the journey of the soul, we embark on the path of life's challenges in search of Self, immortalised in our much-loved fairy stories and in classical texts such as Homer's *Odyssey*. The receptive, intuitive feminine energy, represented by the silver thread, allows us to navigate our way safely through the mortal world into the realms of metaphysical mysteries.

In the myth of *Theseus and the Minotaur*, Ariadne gives Theseus the thread to find his way out of the labyrinth after killing the Minotaur, a metaphor of taking full control in order to slay the shadow aspects of the human psyche. As the gatekeeper of our own soul, we can choose at any time to open or close the door to the inner sanctum of our being. We may decide to open Pandora's Box and descend to the darkest depths, approaching the zenith of all possibility held within our inner realms. To learn the various techniques of frequency shift in the etheric matrix beyond time and space allows us to collapse our perceived reality and tap into the Source of infinite potentiality.

As with Lancelot's quest to save Guinevere, Arjuna's dilemma on the battlefield, Alice in Wonderland's tumble down the rabbit hole and many other legendary tales, the human spiritual journey is symbolic of crossing boundaries. Whether at mundane level or perceived as what Joseph Campbell calls *The Hero's Journey*, we face the frontiers of uncharted regions and discover deeper aspects of our Self. The question is, will we embark on the quest?

The heart resonance of the golden mean is the most powerful harmonic for linking into 'All is One'. So, a pure heart would carry a golden key. By unlocking our energy centres and experiencing the golden light of initiation of the illumined soul, we connect with the higher geometric light frequencies of the matrix – the true meaning of 'enlightenment'. We can then truly be in service to humanity, in a privileged position to help unlock the hearts of others.

Your home is a gift, which as a mirror of your soul reflects back to you aspects of your inner self. It may offer you support and the freedom to travel successfully through life, anticipating your return to a safe and peaceful sanctuary, assured of a warm embrace. On the other hand, it may feel like its walls are hemming you in behind a time worn door with rusty hinges, shackled chains of imprisonment holding you back in life. Only you hold the key to unlock your future waiting to unfold.

Which role in the allegorical drama of life will you choose as you express and act out your dreams and desires? Your home is aware that it too has a journey of evolution embedded in the seed core quintessence of its being. Absorbing and reflecting the consciousness of all, your home patiently awaits acknowledgment and love in the heart coherent relationship that we ultimately all seek.

When we fully comprehend our place in the dynamic of our protective home spaces, in this vast universe in which our soul has chosen to incarnate, we will have arrived at an alchemical understanding of the sacred Golden Vessel, and can hold this precious chalice in our hearts. Within the unified field from which grace descends, all things are possible on the journey of discovering our relationship with the heart of home.

About the Author

Born in Nicosia, Cyprus, Christian left the Island of Aphrodite as a young child when his family emigrated to London. Curious about how things mechanical and electrical worked, he has always been absorbed in exploring the philosophical nature of the universe and the search for the meaning of life.

His breadth of knowledge and understanding comes from a lifetime of learning, delving into the subjects of music, sacred geometry, alchemy, psychology, physics, science, mathematics and cosmology. His study of ancient cultures and world religions include spending time in Greece, much of Europe, America, Canada, Egypt, India, Tibet and China. He is especially interested in the Vedic scriptures, the Sanskrit language and various meditation practices.

As a chartered architect and interior designer, Christian Kyriacou RIBA, MCSD, has run his own professional practice for over 45 years. Practical experience in the building trades at an early age was a good foundation for his later work. Commissions worldwide include airport interiors, restaurants, offices, educational buildings and houses.

He is passionate about fusing classical principles of architecture with contemporary materials and ideologies, incorporating sacred geometry, harmonic proportion, geomancy and the oriental practices of Feng Shui and Vaastu. Co-founder of the London School of Feng Shui, he offers workshops on a wide range of subjects close to his heart. An inspirational speaker, he has appeared on television and radio, and also advises clients and other professionals on architectural projects from the perspective of *The House Whisperer*.

Christian lives in Kingston upon Thames, England, and has three grown-up children. From a Greek musical family, he is never more at home than when surrounded by his many ancient and contemporary musical instruments, composing and playing harmonies that flow through him from the wonders of creation.

www.Kyriacou.com

CPSIA information can be obtained
at www.ICGtesting.com
Printed in the USA
LVOW13s2227190118
563274LV00009B/159/P